Myths, Lies, and Half-Truths

Other Books by Gary DeMar

God and Government: A Bible and Historical Study

God and Government: Issues in Biblical Perspective

God and Government: The Restoration of the Republic

Last Days Madness: Obsession of the Modern Church

Ruler of the Nations

America's Christian History: The Untold Story

Surviving College Successfully: A Complete Manual for the Rigors of Academic Combat

The Reduction of Christianity: A Biblical Response to Dave Hunt

The Debate Over Christian Reconstruction

Christian Reconstruction: What It Is. What It Isn't

To Pledge Allegiance: A New World in View

To Pledge Allegiance: Reformation to Colonization

To Pledge Allegiance: On the Road to Independence

War of the Worldviews

Is Jesus Coming Soon?

Left Behind: Separating Fact from Fiction

Thinking Straight in a Crooked World: A Christian Defense Manual

America's Christian Heritage

The Christian History of America

The Early Church and the End of the World

Liberty at Risk: Exposing the Politics of Plunder

Whoever Controls the Schools Rules the World

Memory Mechanics: How to Memorize Anything

Why the End of the World is Not in Your Future

The Case for America's Christian Heritage

Myths, Lies and Half-Truths

How Misreading the Bible Neutralizes Christians and Empowers Liberals, Secularists, and Atheists

Gary DeMar

AMERICAN VISION
POWDER SPRINGS, GEORGIA

Myth, Lies, & Half Truths

How Misreading the Bible Neutralizes Christians and Empowers Liberals, Secularists, and Atheists

Published by American Vision
Powder Springs, Georgia

ISBN: 0–915815–45–1

Printed in the United States of America

12 11 10 09 7 6 5 4 3

Cover design by Joseph Darnell

American Vision can be contacted in the following ways:

www.AmericanVision.org
info@AmericanVision.org
1-800-628-9460

The American Vision, Inc.
3150-A Florence Rd.
Powder Springs, Georgia 30127

Table of Contents

Preface

First-century believers could have offered tangible evidence that there was little chance for the gospel to have an impact on the *status quo* of religious and civil oppression in their day. How could a small band of men—led by a fisherman (Peter) and a tentmaker (Paul)—living under Roman occupation ever conceive that their circumstances would change enough so that the gospel message would lead to the transformation of the world? To add to the improbability of a world-wide impact, soon after the victorious ascension of Jesus and the outpouring of the Holy Spirit on His disciples, one of their own was killed by a leader of the religious establishment (Acts 7:54–60). What did God do? He converted the man who led the persecution and made him a missionary to the Roman Empire! (9:1–31). After Stephen's death, James, the brother of John, was executed by the local civil governor (12:1–2) and Peter was arrested and thrown in prison. What did God do? Herod "was eaten by worms and died" (12:23). Through tradition we learn that every apostle, with the exception of John, died a martyr. Even so, God's kingdom continued to advance (28:30–31).

The Roman Empire was the major kingdom force in the first century, and the church was relegated to footnote status by the historians of the day. How times have changed. The historians of that era are footnotes in today's textbooks, time is still measured by the birth of Christ—even with the use of BCE (Before the Common Era) and CE (Common Era) by the academic establishment—the Roman Empire is a memory and its remaining buildings are tourist attractions, but the church of Jesus Christ circles the globe. If God accomplished all of this with a few disciples with little or no social influence and no political connections, why does it seem incredible to accomplish something similar with hundreds of millions of believers today? Is the gospel any less effective?

The Vanishing Christian Worldview

In his book *The Vanishing Conscience*, pastor John MacArthur tries to argue that "'Reclaiming' the culture is a pointless, futile exercise. I am convinced," he writes, "we are living in a post-Christian society—a civilization that exists under God's judgment."[1] MacArthur and other Christians believe that such conditions serve as immovable impediments to reformation. Scripture and history are not on his side. The gospel entered a non-Christian society and transformed it. We may live in a post-Christian world, but it wouldn't take much time or effort to reverse the trend. Even Tim LaHaye, co-author of the popular *Left Behind* series that presents a pessimistic view of the future, thinks MacArthur is off base. "Personally," Tim and Beverly LaHaye write, "we have serious problems with that kind of thinking. . . . If we just give up on our country, America may be sentenced to an unnecessary hundred or so years living without the freedom to preach the gospel here or around the world—simply because we gave up on our culture too soon."[2] In their book *Mind Siege*, co-authors David Noebel and LaHaye write the following:

> The Christian life should never be dull or boring. There is plenty to do in all spheres of life. The importance of Christians entering the cultural sphere (art, music, popular entertainment, theater, media, law, religion, education) cannot be overlooked or underestimated.
>
> As Robert Bork makes very clear in his work, conservatives who hold a pro-moral point of view might control the White House and the Congress, but still "they cannot attack modern liberalism in its fortress . . . Hollywood,

> the network evening news, universities, church bureaucracies, the New York Times and the Washington Post." Modern liberals, says Bork, "captured the government and its bureaucracies because they captured the culture."
>
> Christians need to ponder this point carefully. Christian parents need to prepare their sons and daughters to invade the fortress of the left. Someday the major newscasters will retire, and there is nothing amiss in believing that well-prepared Christians can replace them.[3]

Unfortunately, while LaHaye's points are well made, his call for any type of social action cannot be sustained over time because his eschatology, his view of the future, will not allow it. In their book *Charting the End Times*, LaHaye and co-author Thomas Ice write, "we believe that our generation has more signs to indicate that Christ *could* come in our lifetime than any generation before us."[4] They believe that God is "setting the stage"[5] for the "rapture." If this is the case, then MacArthur is right, so why expend energy training Christians to replace newscasters, journalists, college professors, lawyers, educators, and politicians who may not retire for another 20 years? If the stage has been set for the "rapture," and LaHaye is correct in his interpretation of current prophetic events, then he is promoting an activist worldview that is destined to fail no matter how much Christian effort is expended.

LaHaye understands the logical dilemma he has unwittingly created with the publication of his innumerable prophetic writings that reinforce the idea that the time for the "rapture" is indeed near:

> Because present world conditions so closely resemble Bible prophecies of the last days (see 2 Timothy 3:1–7; 2 Peter 3:1–4; Matthew 24:6–7, 37–38), some Christians have concluded that a takeover of our culture by the forces of evil is inevitable. Consequently they do nothing to resist it. They say, "It is necessary that perilous times

> shall come as we approach the end of the age," so they are unwilling to raise their voices in protest.[6]

Having written this in a book dealing with the Christian worldview, LaHaye cannot bring himself to write the same cautionary words in his books dealing with end-time events. In a June 19, 2000, interview with CNN's Larry King, LaHaye said, "In fact, I believe there are a number of signs in Scripture that indicate it's going to come pretty soon. We say maybe within our lifetime."[7] Jerry Jenkins, the co-author of the *Left Behind* series, has a prophetic novel of his own with the title *Soon.* And what is to happen "soon"? The subtitle says it all: *The Beginning of the End.*[8] If prophetic events are going to happen "soon," "within our lifetime," why should anyone plan for even the immediate future and expect any long-term and lasting success?

The LaHayes have always been a bit schizophrenic on the relationship between Bible prophecy and Christian activism. Beverly LaHaye worked to stem the tide of secularism with her effective Concerned Women of America (CWA) organization, and Tim writes his prophetic books against the backdrop of the rising tide of secularism. Even so, I would rather have LaHaye's prophetic schizophrenia than MacArthur's prophetic fatalism.

The Next Christendom?

America could be reduced to a burned out cinder, yet God's Church will still go on. Even world-wide disasters (plagues and world wars) did not mark "the end." As history shows, there have been many who have been premature in writing the obituary of the Church and Christian civilization. The doctrine of the Church is bigger than our nationalist limitations, and it is more powerful and resilient than the most demanding evils. "Over the past five centuries or so, the story of Christianity has been inextricably bound up with that of Europe and the European-driven civilizations overseas, above all in North America. Until recently, the overwhelming majority of Christians have lived in White nations, allowing theorists to speak smugly, arrogantly, of 'European Christian' civilization. . . . Already, today, the largest Christian communities on the planet are to be found in Africa and Latin America,"[9] and we can add, China.

The struggles of these "non-White" nations far outweigh the moral and political struggles we are facing in the United States. They have none of our evangelical infrastructure (a church on every corner), but they seem to be making remarkable evangelical progress. Only time will tell what type of evangelicalism is sprouting and how it will be maintained. As long as the end-time speculative writings of MacArthur and LaHaye are kept at bay and we continue to believe in the power of the gospel, the future looks bright for these burgeoning Christian nations. There may also be hope for America as well.

The structures are in place to turn our nation around. What do we lack? It's not money, people, organization, or skills. We lack motivation, knowledge, and vision. Modern-day American Christianity is not what I bought into when I became a Christian. The first light of the gospel brought a dramatic change in my life. Paul's words about being a "new creature in Christ" (2 Cor. 5:17) were and are real. I believed that what was true for me as an individual was also true for the whole body of Christ. As I've traveled around the United States, I've watched and listened to what passes for the gospel on "Christian" television and radio, frequented Christian bookstores, endured shelves filled with countless books on "relational" Christianity ("What can Jesus do for *me*?"), Christian fiction, end-time novels, and *VeggieTales*[10] and *BibleMan* DVDs. I have often wondered if Christians really understand the true power of the gospel.

I know politics is viewed as a dirty business by many Christians (what isn't?), but it wouldn't take much to reshape the face of Congress. With this accomplished, the make-up of the Supreme Court and the lower courts could also be affected. What would it take? Getting Christians to vote to *limit* the power of civil governments at all levels. The few conservative Christian voices that are struggling in Washington need help. A five to ten percent shift in the balance of power is possible in upcoming elections if Christians will take advantage of the opportunity. LaHaye and Noebel point out that "only 48 percent of Christians bother to vote, even in presidential elections."[11]

The goal, of course, is not to use politics as a club to impose a top-down moral regime on America. Christians must understand that civil government has a very narrow focus and limited jurisdiction. The goal is to get the welfare genie back in its bottle and an activist judiciary returned to Pandora's Box with the lid closed down tight. Politics is not a reforming agent, but it is something that needs reforming. It certainly can inhibit reform by creating draconian laws designed to relativize public discourse on any issue.

We are told that there are no simple answers. As New York University president John Sexton stated: "Our [secular] universities are committed to the deep and nuanced study of humanity. The more sophisticated you are, the more you tolerate ambiguity." The goal of secularism is ambiguity, intellectual as well as moral. That's why when Christians advocate placing the Ten Commandments in a court house, and in granite no less, the political establishment faints in disbelief and awakens in outrage. There is a fear that people might actually obey the Ten Commandments and begin to believe that there is a God, and He's not any of the justices who sit on the Supreme Court. Am I exaggerating? In *Stone v. Graham* (1980), the court wrote, "If the posted copies of the Ten Commandments are to have any effect at all, it will be to induce the schoolchildren to read, meditate upon, perhaps to venerate and obey, the Commandments. However desirable this might be as a matter of private devotion, it is not a permissible state objective under the Establishment Clause." The fear is that people might actually believe that there is a God who demands something of His creatures. What a shocking assertion. How can Christians remain silent and sit still when such nonsense passes as a *Supreme* Court decision? In 1965, Rousas J. Rushdoony spotted the logic of a court that sees itself as the foundation of law:

> If there is no God and no divinely ordained law, then not only does perversion have equal rights with morality, but actually truer rights, because Christian morality is seen as an imposition on and a dehumanization of man, whereas perversion is an act of liberty and autonomy for this school of thought.[12]

As the courts mumble about toleration and diversity, we are beginning to see a pattern: Any laws based on religious assumptions, particularly *Christian* religious assumptions, cannot be *by definition* part of America's legal discourse. So what do we do about this? According to MacArthur, not much. Preach the gospel, to be sure, and hope that this will have a leavening effect on the culture. But even if the country were 80 percent Christian, and this majority decided not to involve themselves in the broader culture, the remaining 20 percent would rule us and in the end deny Christians and everyone else their freedoms.

Notes

1. John F. MacArthur, *The Vanishing Conscience: Drawing the Line in a No-Fault, Guilt-Free World* (Dallas, TX: Word, 1994), 12.
2. Tim and Beverly LaHaye, *A Nation Without a Conscience: Where Have All the Values Gone?* (Wheaton, IL: Tyndale, 1994), 243.
3. Tim LaHaye and David Noebel, *Mind Siege: The Battle for Truth in the New Millennium* (Nashville: Word, 2000), 228.
4. Tim LaHaye and Thomas Ice, *Charting the End Times: A Visual Guide to Understanding Bible Prophecy* (Eugene, OR: Harvest House, 2001), 119.
5. LaHaye and Ice, *Charting the End Times*, 118.
6. LaHaye and Noebel, *Mind Siege*, 237–238.
7. Quoted in Gary DeMar, *Left Behind: Separating Fact from Fiction,* 2nd ed. (Powder Springs, GA: American Vision, [2001] 2009), 208–209.
8. Jerry B. Jenkins, *Soon: A Prophetic Novel* (Wheaton, IL: Tyndale, 2003).

9. Philip Jenkins, *The Next Christendom: The Coming of Global Christianity* (New York: Oxford University Press, 2002), 1–2.

10. Gary DeMar, *MeatyTales: Should Talking Vegetables be Used to Teach the Bible?* (Powder Springs, GA: American Vision, 2009): http://www.americanvision.com/meatytalesebook.aspx

11. LaHaye and Noebel, *The Mind Siege*, 279.

12. Rousas J. Rushdoony, *The Religion of Revolution* (Victoria, TX: Trinity Episcopal Church, 1965), [11].

Introduction

"Have nothing to do with worldly fables fit only
for old women" (1 Tim. 4:7a).

When I was very young, I remember seeing a western on television where a dispute was settled by the answer to a single Bible question. I can't tell you anything else about the show, but that one scene is etched in my mind. Here's the question: "Who cut off Samson's hair?" A smile appeared on the man's face as he confidently responded, "Delilah." No doubt the majority of people would have given the same answer, and they, like the man in the long-forgotten western, would be wrong. A careful reading of the biblical text shows something that surprises a lot of people:

> And she had made him [Samson] sleep on her knees, and called for a *man and had him shave off the seven locks of his hair*. Then she began to afflict him, and his strength left him (Judges 16:19).

While the Samson and Delilah hair removal story is not a central doctrine of the Christian faith, it does demonstrate that if a misreading of the Bible is passed on as fact, with few people ever checking the text for accuracy, then, by default, misinformation or worse (myths, lies, or half-truths) becomes part of the biblical record. This isn't the only bit of biblical misinformation that now plagues the church. Some of these are harmless misreadings of Scripture: the belief that the forbidden fruit was an apple (no fruit is specified), that Jonah was swallowed by a whale (it was "a great fish"), and that angels have wings (they don't). These and other fables parade as facts only because we have heard them for so long and fail to examine "the Scriptures daily, to see whether these things were so" (Acts 17:11). The following questions are designed to test your knowledge of the Bible. No interpretation is needed. These are simple questions of fact alone:

1. The following phrase is found in the Bible: "Ashes to ashes and dust to dust."True or false?[1]
2. Noah's ark landed on Mt. Ararat. True or false?[2]
3. "Pride goes before a fall?" True or false?[3]
4. Complete the following: "The ______________ will dwell with the lamb."[4]
5. Elijah was taken to heaven in a fiery chariot. True or false?[5]
6. How many wise men came to visit Jesus while he lay in the manger?[6]
7. Jesus stumbled and fell while He was carrying His cross. True or false?[7]
8. Where in the Bible is 6-6-6 found?[8]
9. Where in the Bible does it say that Jesus will reign on the earth for a thousand years?[9]
10. What is the biblical definition of "antichrist," and in which book of the Bible is he mentioned the most?[10]

How well did you do? If Christians have adopted myths as truths where little or any interpretation is needed, is it possible that they may have adopted myths as truths in areas where greater study is needed?[11]

"You've Heard It Said"

Jesus encountered a similar problem with those who misread or misunderstood what the Bible actually states. "You have heard that the ancients were told. . ." (Matt. 5:21) and "You have heard that it was said. . ." (5:27) were repeated five times by Jesus in a series of twenty-eight verses. If we were to translate Jesus' words into a contemporary setting, we might hear Him say: "Contrary to what you may have heard, you are mistaken on what you think the Bible says on this issue. You are, therefore, equally mistaken on how these passages should be interpreted and applied. Let Me clear up the confusion for you by directing you to take a closer look at Scripture." Jesus was correcting erroneous beliefs about the Bible. He was not rebuking His listeners for not believing that the Bible is God's infallible and inerrant Word. Jesus touched on four areas:

- An out-of-context reading and application of a text (Matt. 5:21).
- A misreading or an incomplete reading of a text (5:38).
- A misstatement of fact (5:43).
- Faulty reasoning from an incorrectly established premise.

Jesus was not declaring a new set of rules for the church to obey by discounting what had been written in what Christians know as the "Old Testament." He was simply holding His first-century audience accountable for how they were *misreading* Scripture and urging them not to rely on what they had heard was written. For example, if you read Matthew 5:38–40 and compare it to Exodus 21:22, you will notice that Jesus did not replace capital punishment with a turn-the-other-cheek ethic. Exodus 21:22 clearly states that "judges" are to decide what punishment is to be imposed. Victims could not take personal vengeance (cf. Rom. 12:18–21; cf. 13:4). There were some in

Jesus' day who were taking a law that was meant for civil authorities to adjudicate and carry out and were applying it to personal situations. The consequences can be devastating (James 4:1–2). D. A. Carson gives a helpful interpretation of Jesus' words:

> Jesus says something like this: "You have heard that it was said . . . but I tell you. . . ." He does not begin these contrasts by telling them what the Old Testament said, but what they had heard it said. This is an important observation, because Jesus is not negating something from the Old Testament, but something from their understanding of it.
>
> In other words, Jesus appears to be concerned with two things: overthrowing erroneous traditions, and indicating authoritatively the real direction toward which the Old Testament Scriptures point.[12]

These misreadings led to misunderstandings which resulted in creating a mythological tradition that had the effect of nullifying what God's Word actually said and meant. Over time, the traditions were used by religious authorities to supplant the truth and misdirect the people down an unbiblical path. Jesus said the following to the Scribes and Pharisees: "Neglecting the commandment of God, you hold to the tradition of men. . . . You nicely set aside the commandment of God in order to keep your tradition" (Mark 7:8–9).

Like the Bereans of Paul's day (Acts 17:11), Christians should check the veracity of all opinions against the only reliable standard of authority that God has placed in our hands: the Bible. This may mean a change in belief systems for some. There is no novelty in this. God confronted Peter directly about the inclusion of Gentiles into the household of faith (10:9–16). Paul confronted Peter "to his face" on a similar matter (Gal. 2:11–14). There are times when we all need to be knocked off our horse of mistaken opinions (Acts 9:4). "Testing" is a biblical mandate (2 Cor. 13:5; 1 John 4:1).

Contrary to Popular Opinion

Myths, Lies and Half-Truths adopts Jesus' methodology of taking a closer look at God's Word and applies it to erroneous misinterpretations that have resulted in a virtual shut-down of the church's full-orbed mission in the world (Acts 20:27). These traditional but mistaken interpretations and applications of popular Bible texts to contemporary issues have resulted in the Christian faith being "thrown out and trampled under foot by men" (Matt. 5:13). Too many Christians believe, along with a watching world, that the Bible is irrelevant this side of heaven. While the homosexual community is about one percent of the population, it has had and continues to have tremendous impact on our culture and laws. Christians, who make up about 35 percent of the population, seem to have voluntarily abandoned culture and hidden the gospel under a bushel waiting for a rescue from heaven that is always said to be coming "soon." This is the first time in the history of the church that such a minimalized worldview has become so pervasive in the church.

There was a time when the gospel of Jesus Christ touched every area of a person's life and the world in which he lived. This is no longer the case. Certainly the humanists have attempted to bar Christ's words from what is often described as the "secular" realm. But Christians have barred themselves by teaching a one-dimensional gospel. The Bible tells us about the tithe but not about taxes. We've left that to the humanists. A majority of Christians still send their children to the very schools that deny Christ and his Word, and we wonder why the humanists are setting today's cultural agenda.[13]

Our nation is in a crisis. The world is crying out for answers in the face of bewildering and seemingly unsolvable problems. This book demonstrates that the Bible has real answers and shows that the church has been instrumental throughout history in the development of what is uniformly described as a comprehensive Christian worldview.[14]

Neutralized No Longer

In order to demonstrate the validity of Christianity as a religion for all of life, it is necessary to demythologize the misrepresentations that have been nurtured by a bewildering number of unorthodox theologies. These "cherished myths" have had the effect of neutralizing the Word of God as it relates to this world. Christianity has often been accused of being too "otherworldly" in that it has failed to offer viable political, economic, judicial, and social programs for the world order. The teaching of Jesus that his kingdom "is not of this world" has been interpreted to mean that earthly life must merely be endured and that Christians cannot expect to accomplish lasting reform before the return of Christ.

But does the New Testament really offer no guidance for shaping political or economic policy? Does it contain no judicial or social precepts that may be applied in today's society? True, neither Jesus nor Paul spoke in detail of political or economic ideologies. But since both spoke out of a Jewish background and context with "all Scripture" in mind (2 Tim. 3:16–17), direct allusions may have been unnecessary. Christians must understand that their faith is rooted in all the Bible which contains highly specific political, economic, judicial, and social precepts that give guidance to all of life. The fact that such ideals exist as an intrinsic part of Christianity can go a long way toward establishing the credibility of the Christian faith in these areas.[15]

Christianity's failure to be a practical religion in the past 150 years or more has meant the success of a perverted and twisted secularism and an advancing militant Islam that are doing incalculable harm at home and abroad. Humanism and Islam have gained the upper hand by default. The rejection of any type of this-worldly application of the Bible has resulted in the proliferation of a man-centered worldview that has steadily drained the life out of our world and left behind a spiritual vacuum. Will the church of Jesus Christ be ready with biblical answers for the millions who will be ready to follow the light of the gospel of grace and all that it means for their lives this side of heaven as the worldviews of humanism and Islam continue to be exposed as "folly"? (2 Tim. 3:9). Now is the time to make the necessary theological preparations. It is my prayer that this book will help in that task.

Notes

1. False. This phrase in not found in the Bible. It appears in the Anglican *Book of Common Prayer.* The biblical text reads, "By the sweat of your face you will eat bread, till you return to the ground, Because from it you were taken; for you are dust, and to dust you shall return. (Gen. 3:19).

2. False. The ark rested on the "mountains of Ararat": "And in the seventh month, on the seventeenth day of the month, the ark rested upon the mountains of Ararat" (Gen. 8:4).

3. False: "Pride goes before *destruction*, and a haughty spirit before a fall" (Prov. 16:18, KJV). As you can see, it's a "haughty spirit that goes before a fall." The first phrase is confused with the second phrase.

4. "Lion" is incorrect: "And the *wolf* will dwell with the *lamb*, and the leopard will lie down with the kid, and the calf and the young lion and the fatling together; and a little boy will lead them" (Isa. 11:6) and "The *wolf* and the *lamb* shall graze together, and the lion shall eat straw like the ox. . ." (65:25).

5. False. "And it came about when the LORD was about to take up Elijah by a *whirlwind* to heaven, that Elijah went with Elisha from Gilgal" (2 Kings 2:1). A "chariot of fire and horses of fire" separated Elijah and Elisha (2 Kings 2:11)

6. First, the Bible does not tell us the number of magi who visited Jesus. We do know that there were more than one and that they presented Him with three gifts (Matt. 2:11). The inference is, based on the number of gifts, that there were three of them. The wise men are never named, although tradition has them as Caspar, Melchior, and Balthasar. Second, by the time the wise men find Jesus, He is in a house: "And they came into the house and saw the Child with Mary His mother" (2:11). Matthew 2:1 states: "Now after Jesus was born in Bethlehem of Judea in the days of Herod the king, behold, magi from the east arrived in Jerusalem." The magi began their travels from the east after first seeing the star. We do not know how long it took them finally to reach Jerusalem and then Bethlehem, but it was soon after Jesus' birth. For a discussion of this topic, see Floyd Nolen Jones, *The Chronology of the Old Testament: A Return to the Basics*, 15th ed. (Green Forest, AR: Master Books, [1993] 2005), 214–217.

7. We know that Jesus carried His own cross (John 19:17); we also know that Simon was called upon to carry it after Jesus first took it up (Matt. 27:32; Mark 15:21; Luke 23:26); but we can only speculate as to why Simon was asked to bear Jesus' cross.

8. The number of the mark of the beast is not three sixes: "Here is wisdom. Let him who has understanding calculate the number of the beast, for the number is that of a man; and his number is *six hundred and sixty-six*" (Rev. 13:18; also see 1 Kings 10:14).

9. No verse in the Bible specifically states that Jesus will reign on the "earth" for

a thousand years: "And I saw thrones, and they sat upon them, and judgment was given to them. And I saw the souls of those who had been beheaded because of the testimony of Jesus and because of the word of God, and those who had not worshipped the beast or the image, and had not received the mark upon their forehead and upon their hand; and they came to life and reigned with Christ a thousand years" (Rev. 20:4).

10. An antichrist, and there were many in John's day (1 John 2:18), is anyone who "does not acknowledge Jesus Christ as coming in the flesh" (2 John 7). The only other uses of the Greek word "antichrist" are found in 1 John 2:22 and 4:3. The word "antichrist" does not appear in Revelation.

11. Joe Kovacs, *Shocked by the Bible: The Most Astonishing Facts You've Never Been Told* (Nashville: Thomas Nelson, 2008) and J. Stephen Lang, *What the Bible Didn't Say: Popular Myths and Misconceptions About the Good Book* (New York: Fall River Press, [2003] 2008).

12. D. A. Carson, *The Sermon on the Mount: An Exegetical Exposition of Matthew 5–7* (Grand Rapids, MI: Baker Book House, 1978), 39–40.

13. Gary DeMar, *Whoever Controls the Schools Rules the World* (Powder Springs, GA: American Vision, 2007).

14. Gary DeMar, *Thinking Straight in a Crooked World: A Christian Defense Manual* (Powder Springs, GA: American Vision, 2001).

15. Larry Poston, "The Adult Gospel," *Christianity Today* (August 20, 1990), 25.

PART ONE

Christians and the World

1

"The World Is Unimportant"

Myth, Lie, or Half-Truth?: *The world is full of sin. One day God will burn up the world and create a new world. In the meantime, Christians should focus on what's really important—the world above.*

> The Christian is in the world, but not of the world. This constitutes the basis for the perennial problem involved in the discussion of Christian culture. Because believers are not of the world, there have always been many Christians who have taken a negative attitude toward culture. They understand the Christian's calling to consist exclusively in proclaiming salvation through Christ to lost men in a dying world. They see that dying world only as lying under the sentence of death and final judgment. Others, having eagerly accepted the Pauline assurance, "all things are yours," stress the fact that believers have a cultural calling here and now to subdue the earth as members of the human race.[1]

Nikita Khrushchev (1894–1971), Premier of the former Soviet Union, described a time in the Communist republic's history when a wave of petty theft was sweeping through the government-owned plants. To curtail the stealing, guards were placed at factory entrances to watch the laborers as they entered and departed. At the Leningrad timberworks, one of the guards spotted Pyotr Petrovich leaving the yard with a wheelbarrow filled with a bulky sack. A guard became dutifully suspicious.

> "Come on, Petrovich," said the guard. "What have you got there?"
>
> "Just sawdust and shavings," Petrovich replied.
>
> "Come on," the guard said, "I wasn't born yesterday. Tip it out." Out it came—nothing but sawdust and shavings. So he was allowed to put it all back again and go home.
>
> The same thing happened every night all week, and the guard was getting extremely frustrated. Finally, his curiosity overcame his frustration.
>
> "Petrovich," he said, "I know you. Tell me what you're smuggling out of here, and I'll let you go."
>
> "Wheelbarrows," said Petrovich.[2]

Error has been smuggled into the church under the pretense of truth since the beginning of time (Gen 3:1–7). Jesus warned His disciples not to be led astray by traditions that have the effect of setting "aside the commandment of God" (Mark 7:9). Paul cautioned the "elders of the church" at Ephesus that after his departure "savage wolves will come in among you, not sparing the flock; and from among your own selves men will arise, speaking perverse things, to draw away the disciples after them" (Acts 20:17, 29–30). It's no less true today than in John's day that "many false prophets have gone out into the world" (1 John 4:1), many of whom "went out from us" (2:19).

Some are surprised that false doctrines often arise from within the church, "from among your own selves," as Paul warns. That's what makes error insidious; it's promoted by someone from within. Jesus saved His harshest criticism for the religious leaders of Israel for the simple reason that they are religious leaders who carry the weight of authority with their words and actions (Matt. 21:23–46; 23:2–3; James 3:1).

While a false doctrine has the trappings of truth, in terms of what the Bible actually tells us, it is rotten to the core (Matt. 23:25–28). Heresy most often enters the church under the cover of some orthodox position. A grain of truth grows into a mountain of error. Irenaeus, a second-century Christian writer, describes how error is most often covered by a thin veneer of recognizable orthodoxy:

> Error, indeed, is never set forth in its naked deformity, lest, being thus exposed, it should at once be detected. But it is craftily decked out in an attractive dress, so as, by its outward form, to make it appear to be inexperienced (ridiculous as the expression may seem) more true than truth itself.[3]

The claim is often made by some well-meaning Christians that the world and the things in the world are off-limits to Christians; that the best way to live the Christian life is not to get involved in "the world." Holiness is defined by some as a rejection of the world as a place or arena for comprehensive redemption. Others go so far as to argue for a physical escape from this world through some cataclysmic eschatological event like a pretribulational rapture that is always said to be "near."[4] "In doing so they have virtually turned their backs on the world in which they live."[5] These beliefs go counter to the overwhelming biblical evidence that God has made us stewards of His good creation of which one day He will demand an accounting of our actions or inactions (Matt. 25:14–30).

This Is My Father's World

Abraham Kuyper (1837–1920) said, "there is not one inch of creation of which Christ doesn't say 'Mine.'"[6] Kuyper put this message into practice as a church reformer, university founder (Free

University of Amsterdam), journalist (editor of *The Standard*), political leader (the ideological force behind the Antirevolutionary Party), and statesman (premier of the Netherlands). His vision was "that in spite of all worldly opposition, God's holy ordinances shall be established again in the home, in the school, and in the State for the good of the people; to carve as it were into the conscience of the nation the ordinances of the Lord, to which the Bible and Creation bear witness, until the nation pays homage again to God."[7] Too often we find Christians who believe or at least live as if they believe that "there is not one inch of creation of which *Satan* doesn't say 'Mine.'"

Many Christians would think it impossible and even "unspiritual" to have a leadership role in the areas Kuyper considered a necessary part of Christian ministry. Historically, the church did not divide the world into opposing realms, consisting of a good sacred/spiritual realm and a bad secular/material realm. More importantly, the Bible does not divide the world this way. The Bible is concerned about the distinction between good and evil, right and wrong, moral and immoral, whether in the church or in the world, whether material or spiritual.

The biblical doctrine of creation tells us that the created order is an arena for Christian action. God put Adam and Eve in the midst of the garden to "cultivate it and keep it" (Gen. 2:15). A delegated sovereignty had been given to mankind to be caretakers over the created order (1:26). While God reserves ultimate authority and sovereignty for Himself, He delegates a subordinate authority and sovereignty to men and women as stewards. God also sets the rules by which they are to exercise that delegated stewardship and sovereignty. In fact, it was the breaking of these established creation laws that got Adam and Eve exiled from the garden. Gordon J. Spykman describes God's own perspective on the world He created: "Creation . . . was and is and remains God's first and foremost revelation. . . . God did not create junk, and being jealous of his handiwork, He does not discard what He creates."[8]

Maker Of Heaven and Earth

The opening line of the Apostles' Creed tells us that God is the "Maker of Heaven and Earth," of a creation that He Himself describes as being "very good" (Gen. 1:31). The New Testament reinforces the goodness factor of the creation even in its post-fall condition: "For everything created by God is good, and nothing is to be rejected, if it is received with gratitude; for it is sanctified by means of the word of God and prayer" (1 Tim. 4:4–5). God created the world with design and purpose in mind. God is not the world as in pantheism,[9] nor is He indifferent to or distant from the world as with deism. The world is not an emanation from God's being as in New Age humanism. "The creed confesses a living God; no detached spectator on the world and its fate, God is the leading actor. All powerful, he retains and exercises the initiative. This is the most basic theme in the Christian world view."[10]

To be sure, sin has affected the world. Even so, God has not forsaken it, just as He has not forsaken us because of our sin (Rom. 5:6). His redeeming work in and over this world has a transforming effect on all aspects of our fallen domain. God was pleased to dwell in Christ "and through Him to reconcile all things to Himself, having made peace through His blood; through Him, I say, *whether things on earth* or things in heaven" (Col. 1:20). We learn through Scripture that "whatever is born of God overcomes the world; and this is the victory that has overcome the world—our faith" (1 John 5:4). "The Christian's responsibility on earth is to transform the world that 'thy will be done, on earth as it is in heaven' (Matt. 6:10)."[11] Heaven is the pattern, earth is the work in progress.

Because God is the One who brought "heaven and earth" into existence and "upholds all things by the word of His power" (Heb. 1:3), these truths alone should be enough to convince all Christians who recite the opening line of the Apostles' Creed that this world is important and is a legitimate place to work out our salvation with fear and trembling. While evil may exist in this world because of sin, the world in and of itself is not evil. "Whatsoever is evil, is not so by the Creator's action, but by the creature's defection."[12] Therefore, we should be skeptical of any theological position that defames any part of God's good creation by declaring it off-limits to Christians. "There is no nature originally sinful, no substance in itself evil, no being, therefore, which may not come from the same fountain of goodness."[13]

Practicing Pagans

Some Christians have forsaken the biblical doctrine of creation, not as a belief, but as a practical application of how they actually live. They contend that while God created the physical heavens and earth, the created order is an incumbrance, a temporary inconvenience this side of the afterlife. Such beliefs have more in common with pagan religious assumptions than with the Bible. For example, animists are anti-world. They believe that nature is governed by capricious unseen forces that bedevil and disturb the natural order of things. Animists contend that nature is *animated*, alive with unpredictable gods, goddesses, sprites, and evil forces intent on disorder. This has the effect of turning nature into a living essence that is to be feared and placated rather than examined, developed, and probed.

The results of animist belief patterns are evident in that science and technology rarely develop in these cultures beyond some initial discoveries. "Nor could science have originated in India among the Hindus, nor in China among the Buddhists, for both Hinduism and Buddhism teach that the physical world is unreal and that the only reality is that of the world's soul and that the greatest thing anyone has to learn is that the physical world is not real. Therefore, there would have been no point in spending one's life fooling with that which had no reality in the first place."[14]

While Christians don't share the worldview of animists, Buddhists, and Hindus, many who hold anti-world belief patterns do so because of misguided theological perceptions that have the same anti-world effects. The development of culture, art, music, science, literature, medicine would never have developed if Christians had followed an anti-world theology that is still prevalent in much of the world today.[15]

Your World Is Too Small

In 1960, J. B. Phillips wrote a book with a shocking title—*Your God is Too Small.* "For many persons," he pointed out, "the greatest stumbling block to mature faith lies in the fact that they haven't found a God big enough for their needs—big enough to 'account for' life, and to command their respect and worship."[16] What's true of peoples' perception of God is also true about their perception of His creation. Many Christians have shunned involvement in the world beyond personal piety because they misinterpret certain passages about God's creation similar to the way they misinterpret passages about God Himself. If God is ineffectual in His being to accomplish great things for the individual, how could anyone imagine that God could or would accomplish great things for His creation?

This misperception is reinforced by how the word "world" is understood when Christians read that it is under God's condemnation (1 Cor. 11:32) or when Peter speaks of "the corruption that is in the world" (2 Peter 1:4) and the "defilements of the world" (2 Peter 2:20). From these and other similar passages many well-meaning Christians conclude that any contact with the world and the things that operate in the world will have an adverse effect on their relationship with Jesus Christ. Tom Minnery understands the mixed message some Christians get when they read these passages:

> It isn't difficult to see why some people read their Bible and plunge into the world's problems, believing that since Christ loved the world so much, they should develop a love for it as well. On the other hand, it's obvious why some Christians might read the same passages

> and conclude that it is ungodly even to help citizens register to vote.[17]

Much of this misunderstanding comes from reading the Bible in bits and pieces rather than as an integrated whole. In addition, there is the issue of language and the different ways "world" is used in literature. The Bible is literature, and we should expect to find certain literary features[18] among its many stories.[19] Since the Bible uses "world" in a variety of ways and in distinctive contexts, we should not take the way "world" is used in one context and assume that it has the same meaning in every context. For example, the word "lion" refers to both Jesus and Satan but in different ways. The context gives us the proper setting for the correct interpretation. A lion has many attributes, some good (royalty and dignity: Gen. 49:9–10; Num. 23:24; Prov. 28:1) and some bad (ruthlessness and cunning: Psalm 10:9; 22:13). Jesus is the lion from the tribe of Judah (Rev. 5:5), and Satan "prowls around like a roaring lion, seeking someone to devour" (1 Peter 5:8). It's obvious that "lion" is not being used in the same way in both contexts. Satan is described as a "serpent" (Gen. 3:1), and Christians are told to be "wise as serpents" (Matt. 10:16). We can hardly conclude that being "wise as serpents" means we should be like Satan who is said to be liar (John 8:44).

If we follow the logic that some use in reference to "world"—that "world" is always a description of an evil domain to be avoided—then we could make a similar claim regarding the use of serpent and lion. The varied meanings of words and how they are used in specific contexts are keys to understanding any type of literature, including the Bible.

The Bible and the "World"

While the Bible's use of "world" has a number of specialized meanings, in most cases it differs little from the way we use the word in everyday conversation and writing: A Major League "World Series" is a sports competition that can include baseball teams from only two countries (the United States and Canada);[20] the television show "Dave's World" was about the *limited* life and times of comedian Dave Barry; being "on top of the world" has nothing to do with climbing the highest peak of Mt. Everest; Jiminy Cricket's song about it being "a small world after all" is not a description of planetary dimensions; and claiming that "love makes the world go 'round" is hardly an established law of physics. Few people have a problem understanding these varied uses of the word "world" in normal speech because they understand the *context* in which the word is used. The same is true for the way the Bible uses "world." Different contexts can change the meaning of a word. It's the interpreter's task to pay close attention to the subject matter in order to understand what meaning the author has in mind when he uses "world." In John 1:10, "world" is being used three different ways with no confusion.

The World as God's Physical Creation

God's first creative act was the creation of the cosmos, the *physical* world: "In the beginning God created the heavens and earth" (Gen. 1:1). What was God's opinion of His work?: "And God saw all that He had made, and behold, it was very good" (1:31). From the New Testament, we not only know that "the world was made through Him" but that Jesus "was in the world" (John 1:10; cf. Heb. 1:2–3; Col. 1:16). The created order is God's doing, and it plays a significant role in God's providential plan:

> Christ was chosen "before the foundation of the world" (1 Pet. 1:20), and Hebrews speaks of what Christ said when he "came into the world" (Heb. 10:5). Paul says that there are "many different languages in the world" (1 Cor. 14:10). The meaning is straightforward: the reference is to our physical habitat, the earth.[21]

In his address to the Athenian philosophers, Paul drew from the common belief that God "made the world and all things in it" (Acts

17:24). The one, true God, who made the cosmos (17:31) and could save them from their sin.

The Greek word *kosmos* ("world"), from which we get the English words cosmos, cosmic, cosmopolitan, microcosm, and cosmology,[22] can designate the entire created order (Matt. 13:35; 24:21; Luke 11:50; John 17:5, 24), the earth in particular (Matt. 4:8; Mark 14:9; Luke 12:30; John 11:9), a large group (John 12:19), a political/social/religious system (Rev. 11:15), a competing world system (1 John 5:19), and, as we will see, the particular domain of God's redemptive work.

The World as the Object of God's Redeeming Grace

One of the most cherished verses in the Bible is "For God so loved the world, that He gave His only begotten Son, that whoever believes in Him should not perish, but have eternal life" (John 3:16; cf. 2 Cor. 5:19). By understanding the redemptive context of John, the use of "world" is best understood to teach that Jesus' love has no national, racial, or geographical limitations, and that it is not restricted to any one group of people. The Samaritans, who as a group were ostracized by the Jews, were embraced by Jesus. Upon hearing Jesus' redemptive message, they said the following to the Samaritan woman who first met Jesus at the well: "It is no longer because of what you said that we believe, for we have heard for ourselves and know that this One is indeed the Savior of the world" (John 4:42). The "eternal gospel" is to be preached "to those who live on the land, and to every nation and tribe and tongue and people" (Rev. 14:6), that is, to the world.

Prior to Pentecost, the gospel was almost exclusively an Israelite-only message with some exceptions (Matt. 10:5; 15:21–28). A non-Israelite family could be incorporated into Israel by faith (e.g., Rahab's family: Josh. 2:8–14; cf. Matt. 1:5). Under the New Covenant, there is neither Jew nor Gentile (Gal. 3:28) because the dividing wall separating the two worlds was dismantled by Jesus' redemptive work (Eph. 2:11–22). Jesus is now the "Savior of the world."

Jesus' redemptive love extends to Jews (Matt. 15:24), Canaanites (15:22), Samaritans (John 4:42), and Gentiles in general (Matt. 12:18, 21; Luke 2:32; Acts 9:15; 10:45; 11:1, 18). Jesus was "to die for the nation; and not for the nation only, but that He might also gather together into one the children of God who are scattered abroad," that is, His elect from around the world (John 11:51–52; 10:16). This was a novel idea for first-century Jews. Even Peter had to be convinced by God that non-Jews (the world as distinct from Israel) also would share in covenantal blessings through the cross of Christ (Acts 10–11:1–18; 15:1–29; Gal. 2:11–14). This is why Peter could say, "I most certainly understand now that God is not one to show partiality, but in every nation the man who fears Him and does what is right, is welcome to Him" (Acts 10:34b).

The World as Referring to All Without Distinction

The Pharisees were concerned enough about Jesus' impact on the hearts and minds of the Jews, especially in the capital city of Jerusalem, that they issued this frantic warning: "The world has gone after Him" (John 12:19; cf. 7:4; 14:22; 16:21; 18:20). The world in this context means a large group of people and not millions of people from around the globe—not everybody without exception, but everybody without distinction in Israel: young and old, male and female, and Jew and Gentile (12:20). The word "all" is used in a similar way throughout the Bible (e.g., Matt. 3:5; 4:23–24). "For example, Mark 11:32 tells us that 'all men counted that John was a prophet' but obviously only people aware of what was going on could have been intended. In John 8:2 we are told that 'all people came to Him' but we know the Pharisees did not do so. In both cases it would be more appropriate to say 'all kinds of' people."[23] We use "all" in a similar way today.

The World as a Political System

The advance of the gospel throughout the Roman Empire caused enough alarm that some claimed that Jesus' disciples had "upset the world" (Acts 17:6). Although a different word is used for "world" (*oikoumene*), the meaning is similar to *kosmos* in application. In the days of the early church, Roman ideology, military strength, and commerce dominated the Mediterranean world. The inhabited earth, as far as the New Testament writers were concerned, was an alien political and religious world ruled by the Roman Empire (Matt. 24:14; Luke 2:1; 11:27–28).

These gospel opponents understood that an allegiance with Jesus would mean that their divine king, Caesar, could no longer claim the title of *Dominus et Deus*, "lord and god." The competitive threat of Jesus' lordship to the prevailing political kingdom of Rome led to Jason and his associates being charged with anti-kingdom (Roman) activities: "They all act contrary to the decrees of Caesar, saying there is another king, Jesus" (Acts 17:7). The use of "world" in this context means the world of pagan Rome dominated by all of its attendant decadence, including its toleration of occult practices (8:9–11; 13:6–12; cf. 19:19) and worship of rulers (12:20–24).

The World as Antithesis

How can it be "that friendship with the world is hostility toward God" (James 4:4) when we know that "God so loved the world" (John 3:16)? If "world" is given the same meaning in every context in which it appears, then we would have a contradiction. The "world" James is describing is the world of unbelief, not the world as a place, a sphere of influence, or the realm of redemption. The use of *kosmos*, as James describes it, is "a widespread disposition and power in mankind for evil in opposition to God."[24] The Bible uses *kosmos* to characterize what sinful men and women have done with their world and shows its antithesis to God's ideal world and His moral order (1 Cor. 11:32; Eph. 2:2; 1 John 2:15–17).

> The world is in sin and therefore needs to be saved (John 1:20; 3:17; 4:42; 12:47; 16:8). The world is the place of darkness, ethically speaking, into which the light

> (God's holy Son, Jesus Christ) has shone (John 3:19; 8:12; 9:5; 12:46). The world is *spiritually dead* and thus needs life given to it (John 6:33, 51); this clearly demonstrates that "world" cannot be taken in a natural sense, for the world (understood descriptively as the created order) is animated and alive.[25]

Scripture plainly teaches that Christians are to be *in* the world (geographically) but not *of* the world (morally) (John 15:19; 17:14–15, 16, 18; 1 John 2:15). If the world as a place is to be rejected, then God violated His own prohibition by sending His Son into the world and by taking on human flesh and leaving His newly formed body of believers behind to carry out His mission in His name. God does not call on us to escape from the world as a place but to avoid worldliness as a system of belief and competing allegiance. Paul wrote to the Corinthians "not to associate with immoral people" (1 Cor. 5:9). Some took this to mean a complete separation from the world. But this is not what Paul had in mind, "for then you would have to go out of the world" (1 Cor. 5:10). Christians are to remain in the world, while those so-called Christians who practice immorality were to be removed from fellowship (1 Cor. 5:13).

Conclusion

Scripture is our guide as we deal with the world and not the two-dimensional worldview of either secularism (making the world or nature absolute) or pietism (escaping from the duties of this world). God "became flesh and dwelt among us" (John 1:14) in this world! We, as Christ's disciples, are to carry out His mission in the world. Jesus worked in His earthly father's shop as a carpenter, affirming the goodness of the created order and the value of physical labor. He healed the bodies of the infirm. He fed the masses. The Bible calls on us to care for the widow and orphan. This is what it means to be in the world but not of the world.

Notes

1. Henry R. Van Til, *The Calvinistic Concept of Culture* (Grand Rapids, MI: Baker Book House, [1959] 2001), 15.

2. Os Guinness, "The Christian and Society," in James M. Boice, ed., *Transforming Our World: A Call to Action* (Portland, OR: Multnomah Press, 1988), 52.

3. Irenaeus, *Against Heresies* (1.2). Cited in Harold O. J. Brown, *Heresies: The Image of Christ in the Mirror of Heresy and Orthodoxy from the Apostles to the Present* (Garden City, NY: Doubleday, 1984), 6.

4. For an evaluation of this belief, see Gary DeMar, *Last Days Madness: Obsession of the Modern Church*, 4th ed. (Powder Springs, GA: American Vision, 1999); *Left Behind: Separating Fact from Fiction*, 2nd ed. (Powder Springs, GA: American Vision, [2001] 2009) and *Why the End of the World is Not in Your Future: Identifying the Gog-Magog Alliance* (Powder Springs, GA: American Vision, 2009).

5. Os Guinness, *Fit Bodies Fat Minds: Why Evangelicals Don't Think and What to do About It* (Grand Rapids, MI: Baker Books, 1994), 67.

6. Quoted in Douglas Groothuis, "Revolutionizing our Worldview," *The Reformed Journal* (November 1982), 23.

7. Quoted in Douglas Groothuis, *Christianity That Counts: Being a Christian in a Non-Christian World* (Grand Rapids, MI: Baker Books, 1994), 28.

8. Gordon J. Spykman quoted in David T. Koyzis, *Political Visions and Illusions: A Survey and Christian Critique of Contemporary Ideologies* (Downers Grove, IL: InterVarsity Press, 2003), 200, note 21.

9. For the inherent limitations of the pantheistic worldview to explain our world, see Francis A. Schaeffer, *Pollution and the Death of Man* in *The Complete Works of Francis A. Schaeffer: A Christian Worldview*, 5 vols. (Westchester, IL: Crossway Books, 1982), 5:19.

10. Arthur F. Holmes, *Contours of a World View* (Grand Rapids, MI: Eerdmans, 1983), 57.

11. Robert E. Webber, *Common Roots: A Call to Evangelical Maturity* (Grand Rapids, MI: Zondervan, 1978), 205.

12. John Pearson, *An Exposition of the Creed*, 2 vols. 3rd ed. (Oxford, England: Oxford University Press, 1847), 1:79.

13. John Eyre Yonge, *An Exposition of the Apostles' Creed* (London: Hodder and Stoughton, 1887), 27.

14. D. James Kennedy and Jerry Newcombe, *What If Jesus Had Never Been Born?* (Nashville, TN: Thomas Nelson, 1994), 95.

15. Alvin J. Schmidt, *Under the Influence: How Christianity Transformed Civilization* (Grand Rapids, MI: Zondervan, 2001).

16. J. B. Phillips, *Your God is Too Small* (New York: Macmillan, 1960).

17. Tom Minnery, *Why You Can't Stay Silent: A Biblical Mandate to Shape Our Culture* (Wheaton, IL: Tyndale House Publishers, 2001), 87.

18. Leland Ryken, *Words of Delight: A Literary Introduction to the Bible* (Grand Rapids, MI: Baker Book House, 1987) and Leland Ryken and Tremper Longman, III, eds., *A Complete Literary Guide to the Bible* (Grand Rapids, MI: Zondervan, 1993).

19. The use of the word "stories" to describe the biblical narrative in no way diminishes the Bible's revelatory character. "Story" is being used to describe the way God gets His message across. See Richard L. Pratt, Jr., *He Gave Us Stories: The Bible Student's Guide to Interpreting Old Testament Narratives* (Phillipsburg, NJ: Presbyterian and Reformed, [1990] 1993).

20. Little League includes more than 100 countries from around the world. The winning team in America plays the winner of the international competition.

21. David F. Wells, *God in the Wasteland: The Reality of Truth in a World of Fading Dreams* (Grand Rapids, MI: Eerdmans, 1994), 37.

22. Bob Moore and Maxine Moore, *Dictionary of Latin and Greek Origins: A Comprehensive Guide to the Classical Origins of English Worlds* (New York: Barnes & Noble Books, [1997] 2000), 115–156.

23. Arthur C. Custance, *The Sovereignty of Grace* (Grand Rapids, MI: Baker Book House, 1979), 163.

24. B. C. Johanson, "The Definition of 'Pure Religion' in James 1:27 Reconsidered," *Expository Times* 84 (1973), 118–19. Quoted in Peter Davids, *Commentary on James*, New International Greek Testament Commentary (Grand Rapids, MI: Eerdmans, 1982), 103.

25. Greg L. Bahnsen, "The Person, Work, and Present Status of Satan," *The Journal of Christian Reconstruction*, Symposium on Satanism, ed. Gary North 1:2 (Winter 1974), 23–24.

2

"Involvement In The World Is Not 'Spiritual'"

Myth, Lie, or Half-Truth?: *The best way to live a holy life is to avoid contact with the world. To participate in the affairs of this world takes time and energy away from true kingdom work.*

Recently a historian commented on what he had observed of the Christian faith in America: "Socially irrelevant, even if privately engaging."[1]

In Egypt, in the middle of the third century, an ascetic named Antonius secluded himself from the world after being impressed by the story of the rich young ruler (Mark 10:17–27). He sold all his possessions and distributed the money to the poor. "He then said farewell to the world, to relations and friends, and lived alone—first near his home, then in a tomb, later in a disused fort, and finally on a mountain. Twice a year his friends brought him food, which he ate with a little salt. He drank nothing but water. He decided not to comb or cut his hair, except once a year, at Easter. He never took a bath. . . . Antonius, we are told, lived until he was 106 years of age."[2]

There are other accounts of equally misguided "super-spiritual saints." The Stylites lived on pillars (*stylos* is the Greek word for "pillar"). These "pillar saints," as they were called, followed the example of a recluse named Simeon who lived in the fourth century. Simeon's desire to be a super-spiritual saint began when he was a boy. He chose the life of a shepherd in an attempt to give himself the needed solitude to develop true "spirituality." Since the life of a shepherd was not isolated enough to cultivate the true spiritual life he desired, he entered a monastery. In the nine years he spent as a monk, he never once set foot outside the confined space of his room. Seeking even more solitude and "spirituality," Simeon went into the desert, erected a pole nine-feet high, and began his thirty-year perch. "Even then Simeon thought he was too near the earth, and little by little he lengthened the pillar until finally it reached the height of sixty feet."[3] Simeon believed "that by living on the top of a pillar his soul would benefit."[4]

How was Simeon's spirituality better than those who cared for him? His attendants toiled while Simeon enjoyed the fruit of their labor. In reality, Simeon's "spirituality" was worthless *because* it was self-serving. Jesus said it best: "You are the salt of the earth; but if the salt has become tasteless, how will it be made salty again? It is good for nothing any more, except to be thrown out and trampled under foot by men" (Matt. 5:13). It was deception, Paul wrote, to believe that such practices contributed in any way to true spirituality (Col. 2:16–23). The definition of "pure and undefiled religion" is to "visit orphans and widows in their distress, and to keep oneself unstained from the world" (James 1:27). Of course, there is no way to visit orphans and widows if you are perched atop a pole separated from the world where orphans and widows live.

Defilement does not come by way of things but from what's inside a person, from "the things that proceed out of the mouth" which arise "from the heart. . . . For out of the heart come evil thoughts, murders, adulteries, fornications, thefts, false witness, slanders" (Matt. 15:18–19). There isn't a pole high enough to escape the sinfulness of the heart. The Reformers of the sixteenth century understood Christian spirituality "in terms of the vocation of *all* Christians to express their faith in the market-place of life."[5]

How Much of an Example?

Supposedly Jesus was the example of a this-world-denying escapist "spirituality" since He did not marry or own property. "The foxes have holes, and the birds of the air have nests; but the Son of Man has nowhere to lay His head" (Matt. 8:20). The spiritually misguided seem to have overlooked how Jesus blessed the marriage relationship (John 2:1–11), spent time in the homes of his disciples and friends (Matt. 8:14; 9:10, 23; 10:12; 26:6, 18), and never condemned the use of private property, although He did warn of the dangers of riches when they hold a more significant place in the Christian's life than does God Himself (Mark 10:17–31; cf. 1 Tim. 6:10).

Teachers of a false spirituality in the first-century church were "forbidding marriage" and advocating "abstaining from foods, which God has created to be gratefully shared in by those who believe and know the truth" (1 Tim. 4:3–4). Decrees such as "Do not handle, do not taste, do not touch!" were set up by some in the church as obligatory for the practice of a "true spirituality." The Apostle Paul clearly stated that they "have the *appearance* of wisdom in self-made religion and self-abasement and severe treatment of the body, but are of *no value* against fleshly indulgence" (Col. 2:21, 23). In a word, true spirituality is not enhanced by abstaining from God's good creation and those institutions He has ordained for the proper government of the world (e.g., Rom. 13:1–4).

Spirituality is not measured by a withdrawal from the world in any form. Neither is it a sign of spirituality when a Christian has an attitude and philosophy of life that has the same effect on the world as the retreatist actions of Simeon and Antonius. The Christian who claims he is spiritual because he has distanced himself from the world by not getting involved in the reformation process is a spiritual heir of the ineffective "pillar saints." Such practices and attitudes are contrary to the words of Jesus: "Let your light shine before men in such a way that they may see your good works, and glorify your Father in heaven" (Matt. 5:16). The Bible surely tells us that we are not "of the world" (John 17:14), and that we are to "come out from their midst and be separate" (2 Cor. 6:17), but nowhere are we told to retreat from the world, for Jesus has sent us "into the world" (John 17:18). In fact, not being engaged in the world is a sign of judgment:

> Then the sons of Israel did what was evil in the sight of the LORD; and the LORD gave them into the hands of Midian seven years. And the power of Midian prevailed against Israel. Because of Midian the sons of Israel made for themselves the dens which were in the mountains and the caves and the strongholds. . . . Then the angel of the LORD came and sat under the oak that was in Ophrah, which belonged to Joash the Abiezrite as his son Gideon was beating out wheat in the wine press in order to save it from the Midianites (Judges 6:1–2, 11).

Being disengaged from the world, either voluntarily by sitting on a pole, joining a monastery, retreating to the mountains, or hiding from an oppressor as Gideon and David were forced to do (1 Sam. 22:1), is a sign of defeatism and judgment.

True Spirituality

Being "spiritual" does not mean "made up of spirit." "Spirit" is not a ghost-like substance that inhabits the truly "spiritual Christian." The adjective, as in "spiritual man" and "spiritual body," does not mean ethereal, incorporeal, immaterial, otherworldly, or even unworldly as depicted in movies like *The Ghost and Mrs. Muir*, *Ghost*, and *The Sixth Sense*. True spirituality takes form as we live in this world in our own bodies following God's Word in the power of the Holy Spirit:

> To be Spiritual is to be guided and motivated by the Holy Spirit. It means obeying His commands as recorded in the Scriptures. The Spiritual man is not someone who floats in midair and hears eerie voices. The Spiritual man is the man who does what the Bible says (Romans 8:4–8). This means, therefore, that we are supposed to get involved in life. God wants us to apply Christian standards everywhere, in every area. Spirituality does not mean retreat and withdrawal from life.[6]

Spirituality is measured by "good works, which God prepared beforehand, that we should walk in them" (Eph. 2:10). Good works manifest themselves at the personal level as the Christian exhibits the "fruit of the Spirit" (Gal. 5:22–24), at the family level as children obey their parents (Eph. 6:1), at the business level where employers pay a promised wage (Deut. 24:15), at the judicial level where all should be considered equal before the law (Lev. 24:22), and at the civil level where civil governments are paid their due (Matt. 22:21) and do what's right (Rom. 13:4).

We have been redeemed and rescued from the pollution of the world. This does not mean that we are to turn our backs on life. Rather, we are to avoid all participation in the world's uncleanness. "Christians, indeed, as our Lord taught, are the *light of the world*; this they cannot be if their light is hidden or withdrawn. Thus they are to let their light shine before men (Mt. 5:14ff.), though at the same time shunning the depravities of unregenerate society and of unchristian worship."[7]

Inside Out Religion

A prevailing and false understanding of true spirituality is the work of the gospel turned in on itself. To be spiritual, in the modern and corrupt sense, means to *internalize* the effects of the Holy Spirit's regenerating work on the sinner "dead in trespasses and sins" (Eph. 2:1). The weakness of this definition is not that spiritual "renewal starts in the private world, but that *it ends there too*."[8] While there is an internal and spiritual reign of Christ in every believer, there must also be an external expression of that internal faith. This is the Good Samaritan faith where Jesus tells us to "Go and *do* likewise" (Luke 10:37). Jesus does reign in the hearts of His saints. This is a necessary first step:

> The internal, spiritual reign of Christ as Savior and Lord must not be overlooked or minimized in importance. One cannot enter into the kingdom of God apart from spiritual rebirth: "Truly, truly I say unto you, except one be born from above, he cannot see the kingdom of God" (John 3:3). Those who are redeemed have already been transferred into the kingdom of God's beloved Son (Colossians 1:13) and as such appreciate that "the kingdom of God is . . . righteousness and peace and joy in the Holy Spirit" (Romans 14:17).[9]

If the new birth stops with growth on the inside, then it is not true saving faith, just like a light that is hidden under a bushel is not a real light (Matt. 5:14–16). Encouraging someone to be "warmed and filled" is not an expression of true faith (James 2:16). True spirituality is the Christian faith manifested. Jesus exhibited His love for the world in deeds of love and righteousness.

Spiritual Things

As has been pointed out, to be "spiritual" means to be governed by the Holy Spirit in thoughts, words, and deeds. For many, however, spirituality is confined to the individual's personal piety exclusive of any external manifestation that would affect the material world. Biblical language alone mitigates such an interpretation. For example, the devil and his demons are spiritual (non-physical) and evil:

> And I saw coming out of the mouth of the dragon and out of the mouth of the beast and out of the mouth

> of the false prophet, three *unclean spirits* like frogs; for they are *spirits of demons*, performing signs, which go out to the kings of the whole world, to gather them together for the war of the great day of God Almighty. (Rev. 16:13–14).

There are "deceitful spirits" (1 Tim. 4:1), "unclean spirits" (Rev. 18:2), and spirits of "error" (1 John 4:6). There is even "spiritual wickedness" (Eph. 6:12).

On the other hand, Jesus has a body, and He is good, without sin (2 Cor. 5:21). Jesus was raised with a body that could be touched and could eat (John 20:26–29; 21:12–14). Scripture tells us that Jesus shared in "flesh and blood" (Heb. 2:14). Jesus healed physically (Mark 5:29) and also forgave sins (9:5). The test of His true resurrection was its physical nature (John 20:27). He who denies that Jesus Christ has come in the flesh "is the deceiver and the antichrist" (2 John 7; cf. 1 John 4:1–3).

> [Jesus] is today fleshly, earthly, temporal, although [presently] our eyes behold him not. This is the meaning of the Incarnation. The Docetists,[10] embarrassed with the corporeality of the Gospel, attempted to construct a non-material Saviour; later Gnostics[11] argued that only the spiritual (by which they meant the inward, immortal, eternal) aspects of Christ's nature were of saving efficacy.
>
> The early church stoutly rejected this heresy. They defended the fleshly, earthly, and visible aspects of the Messiah. Man beheld his glory (I John 1:4); he was *heard* with human ears and *touched* with human hands (I John 1:1). To be a genuine Christian it was necessary to confess the Messiah had come in the flesh (I John 4:2).[12]

If a person is a Christian, then he or she is animated, made alive, by the Holy Spirit. Being spiritual does not mean that he or she is no longer to be concerned with things related to this world, things we might describe as material. Spirit and matter are not opposites in biblical theology. "Since Greek adjectives ending in *-ikos* [as does the Greek word for 'spiritual'] denote an ethical or dynamic relation, not a material one, *pneumatikos*[13] [spiritual] means 'animated by the spirit' or 'controlled by the spirit.' This 'spirit' refers either to the Holy Spirit or the human spirit as transformed by the divine Spirit."[14]

There is the "Holy Spirit" (e.g., Acts 13:2), a "spirit of truth" (1 John 4:6), "spiritual things" (1 Cor. 9:11), "spiritual food" (10:3), a "spiritual body" (15:44), "spiritual sacrifices" (1 Peter 2:5), "spiritual wisdom and understanding" (Col. 1:9), and "ministering spirits, sent out to render service for the sake of those who will inherit salvation" (Heb. 1:14).

So then, the issue is not spirituality over against non-spirituality. Rather, we must determine whose spirit will be used in determining how we should live *in* the world: The Spirit of God or the spirit of antichrist? This is why John tells us to "test the spirits" (1 John 4:1). Paul admonishes us, "Whether, then, you eat or drink or *whatever you do*, do all to the glory of God" (1 Cor. 10:31).

All areas of life are spiritual, even the realm of politics. "We are so used to thinking of spirituality as withdrawal from the world and human affairs that it is hard to think of it as political. Spirituality is personal and private, we assume, while politics is public. But such a dichotomy drastically diminishes spirituality, construing it as a relationship to God without implications for one's relationship to the surrounding world."[15] Of course, this is what the humanists hope Christians continue to believe as they pursue the realm of politics with a vengeance. "The notion that we can be related to God and not to the world—that we can practice a spirituality that is not political—is in conflict with the Christian understanding of God."[16] God created the realm of politics in the same way that He created the family and church.[17]

The Religion of Secularism

Having dealt with the spiritual side of everything, there is still a worldview that seeks to make absolute the things of this world. A different spirit energizes man without God. This is the religion of humanism called secular*ism*. A "secularist" is someone who "is completely time-bound, totally a child of his age, a creature of history, with no vision of eternity. Unable to see anything in the perspective of eternity, he cannot believe God exists or acts in human affairs."[18] Secularism is the religion of many in our day because they worship the creature rather than the Creator (Rom. 1:25). They make man and this world absolute. There is no God, heaven, or spirit other than the "energy" that resides in man. Man is his own god, and this world is all there is. Whereas Christianity was considered to be the only way to be reconciled with God, the religion of secularism has made the personal God of the Bible irrelevant.

Secularism has replaced God with its own version of the absolute and messianic. It offers a plan of salvation for a lost planet without any regard for anything or anyone greater than man:

> Humanism has become the most messianic of the idolatrous religions of the West. Anthropologist Margaret Mead included in her autobiography a frank acknowledgment that it was a religious belief and called urgently for its spread throughout the world. This is why Milton Friedman described [economist John Kenneth] Galbraith as "a missionary seeking converts." The same urge was behind Erich Fromm's *tour de force*, the transformation of the Old Testament into a defense of radical humanism.[19]

Keeping the dangers of getting involved in this world in mind, let us remember that salvation comes only through the regenerating work of God's Holy Spirit. Nothing in this world can save us. There can be no neutrality here. If the Christian is not involved in the transformation process with the Christian view of spirituality, then be assured that the humanists will be ready with their version. The rise of New Age humanism is one indication that the faltering West is looking for a new spirit to breathe life into the decaying corpse of humanism.[20]

The Privatization of Christianity

The dualism that operated in Germany during Adolf Hitler's rise to power is with us today. There has been "the flight of religion from the world and its realities, a denial of the value of life and a state of detachment and capitulation on the part of religion."[21] The Christian faith is supposedly kept "clean" from the world by not getting involved in the world. The Christian faith, which ought to be recognized as the only life-transforming remedy for our world, is rejected as life's medicine, even by some Christians. The gospel has been reduced to a small compartment within life. Not only is our faith driven back by humanists, but many Christians have forced their faith exclusively into the House of Worship with no exit doors. Even God Himself is privatized. The subject of religion makes many people respond with, "My relationship with God is a private and personal affair." And that's the problem. In her book *Things We Couldn't Say*, Diet Eman describes the following exchange with a Christian just before the invasion of her homeland in the Netherlands by the Nazis:

> Again, a conversation with the doctor. We always come back to the same point: "The church may not mix in politics," he says. And I tell him that when you are a Christian and profess that God is almighty, there is no single area of life from which you can eliminate God.[22]

What effect does an inward, subjective, hyper-spiritualized Christianity have on the world? In May of 2003, the French delegation to the United Nations asserted that the issue of abortion should be based "solely on the basis of public health and not on moral or religious criteria." This is the logical expression of the belief that religion is a private affair that has no impact on the world. Instead of morality, "public health" or "public policy" becomes the new standard. Nazi Germany used the cover of "health" to mask its death policies. The sterilization law—the "Law for the Prevention of Genetically Impaired Progeny"—and the "health in marriage" law of 1935 were used to weed out "undesirable breeders," all for a betterment of Germany:

> These two laws gave the doctors of Germany extraordinary power over the lives of their healthy, law-abiding fellow citizens. This was a power quite beyond the traditional definition of a physician as a man practiced in the art of healing. It is not healing to sterilize a person against his will—it is, in fact, harmful. This is a violation of the Hippocratic Oath.[23]

Abortion in Nazi Germany was allowed "if it was in the interests of racial hygiene,"[24] that is, if it was practiced on non-Aryans to reduce their numbers. This is the secularist religion in action as it supplants the Christian religion's public expression of faith and morality. "Public health" was defined by the Nazis to satisfy the objectives of the Nazi State. If morality is stripped from decision making, then nothing is right or wrong but only convenient and practical.[25] If morality is not anchored in a fixed transcendent standard, then right and wrong are whatever those in power say it is. What's in the best interest of man (humanism) and his time (secularism)? Once again, who defines "best interest"?

Secularism also goes by the name "humanism." Like the secularist, the humanist believes that man and his enterprises are the center of all that is conceived. The benefits must be to man in the here and now without any concern of what man might encounter beyond the grave. There was a time when humanism did not have the negative connotations it carries today. Renaissance humanism emphasized the study of the *humanities*, which included art, music, literature, and culture in general. "As it initially only defined a concern for humanity, many early humanists saw no dichotomy between this and their Christian faith."[26] Gradually humanism has come to mean a naturalistic and materialistic worldview in direct opposition to the Christian worldview. Humanism, like secularism, makes man and his world ultimate. This is why the Bible warns

> against worldliness *wherever* it is found [James 1:27], certainly in the church, and he is emphasizing here precisely the importance of Christian involvement in *social* issues. Regrettably, we tend to read the Scriptures as though their rejection of a "worldly" life-style entails a recommendation of an "otherworldly" one.
>
> This approach has led many Christians to abandon the "secular" realm to the trends and forces of secularism. Indeed, because of their two-realm theory, to a large degree, Christians have themselves to blame for the rapid secularization of the West. If political, industrial, artistic, and journalistic life, to mention only these areas, are branded as essentially "worldly," "secular," "profane," and part of the "natural domain of creaturely life," then is it surprising that Christians have not more effectively stemmed the tide of humanism in our culture?[27]

God created everything wholly good (Gen. 1:31). Man, through the fall, became profane, defiled by sin. Redemption restores both man and creation in Christ. "What God has cleansed, no longer consider unholy" (Acts 10:15; cf. Matt. 15:11; Rom. 14:14, 20). The New Testament in general reinforces the goodness of God's creation: "For everything created by God is good, and nothing is to be rejected, if it is received with gratitude; for it is sanctified by means of the word of God and prayer" (1 Tim. 4:4–5).

Conclusion

The disintegration of culture is the Christian's fault. To blame it on the devil is to justify Eve's words: "The serpent deceived me, and I ate" (Gen. 3:13). The devil did not make us do anything. Of course, God is not to blame. And yet, the way some Christians talk, you would think that God is unable to effect significant change until the devil is out of the way. "I mean, God could do something if He wanted to; so why doesn't He do it?" He has. But too many of us fail to live in the shadow of His finished work. We're still waiting for something else to happen. Who's left to blame? Man and man alone. But what good is man's faith if he hides it under a bushel?

The possibility of the rise of tyranny in a society is in direct proportion to the privatization of the Christian faith and the preoccupation with the irrelevancy of that faith to the larger society. Nazi Germany was no fluke. It can happen again; it can happen here.

Notes

1. Os Guinness, *The Gravedigger File: Papers on the Subversion of the Modern Church* (Downers Grove, IL: InterVarsity Press, 1983), 79.

2. S. M. Houghton, *Sketches from Church History: An Illustrated Account of 20 Centuries of Christ's Power* (Carlisle, PA: The Banner of Truth Trust, 1980), 28.

3. R. B. Kuiper, *"Not of the World": Discourses on the Christian's Relation to the World* (Grand Rapids, MI: Eerdmans, 1929), 27.

4. Houghton, *Sketches from Church History*, 28. Also see Robert J. Morgan, *On This Day: 365 Amazing and Inspiring Stories about Saints, Martyrs, and Heroes* (Nashville: Thomas Nelson, 1997), 5.

5. James M. Houston, "Spiritual Life Today: An Appropriate Spirituality for a Post-Modern World," *The Gospel in the Modern World: A Tribute to John Stott*, eds. Martyn Eden and David F. Wells (Leicester, England: Inter-Varsity Press, 1991), 180.

6. David Chilton, *Paradise Restored: A Biblical Theology of Dominion* (Horn Lake, MS: Dominion Press, [1985] 2007), 3–4.

7. Philip E. Hughes, *Commentary on the Second Epistle to the Corinthians* (NICNT) (Grand Rapids, MI: Eerdmans, 1962), 256.

8. Guinness, *The Gravedigger File*, 78.

9. Greg L. Bahnsen, "This World and the Kingdom of God," in Gary DeMar and Peter Leithart, *The Reduction of Christianity: A Biblical Response to Dave Hunt* (Ft. Worth, TX: Dominion Press, 1988), 351.

10. "Docetism was an ancient heresy that carried Gnostic themes into the Christian church. The specific error of Docetists was to believe that, since the material world by its nature was hopelessly polluted, Jesus only 'seemed' (=*doke* in Greek) to have a real body, to suffer hunger and thirst, to touch the sick, and to suffer as a human being on the cross. Evangelicals indulge a docetic tendency when we think, without qualification, that since 'this world is not my home,' it is of no importance to learn about the world, the structures of human society, and the potential of human creativity." (Mark A. Noll, *The Scandal of the Evangelical Mind* [Grand Rapids, MI: Eerdmans, 1994], 54).

11. "*Gnosticism* refers to a whole range of mystical religions that were practiced widely in the Mediterranean world shortly after the time of Christ. Gnostics differed dramatically among themselves in their beliefs and practices, but they held in common a fear of matter as inherently evil and a tendency toward ethical extremism (either ardent asceticism or wanton licentiousness). They were called Gnostics (=people of special knowledge) because they practiced secret rituals where the supposedly most important knowledge about God and the world was passed along in esoteric formulas from adept to initiate." (Noll, *Scandal of the Evangelical Mind*, 52).

12. P. Richard Flinn, "Baptism, Redemptive History, and Eschatology: The Parameters of Debate," *Christianity and Civilization: The Failure of the American Baptist Culture*, ed. James B. Jordan (Spring 1982), 144–145.

13. The English words pneumonia and pneumatic (pneumatic hammer, pneumatic drill, etc.) are derived from the Greek word *pneuma*, spirit, breath, or air. Bicycle tires that were inflated with air were called "pneumatic tires." See Webb Garrison, *How It Started* (Nashville, TN: Abingdon Press, 1972), 66.

14. Murray J. Harris, *From Grave to Glory: Resurrection in the New Testament* (Grand Rapids, MI: Zondervan, 1990), 402.

15. Glenn Tinder, "Can We Be Good Without God?," *The Atlantic Monthly* (December 1989), 69. This theme is more fully developed in Tinder's *The Political Meaning of Christianity: The Prophetic Stance* (San Francisco: HarperCollins Publishers, 1991).

16. Tinder, "Can We Be Good Without God?," 69.

17. Gary DeMar, *God and Government*, 3 vols. (Powder Springs, GA: American Vision, 1982–1986).

18. James Hitchcock, *What is Secular Humanism?* (Ann Arbor, MI: Servant Publications, 1982), 10–11. Also see R. C. Sproul, *The Consequences of Ideas: Understanding the Concepts that Shaped Our World* (Wheaton, IL: Crossway Books, 2000), 148.

19. Herbert Schlossberg, *Idols for Destruction: Christian Faith and Its Confrontation with American Society* (Wheaton, IL: Crossway Books, [1983] 1993), 273.

20. Gary DeMar, *Thinking Straight in a Crooked World: A Christian Defense Manual* (Powder Springs, GA: American Vision, 2001), 137–198.

21. Dayan I. Grunfeld, "Religion, Law and Life: An Historical Vindication of the Horeb," in Samson Raphael Hirsch, *Horeb: A Philosophy of Jewish Law and Observances*, trans. Dayan I. Grunfeld (New York: Soncino, 1962), cxxxii-cxxxiii.

22. Diet Eman with James Schaap, *Things We Couldn't Say* (Grand Rapids, MI: Eerdmans, 1999), prologue.

23. Hugh Gregory Gallagher, *By Trust Betrayed: Patients, Physicians, and the License to Kill in the Third Reich*, rev. ed. (Arlington, VA: Vandamere Press, 1995), 151.

24. Robert N. Proctor, *Racial Hygiene: Medicine Under the Nazis* (Cambridge, MA: Harvard University Press, 1988), 122.

25. Michelle Hiskey, "Image or morality? Image wins," *Atlanta Journal-Constitution* (May 21, 2003), C2.

26. Os Guinness, *The Dust of Death: The Sixties Counter Culture and How It Changed America Forever*, rev. ed. (Wheaton, IL: Crossway Books, 1994), 20.

27. Albert M. Wolters, *Creation Regained: Biblical Basics for a Reformational Worldview* (Grand Rapids, MI: Eerdmans, 1985), 54.

3

"The Bible is Only Concerned with Salvation"

Myth, Lie, or Half-Truth?: *The concern of Christians is to bring people to Christ. We should not waste time applying the Bible to secular things like education, economics, and politics.*

"The Gospel ... is not confined to a repentance and faith that have no connection with social or civil duties. The Evangel of Christ is an all-embracing theme. It is the vital force in earth and in heaven... The Cross is the centre of the spiritual, and therefore of the material universe." The divine touchstone before which "literature, science, politics, business, the status of society, all charities, all reforms" must be brought to test.[1]

A New York judge used the Bible to determine the amount of bail a former Episcopal church treasurer should pay for embezzling $267,000 from his congregation. Judge Robert Meehan set bail at $534,000, "pointing out that the sum was $2.00 for every $1.00 he allegedly stole. The judge said he chose the bail figure because 'it has a religious message, that if you steal you have to pay back two-fold' [Ex. 22:4, 7]."[2] There were no prisons in Israel. Restitution covered all property crimes. The thief was punished with multiple restitution, and the victim got his property back with an increase.

Contrast the action of Judge Meehan with that of Judge John Vigil who ordered a new sentencing hearing for Robert Harlan who had been convicted of kidnapping, rape, and murder. In the sentencing phase, the jurors had made reference to the Bible during their deliberations about whether to impose the death penalty on Harlan. The judge said this was inappropriate.[3] Bob Grant, who prosecuted the case in 1995, said, "The Bible is part of people's lives. We can't prohibit them from saying 'an eye for an eye' because that is the way they were brought up."[4] Of course, being brought up a certain way does not mean something is morally right. There must be a foundation for why something is right or wrong. What is the foundational moral standard?

If Harlan's death sentence was thrown out because the jurors consulted the principles of the Bible to determine punishment, then why not throw out the conviction as well since the prohibitions against kidnapping, rape, and murder are also found in the Bible. Charles Colson, president of Prison Fellowship, has been calling for the contemporary application of the Bible for prison reform.

> Recently I addressed the Texas legislature.... I told them that the only answer to the crime problem is to take nonviolent criminals out of our prisons and make them pay back their victims with restitution. This is how we can solve the prison crowding problem.
>
> The amazing thing was that afterwards they came up to me one after another and said things like, "That's a tremendous idea. Why hasn't anyone thought of that?" I had the privilege of saying to them, "Read Exodus 22. It is only what God said to Moses on Mount Sinai thousands of years ago."[5]

As these examples demonstrate, there is more to the Bible than being saved and receiving eternal salvation through Jesus' atoning death. While this is the Bible's starting-point message, it is not the end-point. The time should come when every new Christian moves from the milk stage of salvation to the meat stage; from being a student to becoming a teacher (Heb. 5:11–14). Without the Bible as the starting point, morality makes no sense. There is no justification to be moral in a world where life evolved from material elements that neither know nor care about what's moral or immoral.

New Heart–New Life.

In applying all the Bible to all of life, those "dead in trespasses and sins" (Eph. 2:1) must have a "new heart" and a "new spirit" so they can rightly understand God's Word and the world He created for our use (1 Cor. 1:18–25). The "heart of stone" must be removed and replaced with a "heart of flesh," that is, a heart and mind open to God speaking through His Word. This is God's work. God's Spirit must be in us before we can "walk in" His "statutes." The result will be that we "will be careful to observe" His "ordinances" (Ezek. 36:26–27). The New Testament summarizes it this way: "If any man is in Christ, he is a new creature; the old things passed away; behold, new things have come" (2 Cor. 5:17). All of this requires a belief in the sovereign work of God. Only God can make dead men live (John 11:25–26).

In a similar way, only God can bring a dead culture back to life. Cultural "resurrections" are made possible when people are "resurrected" (Eph. 2:6) and then apply their new faith to all of life. "New creatures" (2 Cor. 5:17) mean new societies. Noted scholar and author Rousas J. Rushdoony summarizes it this way:

> The key to remedying the [modern] situation is *not* revolution, nor any kind of resistance that works to subvert law and order. The New Testament abounds in warnings against disobedience and in summons to peace.

> *The key is regeneration, propagation of the gospel, and the conversion of men and nations to God's law-word.*[6]

* * * * *

Clearly, there is no hope for man except in regeneration.[7]

Politics, a conservative economic policy, and other social-oriented agendas are not in and of themselves the answer to man's sinful condition. Because we are sinners, we cannot make proper evaluations of how we ought to live in the world until we have a new heart that guides a new mind. But once this happens, God's Word in all its fullness begins to make sense. We learn to love God's law (Psalm 119:47, 97, 113, 127, 159), because it is "a lamp to [our] feet, and a light to [our] path" (119:105; Prov. 6:23) so that we can shine it on a world that shows the effects of sin.

New Life–New Lifestyle

Zacchaeus not only found Jesus, he also found a new lifestyle. He restored what he had unlawfully taken from others (Luke 19:8; cf. Ex. 22:1; Lev. 6:5; Num. 5:7; 2 Sam. 12:6). His *personal* regeneration had an impact on society. Zacchaeus had used his office as a tax collector and the power of the Roman civil government to line his pockets at the expense of others (Luke 19:1). The encounter with Zacchaeus shows that Jesus' public ministry was the perfect mixture of evangelism and personal and social concern. Jesus went about teaching and preaching (Matt. 4:23; 9:35) and doing good and healing (Acts 10:38). These are examples of Christianity in action in this world this side of heaven.

Similarly, "John the Baptist told tax-gatherers and soldiers not to use their positions to extort money (Luke 3:12–14). When Paul had the opportunity to speak with Felix he talked about 'righteousness, self-control and the judgment to come' (Acts 24:25). James warned the rich of the judgment that must come to those who had defrauded a workman of his wages (James 5:1–6)."[8] The rich were not condemned for being rich but for using their wealth to oppress others.

The first efforts of the early church were to minister to the worldly needs of its members. The gospel included works of mercy, works that had an impact on seemingly mundane issues like seeing that widows were not "being overlooked in the daily serving of food" (Acts 6:1). In our modern welfare-state economy, those least able to care for themselves are most often turned over to government agencies for assistance and made dependents of the State so their last state has become worse than their first (Luke 11:26).

Supposedly these types of "worldly" concerns are the sole province of civil government. This view, however, is not the view of the early church (1 Tim. 5:3). James writes that "pure and undefiled religion" consists of visiting "orphans and widows in their distress" (James 1:27). In the same verse, he exhorts Christians to keep "unstained by the world." Therefore, it cannot be considered "worldly" to be involved in activities that are not solely evangelistic. On the other hand, works of mercy often lead to evangelistic opportunities: "Let your light shine before men in such a way that they may see your good works, and glorify your Father who is in heaven" (Matt. 5:16; cf. James 2:16).

The apostle Paul makes a similar application concerning what a new creature in Christ is to do: "Let him who steals steal no longer; but rather let him labor, performing with his own hands what is good, in order that he may have something to share with him who is in need" (Eph. 4:28). In another place, Paul exhorts Christians to settle disputes by using law courts within the church: "Does any one of you, when he has a case against his neighbor, dare to go to law before the unrighteous, and not before the saints?" (1 Cor. 6:1–11).

Worldview Christianity

The church has a long history of applying all the Bible to all of life. "Throughout American history, the moral principles of Judeo-Christian ethics have been used as one of many effective tools to evaluate and reform a wide variety of social structures, and have continued to be invoked in political debates."[9] This perspective is best exemplified in the life and work of the Puritans who applied the Bible to their vocation, marriage, economics, family, education, politics, social ethics, social action, as well as personal piety, devotion, worship, and theological study, "*a movement in which the Bible was central to everything.*"[10]

America's earliest founders demonstrated their belief in a comprehensive biblical worldview in the educational institutions they established. Harvard College, founded in 1636, had as its goal the following:

> Let every student be plainly instructed, and earnestly pressed to consider well, the main end of his life and studies is, to know God and Jesus Christ which is eternal life (John 17:3) and therefore lay Christ at the bottom, as the only foundation of *all sound knowledge and learning.*

Yale College demanded the same rigorous academic education as Harvard with the Bible as the unshakable and unassailable foundation of knowledge:

> "All scholars shall live religious, godly, and blameless lives according to the rules of God's Word, diligently reading the Holy Scriptures, the fountain of light and truth; and constantly attend upon all the duties of religion, both in public and secret."

There was no true knowledge unless a student compared what he had learned in the world around him to the testimony of Scripture. These early Christian educators were following the instructions laid down in the Bible about loving God with the mind (Matt. 22:37; Deut. 6:1–9; Rom. 12:1–2).

The Bible was the interpretive grid used to study the world and unravel its mysteries. Knowing that God created the world led these Christian students of His creation to believe that they lived in a reasonable and orderly universe. "Christ knew Hebrew and used logical consequences," Samuel Rutherford (*c.* 1660–1661) argued. "Paul quoted the heathen poets, 'in the books of Moses, are secrets of Physick[s], Samuel and Kings introduced man to 'sacred politicks,' and Job taught astronomy. 'The naturall sinlesse knowledge of sciences, arts, tongues [languages]' was, therefore, the candlelight by which Christians studied the Bible."[11] Once elements of the created order, whether studied by Christians or non-Christians, were viewed through the lens of a Christian worldview, all began to make sense.

An example of a Christian who worked to apply the Bible beyond the narrow confines of Christian piety was Cotton Mather (1663–1728). In fact, Mather saw the development of scientific discovery as an outgrowth of his biblical studies. He received his M.A. from Harvard at age 18 and joined his father in his Boston pastorate. He was widely regarded as the most brilliant man in New England. He wrote nearly 500 books and was a Fellow of the Royal Society, a scientific association founded in England in 1660. Scientist as well as pastor, he successfully introduced smallpox inoculation during the 1721 epidemic. Mather "did not share the medieval belief that this world does not matter."[12] For Mather and others like him, having a worldview that had God and the Bible at its center was the only way a person could make sense of the world.

A History of Worldview Christianity

The history of Western civilization is the history of the development and implementation of the Bible to all of life. While a book like James A. Haught's *2000 Years of Disbelief*[13] tries to counter this assertion by claiming that for two millennia no one of any significance believed the truths of the Christian religion, especially in the realm of science, the facts of history demonstrate that *Christian* scientists, explorers, philosophers, artists, inventors, and writers have dominated their fields. Rodney Stark argues there is "no inherent conflict between religion and science" and

"*Christian theology was essential for the rise of science.*" After a thorough study of the Scholastic period, he shows "that the leading scientific figures in the sixteenth and seventeenth centuries overwhelmingly were devout Christians who believed it their duty to comprehend God's handiwork."[14]

Haught makes no mention of Bible-believing scientists Lord Kelvin, Joseph Lister, Johann Kepler, Robert Boyle, and Gregor Mendel; patriot and governor of Virginia Patrick Henry; congressman and author Elias Boudinot whose book *The Age of Revelation* was a direct refutation of Thomas Paine's anti-Christian work *The Age of Reason*; artist and inventor Samuel F. B. Morse who, on May 24, 1844, chose the Bible verse "What hath God wrought?" (Num. 23:23) as the first telegraphic message transmitted over a long distance; airplane inventors Wilbur and Orville Wright;[15] Supreme Court Justice David Brewer who found America to be a "Christian nation"[16] based on his thorough study of the historical record; scholar, Christian apologist, social commentator, and fiction writer C. S. Lewis; social reformer and anti-slavery advocate William Wilberforce[17]; lexicographer Noah Webster, developer of America's first comprehensive dictionary, *An American Dictionary of the English Language* (1828).[18] In addition to Christian scientists, there were people Like Louis Pasteur who believed in God and could not think of studying this world without some knowledge of Him.

In the book *1,000 Years, 1000 People: Ranking the Men and Women Who Shaped the Millennium,*[19] we find a picture quite different from the one painted by Haught. Of the first ten entries, six of the rankings were Christians. Johannes Gutenberg (1394?–1468), inventor of the printing press, is first on the list. The first book that came off his press was the Latin version of the Bible. Christopher Columbus (1451–1506) fills the number two spot. It was Columbus who saw in the Bible a directive to take the gospel—"the Holy Christian Faith"—around the world.[20] He is followed by Martin Luther (1483–1546) who set the Protestant Reformation in motion and whose translation of the Bible into German brought uniformity to the German language. Following him is Galileo Galilei (1564–1642) who systematically attacked the church's reliance on Aristotle's cosmology over against the Bible and changed the way we view the cosmos.[21] Isaac Newton (1642–1727), in addition to his scientific discoveries and laying the foundations for differential and integral calculus, wrote numerous works on Christian theology.[22] One of his most noted works is *Observations Upon Prophecies of Daniel, and the Apocalypse of St. John*, published six years after his death. He is ranked sixth on the list.

> He read the Bible daily throughout his life and wrote over a million words of notes regarding his study of it. Isaac Newton believed the Bible is literally true in every respect. Throughout his life, he continually tested Biblical truth against the physical truths of experimental and theoretical science. He never observed a contradiction. In fact, he viewed his own scientific work as a method by which to reinforce belief in Biblical truth.[23]

Thomas Aquinas (1225–1274), who wrote extensively on the proofs for God's existence, is ranked eighth. He argued that the mind, using reason to think through the reality of God's existence (Isa. 1:18), is a gift given to us by God. It's an attribute that separates us from the animal creation.

We know very little about William Shakespeare's religious views or much else. He is fifth on the list. We do know that he was a member of the Church of England where he and his children were baptized.[24] While Peter J. Leithart correctly notes that there is a "deeply Christian worldview embodied in his plays,"[25] and Louise Cowan maintains that "his perspective was not simply spiritual, but overtly Christian,"[26] we must be careful not to read Shakespeare as a symbolic literary course on the Bible. Even so, "it is seen that Shakespeare drank so deeply from the wells of Scripture that one may say, without any straining of the evidence, without the Bible Shakespeare could not be."[27]

Like Shakespeare, little is known of the specifics of Leonardo da Vinci's religious commitment. We do know, however, that his most memorable art subjects came from the Bible (*Adoration of the Magi, The Baptism of Christ, The Last Supper, The Resurrection of Christ*). Leonardo, ninth on the list, also applied his talents to mathematics, music, anatomy, botany, and engineering. He was the epitome of what it meant to be a Renaissance Man.

Ludwig von Beethoven, who holds the tenth spot, was a Roman Catholic who mistrusted the clergy. While little is known of his religious convictions, "many of his musical works reveal definite Christian imprints. These are plainly evident in *Missa Solemnis* [Solemn Mass] and in *Christ on the Mount of Olives* as well as in other religious compositions."[28]

As these and many other historical examples will show, western civilization cannot be explained without reference to a biblical worldview.

> Modern biographers of scientists seem oblivious to the fact that up to the end of the eighteenth century "most intelligent men, and thus most scientists, held that divine revelation could tell them what had happened in the beginning, how the Creator had so to speak, set the stage of the world which their science was now newly investigating.[29]

Charles Darwin, seventh on the *1,000 Years, 1000 People* list, is the exception that proves the rule. Darwin's radically new secular worldview was a bold attack against what was a prevailing Christian view of origins.[30] Charles Hodge (1797–1878), a theology professor at Princeton Theological Seminary, was the first Christian scholar of distinction to write a comprehensive assessment of Darwinism. In his book *What is Darwinism?*, Hodge concluded simply—"It is atheism." He did not mean by this that "all who adopt [Darwin's] views are atheists; but it means that his theory is atheistic, that the exclusion of design from nature is . . . tantamount to atheism."[31] At the time, few people saw the radical implications of evolution as they are now manifested in education, politics, morality, and science. Many believed then that Darwin's theories could be reconciled with the Bible. Today's prominent evolutionists seek no such reconciliation. They revel in their atheism. Richard Dawkins writes that "Darwin made it possible to be an intellectually fulfilled atheist."[31]

The Bible and All of Life

Henry Morris explains in his book *The Biblical Basis for Modern Science*, that the Bible's approach to worldview issues is comprehensive and includes science, technology, the humanities, commerce, law, civil government, and education, in short, every facet of human culture. As we have seen, there is nothing new in this perspective. It was assumed by most well-read Christians that the Bible applied to all of life:

> [L]ong before [the Great Commission] another great commission was given to all men, whether saved or unsaved, merely by virtue of being men created by God in His image. It also had worldwide scope, and has never been rescinded. It had to do with implementing God's purpose in His work of creation, just as Christ's commission was for implementing His work of salvation and reconciliation.[32]

Morris says that the command to subdue the earth means "bringing all earth's systems and processes into a state of optimum productivity and utility, offering the greatest glory to God and benefit to mankind."[33]

In his introduction to Carl Henry's influential work *The Uneasy Conscience of Modern Fundamentalism*, Harold J. Ockenga expresses a similar emphasis based on Jesus' words that make up the Great Commission:

> A Christian world- and life-view embracing world questions, societal needs, personal education ought to rise out of Matt. 28:18–21 as much as evangelism does. Culture depends on such a view, and Fundamentalism is prodigally dissipating the Christian culture accretion of centuries, a serious sin. A sorry answer lies in the abandonment of social fields to the secularist.[34]

Dominion is an "inescapable concept." Dominion will be exercised by someone, some group, some religion, or some political system. The question is: "What standard will be used to "take dominion"? Rushdoony writes: "Dominion does not disappear when a man renounces it; it is simply transferred to another person, perhaps to his wife, children, employer, or the state. Where the individual surrenders his due dominion, where the family abdicates it, and the worker and employer reduce it, there another party, usually the state, concentrates dominion. Where organized society surrenders power, the mob gains it proportionate to the surrender."[35]

The following list of topics will show that the Bible is more than a book on how we can get to heaven (although it is that). God's Word has much to say about all of life.

The Bible and the Family

- Marriage between a man and a woman (Gen. 1:27–28; Matt. 19:3–12; 1 Cor. 7:2)
- Parental authority (Eph. 6:1–4)
- Inheritance (Prov. 13:22)
- Discipline (Prov. 13:24)
- Education (Deut. 6:1–9; Prov. 22:6)
- Charity (1 Tim. 5:8)
- Care for the aged (1 Tim. 5:3–13)

- Care for orphans and widows (Deut. 14:29; James 1:27)
- Leadership (1 Tim. 3:1–7)

The Bible and Economics

- Debt (Prov. 3:27–28; Rom. 13:8)
- Borrowing (Ex. 22:25; Psalm 37:21; 22:7; Isa. 24:2)
- Lending (Ex. 22:25; Deut. 15:6; Psalm 37:26)
- Interest (Deut. 23:19–20; Prov. 22:26–27)
- Inflation (Prov. 25:4–5; Isa. 1:22–26; Ezek. 22:18–22)
- Helping the needy (Lev. 25:35–37; Deut. 15:7–11; 24:14–15)
- Inheritance (Psalm 17:13–15; Prov. 13:22; 19:14; 20:21)
- Work (Gen. 2:15; 3:19; Ex. 20:8–11; Prov. 10:5; Ecc. 3:13; Acts 16:14; Eph. 4:28; 2 Thess. 3:10–12)
- Wages (Deut. 24:14–15; Jer. 22:13; Luke 10:7; 1 Cor. 9:7–12; 1 Tim. 5:18)
- Employee/employer relations (Lev. 25:53; Prov. 6:6–9; 10:4; 27:18; 28:19)
- Savings (Prov. 6:6–8; 21:20; 28:20; 1 Tim. 6:9)
- Fraud (Eph. 4:28; 1 Thess. 4:6)
- Investments (Psalm 112:5)

The Bible and Civil Government

- Civil authority (Matt. 22:15–22; Rom. 13:1–4; 1 Peter 2:13–17)
- Citizenship (Lev. 24:22; Num. 15:22–30; Acts 22:22–29)
- Bribery (Ex. 23:8; Deut. 10:17; 16:19–20)
- Taxation (1 Sam. 8; Prov. 27:18; Matt. 22:17–21; Luke 3:12–13; Rom. 13:7)
- Military (Num. 1:2–3; 26:2; 31:3–7; Deut. 20:5–8)
- National defense (2 Chron. 26:6–15)
- Civil loyalties (Acts 5:29)
- Ministerial aspect (Rom. 13:4)

The Bible and Law

- Judicial system (Ex. 18; 1 Cor. 6:1–11)
- Laws regarding perverting and obstructing justice (Ex. 23:1–2, 6; Lev. 19:15; Deut. 16:19–20)
- Perjury (Ex. 20:16; Lev. 19:12; Deut. 19:16–20; 1 Tim. 1:10)
- Murder (Ex. 20:13; 21:12)
- Assault (Ex. 21:18–27; Lev. 24:19–20)
- Kidnapping (Ex. 21:16; Deut. 24:7)
- Slander (Lev. 19:16)
- Stealing (Ex. 20:15; 22:1–12)
- Arson (Ex. 22:6)
- Property violations (Deut. 19:14; 1 Kings 21)
- Damages (Lev. 6:1–5; 24:19–20; Ex. 22:4–6)
- Restitution (Ex. 21:18–19, 22–23, 28–30, 32; 22:1–8; Luke 19:8; Eph. 4:28)
- Just weights and measures (Lev. 19:36)

The Bible and Moral Issues

- Abortion (Ex. 21:22–25)
- Homosexuality (Ex. 22:19; Lev. 18:22; 20:13–16; Deut. 23:17; 1 Cor. 6:9; 1 Tim. 1:10)
- Slavery (Ex. 21:16; 1 Tim. 1:10; Rev. 18:13)
- Rape (Deut. 22:25–29)
- Prostitution (Deut. 23:17)
- Incest (Lev. 18:6–18; Deut. 22:30)
- Adultery (Ex. 20:14; Lev. 20:10; Deut. 5:18; 22:22–25)
- Bestiality (Ex. 22:19; Lev. 18:23)

In addition, there are biblical principles related to sanitation (Deut. 23:13), education (Deut. 6:4–9), the environment (Deut. 20:19–20), building safety (Deut. 22:8), and many other worldview categories. If Christians refuse to leaven these areas with the life-transforming work of the gospel, then the world will be leavened with the "leaven of the Pharisees and the leaven of Herod" (Mark 8:15). When the

Word of God is rejected as the standard for godly living in this world, a substitute standard fills the void. The leaven of the Pharisees substitutes the law of God with man-made traditions: Jesus "was saying to them, 'You nicely set aside the commandment of God in order to keep your tradition'" (Mark 7:9). The leaven of Herod places the State over the will of God: "These men who have upset the world have come here also; . . . they all act contrary to the decrees of Caesar, saying that there is another king, Jesus" (Acts 17:7).

In addition to secularism, the world must contend with the leaven of Islam again. Consider that the average age of a convert to Christianity is sixteen, while the average age of a convert to Islam is thirty-one! Why the difference? One of the main reasons for the disparity is the way that Christianity and Islam present their worldview. The older a person gets, the more responsibilities he or she has. For centuries, the church addressed the areas of law, education, and politics, to name only a few fields of concern. Christianity was very much a "this-world religion" as well as being the only way to heaven. Sadly, heaven seems to be the only concern of Christians. Islam, as a rival faith, has supplanted Christianity in the vital area of a this-world application of its understanding of God's word, although in a deeply distorted way:

> Islam is practical. It is considered a this-worldly religion in contrast to Christianity, which is perceived as abstract in the extreme. Muhammad left his followers a political, social, moral, and economic program founded on religious precepts. Jesus, however, is said to have advocated no such program; it is claimed that the New Testament is so preoccupied with his imminent return that it is impractical for modern life.[36]

The renewed advance of Islam can be tied to much of the church's refusal to believe that the public arena is a place of ministry and that God's Word applies to issues beyond personal salvation. For the most part, Christians have failed to be advocates of righteousness in areas beyond personal and familial piety. There has been a steady erosion among evangelicals and fundamentalists over the adoption of a comprehensive biblical worldview. In a December 2003 survey study, the Barna Research Group found that "half of the country's Protestant pastors—51 percent—don't have a 'biblical worldview.'" In addition, "although most people own a Bible and know some of its content, . . . most Americans have little idea how to integrate core biblical principles to form a unified and meaningful response to the challenges and opportunities of life." If a majority of pastors don't believe the Bible applies to all of life, then it's reasonable to assume that the majority of Christians who attend church rarely if ever hear a biblical message that shows a contemporary application of the Bible to all of life.

Our nation was founded on the belief that religion, specifically the Christian religion, undergirds a society. "In the last resort, our civilization is what we think and believe. The externals matter, but they cannot stand if the inner convictions which originally produced them have vanished."[37]

Conclusion

The type of world we live in will only be as good as the people who create it. Family, church, and civil governments reflect self-government, whether good or bad. For example, at the civil level, a nation gets what it votes for. Civil government, no matter how righteously conceived, cannot make people better. Leadership, like water, rises to its own level, the righteousness of the people. The maintenance of good government is dependent on good people who are guided by the Word of God.

A good society comes about through the preaching of the gospel which results in changed hearts and lives. We get good deeds from good people who are willing to apply God's Word to every area of life. We are commanded to show our good works so those without Christ can glorify our God who is in heaven

(Matt. 5:16). If our Christian faith remains solely a private affair, then it is good for nothing, only to be trampled under foot by unbelievers (5:13).

Notes

1. Gilbert Haven, *National Sermons. Sermons, Speeches and Letters on Slavery and Its War. . .* (Boston, 1869), 342–344. Quoted in Timothy L. Smith, *Revivalism and Social Reform in Mid-19th Century America* (Nashville, TN: Abingdon Press, 1957), 36.

2. Edward E. Plowman, ed., *National & International Religion Report* (July 2, 1990), 4.

3. Also see Jean Torkelson, "Case spotlights moral convictions in jury room," *Rocky Mountain News* (May 5, 2003).

4. Associated Press (May 17, 2003). Published in the *Denver Post.*

5. Charles Colson, "The Kingdom of God and Human Kingdoms," *Transforming Our World: A Call to Action*, ed. James M. Boice (Portland, OR: Multnomah, 1988), 154–155.

6. Rousas J. Rushdoony, *The Institutes of Biblical Law* (Phillipsburg, NJ: Presbyterian and Reformed, 1973), 113.

7. Rushdoony, *Institutes of Biblical Law*, 449.

8. Noel Weeks, *The Sufficiency of Scripture* (Carlisle, PA: The Banner of Truth Trust, 1988), 252.

9. Susan Pace Hamill, "An Argument for Tax Reform Based on Judeo-Christian Ethics," *Alabama Law Review* 54:1 (Fall 2002), 3–4. I do not agree with all of Hamill's conclusions or applications of a Judeo-Christian ethic, but her underlying historic claims are correct.

10. Leland Ryken, *Worldly Saints: The Puritans As They Really Were* (Grand Rapids, MI: Zondervan/Academie, 1986), 13.

11. John Coffey, *Politics, Religion and the British Revolutions: The Mind of Samuel Rutherford* (Cambridge, United Kingdom: Cambridge University Press, 1997), 79.

12. Gordon W. Jones, "Introduction," Cotton Mather, *The Angel of Bethesda: An Essay Upon the Common Maladies of Mankind* (Barre, MA: Barre Publishers, [1724] 1972), xi.

13. James A. Haught, *2000 Years of Disbelief: Famous People with the Courage to Doubt* (Amherst, NY: Prometheus Books, 1996).

14. Rodney Stark, *For the Glory of God: How Monotheism Led to Reformations, Science, Witch-Hunts, and the End of Slavery* (Princeton, NJ: Princeton University Press, 2003), 123. See the "Roster of Scientific Stars" on pages 198–199. Also see, George Mulfinger and Julia Mulfinger Orozco, *Christian Men of Science: Eleven Men Who Changed the World* (Greenville, SC: Ambassador Emerald International, 2001).

15. After a successful demonstration of flight while in France, Wilbur was asked if he would fly the machine the next day. "Wilbur told him no. Tomorrow was a Sunday and he would not break the Sabbath." (Barry Combs, with Martin

Caidin, *Kill Devil Hill: Discovering the Secret of the Wright Brothers* [Boston: Houghton Mifflin Co., 1979], 281).

16. David J. Brewer, *The United States: A Christian Nation* (Philadelphia, PA: John D. Winston, 1905). Reprinted by American Vision (Powder Springs, Georgia) in 1996.

17. John Pollock, *Wilberforce* (Belleville, MI: Lion Publishing Co., 1977); Kevin Belmonte, *Hero for Humanity: A Biography of William Wilberforce* (Colorado Springs, CO: NavPress, 2002); Kevin Belmonte, *A Journey Through the Life of William Wilberforce* (Green Forest, AR: New Leaf Press, 2007); Ted Baehr, Susan Wales, and Ken Wales, *The Amazing Grace of Freedom: The Inspiring Faith of William Wilberforce* (Green Forest, AR: New Leaf Press, 2007).

18. Harlow Giles Unger, *The Life and Times of Noah Webster: An American Portrait* (New York: John Wiley & Sons, 1998).

19. Agnes Hooper Gottlieb, Henry Gottlieb, Barbara Bowers, and Brent Bowers, *1,000 Years, 1000 People: Ranking the Men and Women Who Shaped the Millennium* (New York: Kodansha International, 1998).

20. Christopher Columbus, "The Log of Christopher Columbus," in *The Log of Christopher Columbus*, trans. Robert H. Fuson (Camden, ME: International Marine Publishing Co., 1987), 51. Historians still teach that Columbus wanted to prove that the world was round in an age when the best scholars, mostly trained by the church, believed it was flat. No one in Columbus' day believed the earth was flat, but there was disagreement on how big around the earth was. On the flat-earth myth, see Stark, *For the Glory of God*, 121–122; Jeffrey Burton Russell, *Inventing the Flat Earth: Columbus and Modern Historians*; Gary DeMar and Fred Young, *A New World in View* (Powder Springs, GA: American Vision, 1996), chap. 8; Gary DeMar, *America's Christian History: The Untold Story*, 2nd ed. (Powder Springs, GA: American Vision, 1997), appendix C; Richard E. Rubenstein, *Aristotle's Children: How Christians, Muslims, and Jews Rediscovered Ancient Wisdom and Illuminated the Dark Ages* (Orlando, FL: Harcourt, Inc., 2003), 271–272. Even Christians have been duped by historical mythology about a flat earth: "When Christopher Columbus set out to prove that the earth is round, many rejected the idea as ludicrous, despite a wealth of evidence that he was right." (Joe Boot, *Searching for Truth: Discovering the Meaning and Purpose of Life* [Wheaton, IL: Crossway Books, 2003], 25).

21. Nancy R. Pearcey and Charles B. Thaxton, *The Soul of Science: Christian Faith and Natural Philosophy* (Wheaton, IL: Crossway Books, 1994), 38–39 and Philip J. Sampson, *6 Modern Myths About Christianity and Western Civilization* (Downers Grove, IL: InterVarsity Press, 2001), chap. 1.

22. Stark, *For the Glory of God*, 167–172.

23. Arthur B. Robinson, "Introduction," in Isaac Newton, *Observations Upon Prophecies of Daniel, and the Apocalypse of St. John* (Cave Junction, OR: Oregon Institute of Science and Medicine, [1733] 1991), viii–ix.

24. Ronald Mushat Frye, *Shakespeare and Christian Doctrine* (Princeton, NJ: Princeton University Press, 1963), 3.

25. Peter J. Leithart, *Brightest Heaven of Invention: A Christian Guide to Six Shakespeare Plays* (Moscow, ID: Canon Press, 1996), 7.

26. Louise Cowan, "The Importance of the Classics," in Louise Cowan and

Os Guinness, eds., *Invitation to the Classics: A Guide to Books You've Always Wanted to Read* (Grand Rapids, MI: Baker Books, 1998), 19.

27. William Burgess, *The Bible in Shakespeare: A Study of the Relation of the Works of William Shakespeare to the Bible* (Chicago, IL: The Winona Publishing Co., 1903), xiii.

28. Alvin J. Schmidt, *Under the Influence: How Christianity Transformed Civilization* (Grand Rapids, MI: Zondervan, 2001), 329.

29. Schmidt, *Under the Influence*, 243.

30. Charles Hodge, *What is Darwinism? And Other Writings on Science and Religion*, eds. Mark A. Knoll and David N. Livingstone (Grand Rapids, MI: Baker, 1994).

31. Richard Dawkins, *The Blind Watchmaker: Why the Evidence of Evolution Reveals a Universe Without Design* (New York: W.W. Norton & Co., 1986), 6. For an assessment of the weaknesses of modern-day evolutionary theory, see Michael J. Behe, *Darwin's Black Box: The Biochemical Challenge to Evolution* (New York: The Free Press, 1996) and Thomas Woodward, *Doubts About Darwin: A History of Intelligent Design* (Grand Rapids, MI: Baker, 2003).

32. Henry M. Morris, *The Biblical Basis for Modern Science* (Grand Rapids, MI: Baker Book House, 1984), 41. "The responsibility of administering capital punishment is the greatest responsibility of human government. It implicitly entails the obligation also to control those human actions which, if unchecked, could easily (and often do) lead to murder (e.g., robbery, adultery, slander, greed). The dual role of government is that of both protection and punishment—protection of the lives, property, and freedoms of its citizens, and just retribution on those citizens who deprive other citizens of life, possessions, or liberty" (45–46).

33. Morris, *The Biblical Basis for Modern Science*, 41.

34. Harold J. Ockenga, "Introduction," in Carl F. H. Henry, *The Uneasy Conscience of Modern Fundamentalism* (Grand Rapids, MI: Eerdmans, [1947] 2003), xxi.

35. Rushdoony, *The Institutes of Biblical Law*, 448.

36. Larry Poston, "The Adult Gospel," *Christianity Today* (August 20, 1990), 24.

37. Paul Johnson, *The Enemies of Society* (New York: Atheneum, 1977), 117.

PART TWO

Christians and Morality

4

"You Cannot Legislate Morality"

***Myth, Lie, or Half-Truth?:** Christians should remind themselves that morality is a personal matter and should not be imposed on others. People should not be made to feel uncomfortable by being told that there are moral absolutes.*

What Moses brought down from Mt. Sinai were not the Ten Suggestions. They are commandments. *Are*, not *were*. The sheer brilliance of the Ten Commandments is that they codify in a handful of words acceptable human behavior, not just for then or now, but for all time. Language evolves. Power shifts from one nation to another. Messages are transmitted with the speed of light. Man erases one frontier after another. And yet we and our behavior and the commandments governing that behavior remain the same.[1]

"Ladies and Gentlemen, young and old. This may seem an unusual procedure, speaking to you before the picture begins, but we have an unusual subject: the birth of freedom. The story of Moses." These are the words of Cecil B. DeMille. Those who watch *The Ten Commandments* (1956) on television rarely get to see DeMille appear on stage before the movie begins. DeMille considered the topic of freedom under God's law to be the movie's most important message. In his rare on-screen appearance, he explained his reason for producing *The Ten Commandments*:

> The theme of this picture is whether men ought to be ruled by God's laws or whether they are to be ruled by the whims of a dictator like Rameses. Are men the property of the State or are they free souls under God? This same battle continues throughout the world today.

The official Souvenir Book produced at the time the movie was released, expressed DeMille's understanding of the importance of God's revealed law: "The Ten Commandments are not rules to obey as a personal favor to God. They are fundamental principles without which mankind cannot live together." *The Ten Commandments* was first produced by DeMille in 1923 as a silent film. In his autobiography, he sets forth the underlying worldview of the film: "The modern story is of two brothers, one of whom keeps the Commandments while the other breaks them all and is in the end himself broken by his defiance of the Law. Retribution comes upon him not as a vengeful visitation of an arbitrary God: rather it grows inevitably out of his own acts, for the moral law is as much a part of the structure of the universe as the law of gravity."[2]

No Escape from Morality

All law is a reflection of some moral code. Rev. Bo Turner, pastor at Tallulah Falls Baptist Church in Barrow County, Georgia, objected to posting the Ten Commandments in government buildings because such laws assume a moral point of view "to tell you how you should live."[3] There are tens of thousands of laws on the books that tell each and every one of us how we should live—from how fast we can drive our cars to how much money we have to pay in taxes.

In each case, we are being controlled, and someone else's concept of morality is being imposed on us.

Laws against theft and murder are legislated, and they reflect some moral code. There are few people who would object to laws being made that would punish thieves and murderers. And yet, such laws impose a moral system on all of us. Although thieves and murderers might object, no one is calling for these laws to be rescinded because they "legislate morality." Some critics of a religious basis for laws against murder and theft claim that "they or something like them are the basis of every other system of laws too. . . . The Ten Commandments, in this respect, are neither unique in themselves nor uniquely American."[4] Should laws be respected and followed just because people generally agree that they should be laws? Why is a law a law? How does one account for a law's ultimate validity? These are questions that secularists and materialists cannot answer without being inconsistent with their operating assumptions about the origin of the universe.

At one time there was a general moral consensus that abortion and homosexuality were morally wrong. Now the moral climate has shifted. Abortion has been legalized. What once constituted murder now is considered a cherished right that should be protected by law. With the moral universe now turned upside down, pro-abortion advocates believe it is *immoral* to deny a woman a right to an abortion. They work to impose laws on the whole society to protect the "moral rights" of those who want abortions. Constitutional scholar Archie Jones argues there is no way to escape legislating morality:

> Every system of government exists to produce or enforce certain laws, and every law necessarily entails a set of moral assumptions. All morality—even that which is usually supposed to be, or touted as being, based upon an "irreligious" or "anti-religious" philosophical foundation—is ultimately religious in its nature, since it is founded upon a set of pretheoretical presuppositions,

> fundamental assumptions about the nature of reality, about God, man, and things, which are taken on (a usually unacknowledged) faith. In this deepest sense, then, the question for every legal system is not whether it will be based upon "religion" but rather which religion or religious philosophy will be its foundation?[5]

When one concept of what's right or wrong is set against another in the debate over legislation, an appeal to morality is inevitably used. Advocates for the homeless might argue, "It is immoral to have people living in cardboard boxes or in abandoned automobiles when there is so much wealth in a country like the United States." Advocates of peace make arguments like the following: "U.S. taxpayers are paying $15.7 billion for nuclear weapons in fiscal 2004. Georgia taxpayers have run up $403.9 million of that tab. For that same amount of money, 221,342 Georgia children could receive health care."[6] It's immoral, the authors imply, to make bombs when there are so many needy people in the world. The amount of money spent on munitions could go a long way in helping the poor. During the healthcare debate of 2009, many argued that healthcare is a moral issue. Mark Halperin, editor-at-large and senior political analyst for *Time* magazine told CNN's Lou Dobbs, "We're the only industrialized democracy that doesn't cover every citizen" and "that is immoral."

Everybody uses moral arguments to make a case for personal or legislative cause. "[L]eftists in many a Western country speak of a *duty, a moral obligation* on the part of the richer nations toward those less well off (just as richer individuals ought to aid poorer ones)."[7] So then, it's not a question of whether morality will be legislated, but whose view of morality will be legislated?

Legislating morality is an inescapable concept, contrary to the protestations of some. Dexter Chambers, the communications director for the Atlanta City Council, claims that he is against legislating morality: "I do not believe in imposing my morals on anyone else or anyone else imposing their morals on me."[8] But the City Council imposes someone's view of morality on the people of the city of Atlanta on a regular basis. Some people like the Council's rulings, and some do not, but there's no escaping the fact that the morality is being legislated.

Whose Morality?

"In a scene from the recent Western, 'Silverado,' set before law and order reached the frontier, an old black homesteader is murdered by ruthless cattle ranchers. When the old man's son discovers the body he says sorrowfully, 'This ain't right.'"[9] But why "ain't" it right? What is the basis for a law that makes it right or wrong? How do we account for what's moral? Ted Turner, a self-professed humanist and religious skeptic, does not deny that there needs to be a moral code. In fact, in his rejection of the biblical Ten Commandments, he came up with his own set of "ten commandments." At the 1988 National Press Association meeting, Turner proposed a moral code based on what he believed should be a new set of rights and wrongs:

> We're living with outmoded rules. The rules we're living under is [sic] the Ten Commandments, and I bet nobody here even pays much attention to 'em, because they are too old. When Moses went up on the mountain, there were no nuclear weapons, there was no poverty. Today, the commandments wouldn't go over. Nobody around likes to be commanded.

Had Turner read the Ten Commandments before he made this claim? Does he really want us to believe that laws against theft, murder, and lying are "outmoded rules"? I wonder how he would respond if some of his employees stole from him or killed one of his children? If people don't like to be commanded under the "outmoded rules" called the "Ten Commandments," then they won't want to be commanded under anyone's proposed substitutes.

Turner has suggested replacing the Ten Commandments with "Ten Voluntary Initiatives," some of which include helping the downtrodden, to love and respect planet Earth, to limit families to two children or no more than one's nation suggests, and to support the United Nations. What happens when someone else comes along and advocates another set of laws? More fundamentally, if there is no God, then nothing is really right or wrong.[10] Law is only for the moment.

We can't live without rules and a moral code. Even humanists like Turner acknowledge this. Anyway, there was poverty in Moses' day, and the law that came from God to Moses on Mount Sinai set forth detailed solutions on how to deal with poverty. The Bible also has a lot to say about helping the downtrodden, especially widows and orphans (Deut. 14:29; James 1:27), and taking money from the rich and distributing it to the poor is not one of the solutions.

Morality must have an objective reference point that applies to all equally, to civil officials as well as citizens. Should we appeal to the latest polling statistics to determine right from wrong? Is the Supreme Court the final appeal? In 1986, the Supreme Court ruled, in a 5–4 decision, that states could outlaw the practice of sodomy. In 2003, the court reversed itself in a 6–3 decision wiping out all anti-sodomy laws. What happened in a period of less than twenty years that a prohibition became a fundamental right? Which decision from the Court is right and why? Why should we listen to Ted Turner and not someone like Adolf Hitler? Harold O. J. Brown asks it this way:

> If there are no laws made in heaven, by what standards should human society organize itself? We do need laws by which to organize and structure our lives, but if God has not given them, where shall they come from? There is only one answer: We must make them ourselves. Of course, if we make our own laws they will have no more authority or force than what we ourselves possess and can assert by

> means of the power at our disposal. In other words, law comes to represent not the will of the Creator but the will of the strongest creatures. This became the widespread view, sometimes unexpressed but frequently explicit, of most Western societies in the first part of the twentieth century. America's great legal statesman, Oliver Wendell Holmes Jr., thought no differently in this respect from the great dictator, Adolf Hitler. Both of them believed that laws simply represent the will of the dominant majority. Holmes was a courteous, urbane, sophisticated gentleman, but his idea of law would have offered no opposition to the enactments of Hitler, who for a time reflected the will of Germany's dominant majority.[11]

Supreme Court Justice Ruth Bader Ginsburg declared that the court's most recent rulings were based on international law. But this only pushes the reference point for law back a step. What is the foundation for morality among foreign courts? Justice Antonin Scalia wrote in his dissent in the *Lawrence v. Texas* (2003) sodomy case that the court should not "impose foreign moods, fads, or fashions on Americans."[12]

Autonomy as Law

What people often object to is the legislation of morality that affects them personally. Some women want abortion to be legal so they can choose the procedure if a birth control device fails. They object to any legislation that would make abortion illegal and infringe on their personal choices, even if it means killing a pre-born baby. But these same abortion proponents would not want legislation that allowed husbands to beat their wives. They would want anti-wife-beating legislation imposed on their husbands. Proponents of abortion would object to this analogy because a "fetus" is not a person that can be hurt, while a wife is a human being capable of being hurt. The claim of moral libertarians is a person can do what he or she wants as long as the action does not hurt anyone else. Why is it wrong to hurt someone else? From where does this moral norm originate? Who defines hurt? Isn't a pre-born baby hurt in an abortion? Abortionists say no because the "fetus" or "body part"[13] is not a baby until it's born. Who says? Those who push this line of thinking pressure legislatures and the courts to impose *their view* of life, morality, and hurt on society.

> The statement, "You can't legislate morality," is a dangerous half-truth and even a lie, because *all* legislation is concerned with morality. Every law on the statute books of every civil government is either an example of enacted morality or it is procedural thereto. Our laws are all moral laws, representing a system of morality. Laws against manslaughter and murder are moral laws; they echo the commandment, "Thou shalt not kill." Laws against theft are commandments against stealing. Slander and libel laws, perjury laws, enact the moral requirement, "Thou shalt not bear false witness." Traffic laws are moral laws also: their purpose is to protect life and property; again, they reflect the Ten Commandments. Laws concerning police and court procedures have a moral purpose also, to further justice and to protect law and order. Every law on the statute books is concerned with morality or with the procedures for the enforcement of law, and all law is concerned with morality. We may disagree with the morality of a law, but we cannot deny the moral concern of law. Law is concerned with right and wrong; it punishes and restrains evil and protects the good, and this is exactly what morality is about. It is impossible to have law without morality behind the law, because all law is simply enacted morality.[14]

Even the moral anarchist wants laws protecting him so he can be a moral anarchist. There's the case of Armin Meiwes, a German computer expert, who was charged with killing and eating the flesh of an Internet acquaintance. The defense of Meiwes is straightforward and simple. His supposed victim *wanted to be killed and eaten*. Meiwes advertised for a young man for "slaughter and consumption." He received 400 responses. What's a prosecutor to do? The willing participant consented to the "slaughter and consumption." There were no victims if libertine morality is valid and there is no higher law. Even so, prosecutors "filed murder charges, despite concluding the killing had the victim's consent." Based on what? According to Meiwes' testimony, "My friend enjoyed the dying."[15] The attorneys for Meiwes say it was a mercy killing. "It isn't as if I killed anyone against their will," Meiwes argued.[16] The fact that the "victim" consented means that no crime was committed.[17]

The Bible and Morality

God's standard of justice is the same for all His creatures, whether Jew or Gentile, believer or unbeliever. This even includes individuals and nations which do not acknowledge God as Lord and King. Sodom and Gomorrah enjoyed no such exemption from God's law: "Now the men of Sodom were wicked exceedingly and sinners *against the LORD*" (Gen. 13:13). This corrupt city was destroyed for breaking God's law in a civilization-destroying way: in particular, the sin of homosexuality (Gen. 19:4–5; Lev. 18:22; 20:13).[18] Jesus considered the twin cities of Sodom and Gomorrah as the epitome of moral degradation (Matt. 10:15; 11:23; Luke 10:12; 17:29). Jonah went to preach to the non-Israelite city of Nineveh because of its national sins. If the Ninevites were not obligated to keep the law of God, then how could they be expected to repent, and why was God about to judge them? (Jonah 3).

The stranger, an individual *outside* the covenant community of Israel, was obligated to obey the law of God: "There shall be one standard for you; it shall be for the stranger as well as the native, for I am the LORD your God" (Lev. 24:22; cf. Num. 15:16; Deut.

1:16–17). God's law was being "imposed" on them. Failure to comply meant judgment, both temporal and eternal.

The law as given to Israel was a standard for the nations surrounding Israel as well. When these nations heard of the righteous judgments within Israel, they would remark with wonder: "Surely this great nation is a wise and understanding people" (Deut. 4:6). The psalmist proclaims to the kings and judges of the earth "to take warning . . . and worship the LORD with reverence. . ." and to do "homage to the Son" (Psalm 2:10–11).

> It is striking how frequently the other nations are called upon in the Psalms to recognize and to honor God, and how complete is the witness of the prophets against the nations surrounding Israel. God does not exempt other nations from the claim of his righteousness; he requires their obedience and holds them responsible for their apostasy and degeneration [e.g., Amos 1:3–2:5].[19]

Isn't this the imposition of God's morality on the world? Why would God exempt some nations from following His moral laws and obligate other nations?

Under the New Covenant

The New Testament presupposes the validity of the imposition of God's moral code on the world. John the Baptist used the law of God to confront Herod—an Idumean—in his adulterous affair: "Herod . . . had John arrested and bound in prison on account of Herodias, the wife of his brother Philip, because he had married her. For John had been saying to Herod, '*It is not lawful for you to have your brother's wife*'" (Mark 6:17–18; Lev. 20:10; Deut. 22:22).

The psalmist declares that he will speak of God's "testimonies before kings, and shall not be ashamed" (Psalm 119:46). These testimonies are the "commandments" which he loves (119:47). Similarly, Jesus tells His disciples that persecution will give them an opportunity to speak "before governors and kings . . . as a testimony to them and to the Gentiles" (Matt. 10:18).

Notice what John the Baptist told some civil servants who approached him regarding their obligations to the law of God: "Some tax-gatherers also came to be baptized, and they said to him, 'Teacher, what shall we do?' And he said to them, 'Collect no more than what you have been ordered to.' And some soldiers were questioning him, saying, 'And what about us, what shall we do?' And he said to them, 'Do not take money from anyone by force, or accuse anyone falsely, and be content with your wages'" (Luke 3:13–14). John was not appealing to them on the basis of some "neutral" or "natural" law; instead, he referred them to the sixth, ninth, and tenth commandments of the Decalogue (Ex. 20).

Christians are obligated to inform those who rule in the civil sphere of the demands of the law and the consequences of disobedience. There is no area of life where man is exempt from the demands of the law of God. In Romans 13, the civil magistrate is said to be a "minister of God" who has the responsibility and authority to punish evildoers. As God's servants they are obligated to rule God's way and to impose His law in those areas where the Bible gives the civil magistrate jurisdiction. Just as a minister in the church is obligated to implement the law of God as it touches on ecclesiastical matters, a civil servant must implement the law of God as it relates to civil affairs. The determination of good and evil must derive from some objective standard. If the magistrate does not impose God's law, then he will impose his own law or the law of those who have the greatest influence.

Paul ends the section dealing with the civil magistrate by using the Ten Commandments, and proceeds to tell us that they are summed up as, "You shall love your neighbor as yourself" (Rom. 13:9). But this isn't something unique to the New Testament. Paul quotes from Leviticus 19:18 for his summary of the law. Now, some might want to maintain that a summary ethic of love *supplants* and *replaces* the law it summarizes. But a summary does not nullify what it summarizes. Does a summary at the end of a chapter in a book nullify and supplant what it summarizes? Of course not. In the same way, love as the summary of the law does not nullify the details of what it summarizes.

Others might want to maintain that love is our sole guide when it comes to ethical behavior since Paul says that "he who loves his neighbor has fulfilled the law" (Rom. 13:10). But the question remains: How do you know when you are loving your neighbor? Again, love without specifics becomes arbitrary. Love must be defined objectively. The law gives definition to love. Besides, did not Paul "confirm" the law (3:31) which was "holy, just, and good"? (7:12, 14).

The redemptive work of Jesus does not free us from an obligation to keep the moral law—including the social application of the law—laid down in the Bible. Scripture shows no instance of an individual, Christian or pagan, who is no longer required to keep the laws outlined in Scripture. Christians are freed from the "curse of the law" (Gal. 3:13), but not from the demands of the law: "Do we then nullify the Law through faith? May it never be! On the contrary, we establish the Law" (Rom. 3:31).

What Should Not be Legislated

Of course, there is no way that laws can be imposed to make people good. In this sense, it's true that morality cannot be legislated. But making people good is not the function of law. Law, in the biblical sense, is designed to restrain people from doing evil, protect life and property, and set limits for punishment when a violation occurs. This is why the Bible tells us that the "law is good" (1 Tim. 1:8–11). But to say that law cannot be legislated in any sense is nonsense.

> The old canard "you can't legislate morality" is a dangerous myth. The law is a body of rules regulating human behavior, which reflects society's view of right and wrong. Statutes prohibiting murder, for example, reflect the moral judgment that human life has intrinsic dig-

> nity. The law both reflects moral values and is a moral teacher.[20]

The law, even with the best intentions in mind, cannot make someone good. Although, if punishment follows the breaking of the law, another individual, seeing that there is punishment (either multiple restitution or death) might be deterred from attempting the same criminal act. Law was never designed to turn devils into angels, "For if righteousness comes through the Law, then Christ died needlessly" (Gal. 2:21). R. C. Sproul explains the proper way to understand the use of the law:

> The phrase "you can't legislate morality" has undergone a strange evolution in meaning. Originally the expression meant a person's behavior cannot automatically be altered by simply passing laws; legislation doesn't stop people from doing what they are determined to do. The contemporary meaning of the phrase is that it is wrong or illegitimate to enact legislation that restricts moral behavior. This is a ridiculous notion.[21]

An additional point needs to be made. There are numerous prohibitions in Scripture, but many of them do not have ecclesiastical or civil sanctions attached to them. Sins of the heart are not crimes. Coveting, for example, is a sin, but it is not a crime. If covetousness leads to theft, then civil sanctions can be applied for the act of theft but not the covetousness that led to the theft. Some acts of disobedience are best handled by the church and her courts (Matt. 18:15–20; 1 Cor. 6:1–11). Families are also governments that have jurisdictional authority to handle family disputes.[22] This is an argument against so-called hate-crime legislation where additional sanctions are imposed because of the supposed intent of the lawbreaker. Intent is God's domain not that of the courts except in the case of pre-meditation.

"Judge Not!"

How many times have you heard people fault Christians for "judging" others on moral issues? These "non-judgers" want to have it both ways. They want to deny Christians the right to judge behavior they believe is immoral while maintaining their freedom to judge the judging done by Christians. Christians are viewed as hypocrites for using the Bible to judge when the Bible commands them not to judge. The Bible, like any book, can be made to say anything if verses are interpreted with no regard to their original context. For example, the Bible says:

- Judas "went away and hanged himself" (Matt. 27:5).
- "Go and do the same thing" (Luke 10:37).
- "What you do, do quickly" (John 13:27).
- Because "there is no God" (Ps. 14:1).

Each text is true and understandable in its proper context. Strung together with no consideration of context perverts the meaning of the individual verses. The Bible says "There is no God." But the context tells us that it's "the fool" who "says in his heart" "there is no God" (Psalm 14:1; 53:1). The problem with the contextless methodology does not lie with the Bible but with its interpreters. Even some Christians fail to understand what Jesus was getting at when He warned us not to judge:

> As parents, we teach our children not to be critical of or judge another child based upon physical appearance—i.e., weight, color of hair, skin color, etc. On the other hand, we do teach our children not to associate with another child, or anyone for that matter, involved in drugs because drugs are harmful and illegal. We tell our children to judge illegal behaviour as wrong! The Bible even takes this idea of judging one step further by commanding us to reprove or correct that which is wrong (see Eph. 5:11).[23]

Erwin Lutzer calls on us to "consider the immediate context of Jesus' words. 'Do not give dogs what is sacred; do not throw your pearls to pigs. If you do, they may trample them under their feet, and then turn and tear you to pieces' (v. 6). How could we possibly obey these instructions unless we learned to recognize dogs and pigs?"[24] By judging in terms of "righteous judgment," we can develop the ability to identify theological and immoral "dogs" and "pigs" and respond appropriately.

The apostle Paul warned the elders at Ephesus to "be on guard for yourselves and for all the flock" because "savage wolves will come in among you, not sparing the flock; and from among your own selves men will arise, speaking perverse things, to draw away the disciples after them" (Acts 20:29). How would these elders know what a theological wolf was unless they had the obligation and authority to judge? Without being able to judge, there is no way to "test the spirits," identify "false prophets" (1 John 4:1), establish a judicial case against law breakers (1 Cor. 5:1), or to determine if *any* behavior is immoral and deserving of sanctions.[25]

After the defeat of Adolf Hitler's Third Reich, a war crime tribunal was set up in Nuremberg, Germany. The purpose, of course, was to judge those who had participated in the grossest of atrocities, the planned extermination of the Jewish race. But there was a problem. What standard would be used? John Warwick Montgomery describes the moral dilemma in which the prosecutors found themselves:

> When the Charter of the Tribunal, which had been drawn up by the victors, was used by the prosecution, the defendants very logically complained that they were being tried by *ex post facto* laws; and some authorities in the field of international law have severely criticized the allied judges on the same ground. The most telling defense offered by the accused was that they had simply followed orders or made decisions within the framework

> of their own legal system, in complete consistency with it, and that they therefore could not rightly be condemned because they deviated from the alien value system of their conquerors. Faced with this argument, Robert H. Jackson, Chief Counsel for the United States at the Trials, was compelled to appeal to permanent values, to moral standards transcending the life-styles of particular societies—in a word, to a "law beyond the law" of individual nations, whether victor or vanquished.[26]

If the "judge not" concept were taken to its logical conclusion, every court room in the country would have to shut down, every judge laid off, and all attorneys sent packing. This says nothing of the Supreme Court and Congress, two institutions that deal with judgment on a national scale. Even the Nuremberg Trials in their prosecution of war criminals would have had no moral or legal legitimacy.[27]

Avoiding the Double Standard

Jesus said "Do not judge lest you be judged" (Matt. 7:1; Luke 6:37). But He also said, "Judge with righteous judgment" (John 7:24). These are not contradictory statements since the context of Jesus' words in Matthew 7:1 tells us what He means by "not judging" and what it means to judge with "righteous judgment." Jesus was condemning those who judge using two standards of morality, one standard for the judge and another for the accused. The Bible maintains, a principle first set forth in the Old Testament, that the standard of judgment must be distributed equally and used without favoritism (James 2:1–13):

- "You shall do no wrong in judgment, in measurement of weight, or capacity" (Lev. 19:35).
- "There is to be one law and one ordinance for you and for the alien who sojourns with you" (Num. 15:16).

- "You shall appoint for yourself judges and officers in all your towns which the LORD your God is giving you, according to your tribes, and they shall judge the people with righteous judgment" (Deut. 16:18).
- "You shall not have in your bag differing weights, a large and a small" (Deut. 25:13).

Judging with two standards of justice brings about reciprocal judgment: "For in the way you judge, you will be judged; and by your standard of measure, it shall be measured to you" (Matt. 7:2). Jesus opposes *the way* in which some people judge, not judgment itself.

In essence, no one is above the law, not even those who make and enforce it. The Pharisees were blatant violators of the law regarding judging: "They tie up heavy loads and lay them on men's shoulders; but they themselves are unwilling to move them with so much as a finger" (Matt. 23:4). Governments are notorious for using a double moral standard. "A 1994 decree by Attorney General Janet Reno officially exempted federal prosecutors from the ethics guidelines that state bar associations required of all lawyers regarding contacting defendants directly without their lawyers present."[28]

Many homosexual advocates reject arguments by opponents of homosexual marriages because their opposition relies on religious principles found in the Bible. At the same time, they claim that "homosexuality is hard-wired into men and women" by *God*: "God in his infinite wisdom made some of us gay, some of us straight."[29] They can't have it both ways, rejecting what God says about homosexual behavior and then arguing that God made them homosexual. There is an obvious contradiction in logic. A homosexual marriage advocate argues, "If God were against homosexuality, he would not have created homosexuals."[30] I wonder if child molesters, rapists, adulterers, thieves, and pedophiles are permitted to argue in the same way?

Our world could not function without the ability to judge. The question a society must ask is this: What standard will be used in making judgments?[31] Until this question is answered biblically and rationally, our nation will continue down the slope of moral anarchy.

Defining Deviancy Down

Today's defenders of a "judge-not" worldview have, in the words of Daniel Patrick Moynihan, "defined deviancy down"[32] so that what was morally shocking twenty years ago is acceptable, or at least tolerated, behavior today. Robert Bork, explains the phenomenon:

> Emile Durkheim, a founder of sociology, posited that there is a limit to the amount of deviant behavior any community can "afford to recognize." As behavior worsens, the community adjusts its standards so that conduct once thought reprehensible is no longer deemed so."[33]

What's true in politics is doubly true in the entertainment business. To get ahead, like in politics, there is only one commandment to follow: "If you won't judge me, I won't judge you." When Roman Polanski was arrested in 2009 for the rape of a thirteen-year-old girl in 1977, many in Hollywood came to his defense. Why would they do this? "They're terrified to judge Polanski because they don't want to open that door. If 'judgment' is allowed in the room, it could turn on them."[34]

There's a long history of this type of thinking. In 1922, *The Sins of Hollywood* was a sensational exposé of the burgeoning film industry that author Ed Roberts, a former editor of *Photoplay Journal*, claimed "had free play" that "made the scarlet sins of Sodom and Babylon, of Rome and Pompeii fade into a pale, pale yellow." Consider the following from the well-informed author:

> Not so long ago a certain popular young actress returned from a trip. She had been away for ten days. Her friends felt that there ought to be a special welcome awaiting her. Rostrand [Roscoe "Fatty" Arbuckle], a famous comedian,

> decided to stage another of his unusual affairs. He rented ten rooms on the top floor of a large exclusive hotel and only guests who had the proper invitations were admitted.
>
> After all of the guests—male and female—were seated, a female dog was led out into the middle of the largest room. Then a male dog was brought in. A dignified man in clerical garb stepped forward and with all due solemnity performed a marriage ceremony for the dogs.
>
> It was a decided hit. The guests laughed and applauded heartily and the comedian was called a genius. Which fact pleased him immensely. But the "best" was yet to come.
>
> The dogs were unleashed. There before the assembled and unblushing young girls and their male escorts was enacted an unspeakable scene. Even truth cannot justify the publication of such details.[35]

The book was determined by a court to be "too scurrilous" to be sent through the United States Post Office. There were suspicions that the Hollywood studios had something to do with suppressing the book because it revealed too much about the operation of their business:

> Any publication that attempted to reveal the real conditions—to cleanse the festering sores—was quickly pounced upon as an "enemy of the industry"—A subsidized trade press helped in this work! Any attempt to bring about reform was called "hurting the industry." It was the lapses and laxities of the producer that precipitated the censorship agitation—that led a nauseated nation, determined to cleanse the Augean stables of the screen, into the dangerous notion of censorship—almost fatally imperiling two sacred principles of democracy—freedom of speech and freedom of the press![36]

What was done behind closed doors and kept hidden by the studios is now done in public for the world to see. Entire magazines are devoted to the sins of Hollywood, except the sins are now considered to be virtues to be imitated by young girls who see no problem of having babies out of wedlock. There are conservatives in Hollywood, but they are few and far between. There are lesser knowns who won't come out of the conservative closet for fear of being forever blacklisted.

Country singer Reba McEntire was interviewed in a homosexual publication about her views on homosexuality. "I just try not to judge," Reba said. "Don't judge me, and I won't judge you. And that's what it says in the Bible—'Don't judge.'" So if McIntire's husband ran off with another woman or man, would she be permitted to judge him based on her view of the Bible? If her accountant stole from her, could he be judged?

Notes

1. Ted Koppel, *The Last Word,* Commencement Address at Duke University, Durham, North Carolina (May 10, 1987). Quoted in Robert H. Bork, *The Tempting of America: The Political Seduction of the Law* (New York: The Free Press, 1989), 164.

2. Cecil B. DeMille, *The Autobiography of Cecil B. DeMille,* ed. Donald Hayne (Englewood Cliffs, NJ: Prentice-Hall, Inc., 1959), 251.

3. Quoted in Plott Brice, "It's not religion, it's a control issue," *The Atlanta Journal-Constitution* (November 16, 2003), A12.

4. David Rensberger, "Commandments force-fed," *The Atlanta Journal-Constitution* (October 3, 2003), A19. As has been mentioned, all laws are "force-fed." They wouldn't be laws if they weren't.

5. Archie P. Jones, "Christianity and the First Amendment: The Truth about the Religion Clauses of the Constitution," (unpublished manuscript), 3.

6. Nan Grogan Orrock and Regina Thomas, "Nuclear nightmare must not be relived," *Atlanta Journal-Constitution* (August 6, 2003), A11

7. Erik von Kuehnelt-Leddihn, *Leftism Revisited: From de Sade and Marx to Hitler and Pol Pot* (Washington, D.C.: Regnery Gateway, 1990), 303.

8. Quoted in Gayle White, "Vatican condemns same-sex unions," *The Atlanta Journal-Constitution* (August 1, 2003), B5.

9. R. C. Sproul, "Creating Justice," *Eternity* (Nov. 1986), 19.

10. Arthur Leff, "Unspeakable Ethics, Unnatural Law," *Duke Law Journal* (December 1979), 1229–1249.

11. Harold O. J. Brown, *The Sensate Culture: Western Civilization Between Chaos and Transformation* (Dallas, TX: Word, 1996), 88.

12. The material on Ginsburg and Scalia is taken from Gina Holland, "Ginsburg: International Law Shaped Court Rulings," Associated Press (August 2, 2003).

13. Matt Apuzzo, "Connecticut Supreme Court: Fetus is Body Part," *Washington Post* (May 7, 2003). "Defense attorney Paula Waite said if the fetus is its own life form, the state's abortion laws are in question. If the fetus is a body part, laws increasing the penalty for assaulting a pregnant woman could be jeopardized."

14. Rousas J. Rushdoony, *Law and Liberty* (Tyler, TX: Thoburn Press, [1971] 1977), 1–2.

15. Inge Treichel, "Cannibalism suspect says victim wanted to be eaten," *The Atlanta Journal-Constitution* (December 4, 2003), C2. See Nathan Constantine, *A History of Cannibalism: From Ancient Cultures to Survival Stories and Modern Psychopaths* (Edison, NJ: Chartwell Books, 2006).

16. "Perspectives," *Newsweek* (August 4, 2003), 21.

17. Smita Nordwall, "German man confesses to cannibalism," *USA Today* (December 4, 2003), 17A.

18. Greg L. Bahnsen, *Homosexuality: A Biblical View* (Grand Rapids, MI: Baker Book House, 1978) and James B. DeYoung, *Homosexuality: Contemporary Claims Examined in Light of the Bible and Other Ancient Literature and Law* (Grand Rapids, MI: Kregel, 2000)

19. J. H. Bavinck, *An Introduction to the Science of Missions* (Nutley, NJ: Presbyterian and Reformed, 1960), 12–13.

20. Charles Colson, "Half-Stoned Logic," *Christianity Today* (March 5, 1990), 64.

21. R. C. Sproul, *Abortion: A Rational Look at an Emotional Issue* (Colorado Springs, CO: NavPress, 1990), 90–91.

22. For a discussion of multiple governmental roles, see Gary DeMar, *God and Government: A Biblical and Historical Study*, rev. ed. (Powder Springs, GA: American Vision, [1982] 1990).

23. Cathy Mickels and Audrey McKeever, *Spiritual Junkfood: The Dumbing Down of Christian Youth* (Mukilteo, WA: WinePress Publishing, 1999), 220.

24. Erwin W. Lutzer, *Who Are You to Judge?: Learning to Distinguish Between Truths, Half-Truths and Lies* (Chicago: Moody Press, 2002), 39.

25. Paul Copan, *"True For You, But Not For Me": Deflating the Slogans that Leave Christians Speechless* (Minneapolis, MN: Bethany, 1998), 32.

26. John Warwick Montgomery, *The Law Above the Law* (Minneapolis, MN: Dimension Books/Bethany Fellowship, 1975), 24–25.

27. The moral foundation of the Nuremberg Trials was based on the belief that there was a transcendent natural law common to all cultures. "The point is that, without its acceptance, positive International Law lacks its solid foundation and loses its practical meaning. Furthermore, it remains clear that the general principles of International Law coincide with those of the natural law and that among them the principle of good faith is paramount." (Kurt Von Schuschnigg, *International Law: An Introduction to the Law of Peace* [Milwaukee, WI: The Bruce Publishing Co., 1959], 10). What secular natural law advocates do not want to admit is that Charles Darwin's evolution model, adopted as fact by the four prosecuting nations and those standing trial for war crimes, destroyed the

possibility that there can be a natural law. In principle, the Nuremberg tribunal was based on *ad hoc* law.

28. James Bovard, *Freedom in Chains: The Rise of the State and the Demise of the Citizen* (New York: St. Martin's Press, 1999), 166.

29. Lorraine Dusky, "Constitutional proposal helps homophobia thrive," *USA Today* (July 10, 2003), 13A.

30. Gregory Marholin, "Don't allow gay-marriage foes to win," *The Atlanta Journal-Constitution* (January 1, 2004), A13.

31. Gary DeMar, "The End of Law," *Liberty at Risk: Exposing the Politics of Plunder* (Powder Springs, GA: American Vision, 2003), 191–202.

32. Daniel Patrick Moyniham, "Defining Deviancy Down," *American Scholar* (Winter 1993).

33. Robert H. Bork, *Slouching Towards Gomorrah: Modern Liberalism and American Decline* (New York: Regan Books, 1996), 3.

34. John Nolte, "When You've Lost Eugene Robinson: 'Hollywood's Shame,'" Big Hollywood (October 2, 2009): http://tinyurl.com/ybljsa6.

35. Ed Roberts, *The Sins of Hollywood: An Expose of Movie Vice* (Hollywood Publishing Company, 1922): http://www.digitalhistory.uh.edu/historyonline/film_censorship.cfm

36. Roberts, *The Sins of Hollywood.*

5

"Christians Should Remain Neutral"

Myth, Lie, or Half-Truth?: *When discussing issues like politics, law, and education, religious considerations should not be brought into the discussion.*

There is not a square inch of ground in heaven or on earth or under the earth in which there is peace between Christ and Satan.... No one can stand back, refusing to become involved. He *is* involved from the day of his birth and even from before his birth. Jesus said: "He that is not with me is against me, and he that gathered not with me scattereth abroad." If you say that you are "not involved" you are in fact involved in Satan's side.[1]

Homosexual activist Matt Foreman of the National Gay and Lesbian Task Force was appalled when former President George W. Bush described homosexual activity as "sinful" and rejected the legal push for homosexual marriages. Foreman said that the president has a right to his religious views, "but it is unbecoming of the president of the United States to characterize same-sex couples as 'sinners.'"[2] Foreman is maintaining that the president can have *personal* moral opinions, but those *personal* moral opinions should be restricted to opinions only. The underlying claim is that the president should remain "neutral" on moral issues when they conflict with how others believe and behave. Would Foreman hold the same opinion if the president had stated, following his own religious views, that those who practice racism and bigotry are "sinners"?

How can anyone be neutral about anything? God always requires us to make a decision, even if a decision leads to unpopular results. You are either for Christ or against Him (Matt. 12:30). A decision has to be made. Joshua put it like this to his fellow-Israelites: Either serve Jehovah or serve the gods of your fathers. There is nothing in between these two choices. To "forsake the LORD is to serve other gods" (Joshua 24:16). It's either God or Baal. Christ or Satan.

Elijah asks it this way: "How long will you hesitate between two opinions? If the LORD is God, follow Him; but if Baal, follow him" (1 Kings 18:21). What if the people had decided that they would serve neither Jehovah nor Baal? Their supposed claim of neutrality would have been a decision *against* Jehovah because pro-Baalists would fill the spiritual and moral vacuum left by those claiming neutrality.

United States District Judge Myron Thompson ruled on September 4, 2003, that the removal of the Ten Commandment memorial from the Judicial Building in Montgomery, Alabama, did not violate the Constitution. "The empty space or 'nothingness' in the rotunda of the Judicial Building is neither an endorsement of 'nontheistic belief' nor a sign of disrespect for Christianity or any other religion," Thompson wrote. "Rather, it demonstrates governmental neutrality toward religion."[3] This is impossible logic. If a religious display of law like the Ten Commandments is prohibited by law to be displayed in a government building, then that's an action *against* the religious display of law. How can that be neutrality? The judge's ruling is implicit atheism.

What about the argument that no religious argument can be made on any moral issue? Like Judge Thompson's argument, the alternative is atheism, and atheism is not neutral. Atheism is an inverted religion that makes man the basis for what's ultimately true and good. The history of atheism is a record of meaninglessness[4] and genocide[5] on a massive scale, as D. James Kennedy argued in *What If Jesus Had Never Been Born?*:

> Mao killed about 72 million human beings from 1948 to 1976. When we add the 40 million Stalin is responsible for, we come to a number of 112 million. Throw in Hitler's 15 million (not counting the devastating war he started!), and we come to about 127 million. Add other killings by other atheistic and totalitarian states—as a result of their atheistic ideology—you come up with a number of more than 130 million.[6]

Alexander Solzhenitsyn's "estimates reach as high as sixty million" deaths just during Josef Stalin's reign of terror.[7] Indifference to these atrocities in the name of neutrality would have been an equal atrocity.

The claim of neutrality by Christians is judged harshly in the Bible: "I know your deeds, that you are neither hot nor cold; I would that you were cold or hot. So because you are lukewarm, and neither hot nor cold, I will spit you out of My mouth" (Rev. 3:15–16). Standing in the middle of a moral position is not neutrality. David Chilton writes:

> The Laodicean church brings neither a cure for illness nor a drink to soothe dry lips and parched throats. The sort of Christianity represented by Laodicea is worthless. The church provided neither refreshment for the spiritually weary, nor healing for the spiritually sick. It was totally ineffective, and thus distasteful to its Lord. Thus, says [Robert] Mounce, "the church is not being called to task for its spiritual temperature but for the barrenness of its works."

> This explains Christ's statement: *I would that you were cold or hot.* He is not saying outright apostasy is preferable to middle-of-the-roadism; rather, He is wishing that the Laodicean Christians would have an influence upon their society.[8]

The modern church that refuses to take a stand against the evils of the day is good for nothing. In the gospels, Jesus explains it this way: "You are the salt of the earth, but if the salt has become tasteless, how will it be made salty again? It is good for nothing any more, except to be thrown out and trampled under foot by men" (Matt. 5:13). Supposed neutrality is a lamp that's put "under the peck-measure" that leaves the house in perpetual darkness (5:15) and a city's light that's hidden so it does not serve as a beacon to weary travellers (5:14).

Even One Who Hates You

If a passerby refuses to help an accident victim who is bleeding profusely, he cannot claim neutrality. Even if he decides neither to walk away nor make an effort to help, he is not being neutral. Standing at the scene and watching a person die is not neutrality. The bystander's inaction has worked to do harm to the accident victim. Consider what Scripture says about an individual's responsibility in the care of a neighbor's animal.

> You shall not see your countryman's ox or his sheep straying away, and pay no attention to them; you shall certainly bring them back to your countryman. . . . You shall not see your countryman's donkey or his ox fallen down on the way, and pay no attention to them; you shall certainly help him to raise them up (Deut. 22:1, 4).

The passage stipulates that "anything lost by your countryman" is to be returned (22:3). The Bible goes still further: "If you meet your *enemy's* ox or his donkey wandering away, you shall surely return it to him. If you see the donkey of one who *hates you* lying helpless under its load, you shall refrain from leaving it to him, you shall surely release it with him" (Ex. 23:4–5). Now, what's true for the *animals* of our neighbors certainly holds true for our *neighbors* who are created in the image of God.

In addition, as the above passages show, there is no possibility of neutrality even in dealings with our enemies! "It is not unreasonable to assume," Rousas J. Rushdoony concludes, "that the penalty for the inactive bystander was like that of the false witness (Deut. 19:18, 19); the inactive bystander is also a kind of witness, and one who consents to the crime by his failure to act. The inactive bystander is thus an accomplice, an accessory to the crime, and liable to the penalty of the crime."[9]

Silence Would *Not* Have Been Golden

What if Mordecai and Esther had tried to claim a neutral position when they learned of Haman's plot against the Jews? Silence, supposed neutrality, was not an option, a point that Mordecai was quick to make:

> Do not imagine that you in the king's palace can escape any more than all the Jews. For if you remain silent at this time, relief and deliverance will arise for the Jews from another place and you and your father's house will perish. And who knows whether you have not attained royalty for such a time as this? (Esther 4:13–14).

Esther could have remained silent, and it may have happened that she and her family would have escaped Haman's scheme. But it was only a matter of time before he would have come after her. Her status as royalty would not have saved her for long. She risked death by approaching the king only because she realized that silence was not neutrality.

Esther made a direct plea to the king (7:1–6) over against his initial agreement to Haman's plan (3:10–15), a law that, technically, could "not be repealed" (1:19; 8:8). As a result, the king had Haman hanged in the place of Mordecai, Haman's intended victim. The law calling for the extermination of the Jews was repealed (8:3–14). Esther received "the house of Haman" (8:1) and Mordecai was promoted (8:2, 15).

What would have happened if Esther and Mordecai had chosen the path of supposed neutrality? The Jewish people would have suffered greatly, although God would have raised up another "savior" who would not have remained silent. "Relief and deliverance . . . for the Jews would have arisen "from another place" to rescue God's people. This shows that God is never neutral for the simple reason that it's an impossible position to take.

The Samaritan Factor

The New Testament does not accept neutrality as a Christian response to man and his world. A fellow-Jew, beaten, robbed and left for dead, is ignored by a priest and a Levite. These "religious" men, in order to protect themselves from ceremonial uncleanness, "passed by on the other side" (Luke 10:32). Isn't this similar to today's claim of neutrality in the social and political realms by many Christians who want to protect their "spirituality" or their church's tax-exempt status? To be involved in such secular issues like voting against men and women who support abortion and homosexuality—two grievous sins that destroy pre-born human beings and disrupt and ravage the God-ordained family—would mean spiritual defilement. To work for a political candidate would mean less time spent on witnessing, Bible study, prayer, and church services.

Some might want to assert that while *personal* social activism is permitted, *political* social activism is neither mandated, encouraged nor approved by Scripture. It is in politics that Christians are to remain neutral. The Bible mandates, approves, and encourages both social and political activism. Our failure to involve ourselves means that we neglect Jesus' instruction to the lawyer who asked Jesus about the identity of his neighbor:

> "Which of these three do you think proved to be a neighbor to the man who fell into the robbers' hands?" And he said, "The one who showed mercy toward him," And Jesus said to him, "Go and do the same thing" (Luke 10:36–37).

Political decisions, unlike the single decision of the priest, Levite, and Samaritan, affect millions of citizens. The pregnant woman is our neighbor. The unborn child is our neighbor. More than one million pre-born babies are killed each year in the United States. To choose neutrality and base it on the teaching of the Bible is to go against the "go-and-do-likewise" ethic given to the lawyer who asked about the identity of his neighbor. How can we say that we are acting as Christians—in the name of neutrality—when we allow legislation to pass that permits a doctor to do harm either to a mother or an unborn child?

Remaining silent over the sodomy issue is equally unbiblical. A young boy or girl who is seduced by a homosexual will most often be enticed by those who have embraced the homosexual lifestyle. Is it neutrality when we allow for the legalization of a form of sexual perversion (sodomy) that the Old Testament says deserves the death penalty? (Lev. 18:22). Neutrality led to the destruction of Sodom when tolerance for the evils of consensual homosexual activity led most in the city to turn a blind eye to acts of homosexual rape (Gen. 19:1–13).

The lifestyle of Sodom is not that far removed from our day. Film director Roman Polanski admitted drugging and raping a thirteen-year-old girl. He fled the United States before sentencing and hid out in Europe. In 2009 he was captured in Switzerland so he could be sent back to America to answer for his admitted criminal behavior. Many in Hollywood are "rallying behind the fugitive filmmaker. Top filmmakers are signing a pro-Polanski petition, Whoopi Goldberg says the director didn't really commit rape, and Debra Winger complains 'the whole art world suffers' in such arrests."[10] Soon after Polanski's arrest, nearly 150 prominent entertainment notables had taken up Polanski's cause.

Neutrality and Its Fruit

The perpetuation of the neutrality myth has been used by secular humanists to keep Christians out of the arena where social policy is affected, allowing Christians an ineffectual privatized religion. Christians who assert that neutrality is the biblical way have much in common with the humanists. Christians are told, "You can be involved in social issues, but you cannot bring in your religious convictions. You must be morally neutral, especially if your moral views are based in any way on religious convictions." The assumption is that those who are formulating public policy issues are also being neutral. But they are not. Attorney Vernadette Ramirez Broyles exposes the mythology behind moral neutrality:

> Those who marginalize people with deeply held religious views from public participation are attempting to transform America into a society where only one source of argumentation is accepted. Those acceptable arguments, of course, are grounded in the set of deeply held beliefs that social liberals most often esteem—secular moral (or humanist) philosophy.
>
> Liberals typically protest that they are simply preaching tolerance of everyone's point of view. But liberal senators opposing confirmation of devout Catholic judges and advocates of "gay marriage" must recognize that they too are proselytizing their own brand of religion and morality. Their objection to a nominee's religious beliefs and their views on marriage are also inevitably informed by their own beliefs regarding God, religion and the nature of man.[11]

Everybody looks at the world in non-neutral terms. Some worldview—a set of ultimate assumptions about reality[12]—is used to evaluate every fact and idea that comes our way. Social policies are determined by these ultimate assumptions. Everybody evaluates life from a certain religious point of view in terms of what he or she considers to be the ultimate authority, whether it's, God, man, the State, experience, pragmatism, reason, or the will of the people. In fact, denying God's Word a place in public policy discussions because it assumes a religious presupposition is an action *against* God and His Word, and, therefore, far from being neutral.

Here is how one editorial writer describes the way neutrality should operate: Christians can "rant and rave against humanism and feminism and any other 'ism' on Sunday, come Monday, the children belong in school."[13] According to this line of reasoning, Christians should refrain from expressing their religious convictions in a public school classroom and by extension any cultural or political setting where ideas are debated and legislation could be the result. On Sunday, children get religious instruction that should go no further than the four walls of the church and has no greater purpose than personal piety. On Monday through Friday, when children are isolated in the public (government) school classroom, we are to believe that children receive a "value-free" (neutral) education devoid of the opinions of teachers, textbook publishers, and the educational establishment.[14]

Attempts to provide a value-free, supposedly neutral, way of dealing with social issues demonstrate that we have raised a throng of "moral illiterates." In our desire to be neutral, really, "morally autonomous,"[15] we have pushed a generation of young people into the arms of immorality by default. Are we surprised when studies show there has been a rise in teen prostitution among children from middle- to upper-middle-class homes? Child advocates are puzzled by girls "who aren't forced into prostitution but instead appear to sell themselves for thrills, or money, or both. Richard Estes, a University of Pennsylvania researcher, says so-called designer sex is becoming more common in cities across the country."[16] The drift toward moral indifference has been noted by cultural trend watchers:

> When confronted with questions of right and wrong, many more youngsters are guided by what gets them ahead or what makes them feel good than by what their parents or religious authorities say, according to an ongoing study of moral development.[17]

This is the fruit of the humanist insistence that when it comes to morality, parents, teachers, and ministers should remain "neutral" and let children make up their own mind on moral questions. They have. "Overall, 21 percent of elementary-school youngsters told researchers they would try to copy answers or glance at another student's test." The percentages do not get any better as children get older. "Sixty-five percent of high school students said they would cheat on a test if they didn't know the answers." The conclusion of the study?: "There is no one underlying set of assumptions that guides the moral life of American children." We should not be surprised, since moral education has been rejected in favor of moral neutrality. Moral neutrality has brought about "moral illiteracy," which has produced *im*morality.

A Change in Moral Perception

Kay Haugaard has taught creative writing since 1970. As with most of her classes, students read and discuss Shirley Jackson's short story "The Lottery." Jackson's lottery isn't about winning millions of dollars by picking the right Lotto numbers; it's about human sacrifice that a small town accepts and takes part in with no questions asked. Of course, the premise is absurd. Or is it? As the years of teaching this story have passed, Haugaard began to see a change in the moral perceptions of her students. Their views on right and wrong had been dulled by the rhetoric of moral neutrality, "the danger of just 'going along' with something habitually, without examining its rationale and value."[18] Haugaard's closing comments are chilling:

> No one in the whole class of more than twenty ostensibly intelligent individuals would go out on a limb and take a stand against human sacrifice.
>
> I wound up the discussion. "Frankly, I feel it's clear that the author was pointing out the dangers of being totally accepting followers, too cowardly to rebel against obvious cruelties and injustices." I was shaken, and I thought that the author, whose story had shocked so many, would have been shaken as well.
>
> The class finally ended. It was a warm night when I walked to my car after class that evening, but I felt shivery, chilled to the bone.[19]

We've become a nation of moral bystanders. Deep down we know certain behaviors are wrong, but we've been cajoled into believing that nothing can be said in objection to the new amoral climate. If we do react, we are labeled "intolerant" and "insensitive" to different "lifestyle choices." Christians are told they are not being "loving" when they offer an opposing opinion on moral questions. The change in moral perceptions and attitudes has been stunning. "After the horrendous crime against the World Trade Center towers on September 11, 2001, a young Yale student has this observation: 'Absent was a general outcry of indignation . . . [M]y generation is uncomfortable assessing, or even asking, whether a moral wrong has taken place.'"[20]

The Goal is Neutralization

While Christians line up behind the neutrality doctrine, the humanists are establishing their agenda in violation of their rhetoric that everyone should be neutral. How do they get away with it? A more basic question should be, Why do we let them get away with it? Christians dutifully believe the secularist's version of neutrality, believing that it is a biblical and constitutional principle, and then wonder why every competing worldview finds its way into the classroom except biblical Christianity. Charles Colson describes the outlandish but predictable results:

> A friend I greatly respect was speaking, citing one example after another. They were bizarre stories: like the high-school students informed that they could not wear their Fellowship of Christian Athletes T-shirts to school (though satanic T-shirts were okay); or the court decision forcing Zion, Illinois, to change its 88-year-old city seal because it included religious symbols. Or the fact that *The Last Temptation of Christ* was shown in an Albuquerque high school, while the Genesis Project's *Jesus* film, whose script is all Scripture, would not be allowed near school grounds.[21]

This is how the neutrality game is played: Christian, you remain "neutral" so we humanists can implement our version of what's right and wrong, and then we will compel you to live under our set of rules. The State becomes the agent of reform for those who champion the neutrality theory for everyone but themselves. It's no wonder that Harvey Cox described secular humanism as "a dangerous ideological system because it 'seeks to impose its ideology through the organs of the State.'" According to Cox, "secular humanism has no tolerance and is opposed to other religions, it actively rejects, excludes and attempts to eliminate traditional theism from meaningful participation in the American culture."[22] So the Boy Scouts are not permitted to use a public park in San Diego, California, because they require members to believe in God, and actor and director Mel Gibson gets hammered by media critics when he produces a movie called *The Passion of the Christ* (2004),[23] a mostly accurate depiction of the crucifixion of Jesus. Is it being neutral when the Boy Scouts are taken to court and denied the use of the park? Is it being neutral to attack Gibson's *The Passion of the Christ* but support Martin Scorsese's *The Last Temptation of Christ*, calling its production and release "freedom of expression"?[24] Bishop Charles J. Chaput of the Catholic Archdiocese of Denver, wrote in the *Denver Catholic Register* about the criticism swirling around *The Passion of the Christ*, "When the overtly provocative 'The Last Temptation of Christ' was released [in 1988], movie critics piously lectured Catholics to be open-minded and tolerant. Surely that advice should apply equally for everyone."[25] But it doesn't. Those who claim to be neutral, aren't, and we shouldn't expect them to be, because Christians aren't neutral and should never claim to be.

The Neutrality "Logic"

According to a radio editorial some years ago, "a man's religion and the strength of his conviction are his own personal matter" and therefore "religion should not interfere with politics."[26] Regrettably, many churches during Hitler's rise to power accepted the argument that religion and morality should be separated from politics based on the neutrality claim. "Religion was a private matter," historian Richard V. Pierard writes, "that concerned itself with the personal and moral development of the individual. The external order—nature, scientific knowledge, statecraft—operated on the basis of its own internal logic and discernable laws."[27] For the German Christians, morality was a personal not a public or political matter.

The church's sole concern and domain was with a person's *spiritual* life. "The Erlangen church historian Hermann Jorda declared in 1917 that the state, the natural order of God, followed its own autonomous laws while the kingdom of God was concerned with the soul and operated separately on the basis of the morality of the gospel."[28] It was because of this disjunction—built on the myth of neutrality—that Hitler hoped to carry out his devilish schemes unhindered by religious arguments and pressures. Not everyone succumbed to the neutrality logic. The "Confessional Church" took a different, non-neutral, position:

> [It] opposed the Nazification of the Protestant churches, rejected the Nazi racial theories and denounced the anti-Christian doctrines of [Alfred] Rosenberg and other Nazi leaders. In between lay the majority of Protestants, who seemed too timid to join either of the two warring groups, who sat on the fence and eventually, for the most part, landed in the arms of Hitler, accepting his authority to intervene in church affairs and obeying his commands without open protest.[29]

Those "who sat on the fence," having fallen for the neutrality myth, supported Hitler by default. While they did not openly join with the "German Christians," a pro-Hitler alliance of ministers and churches, their inaction, their supposed neutrality, "landed them in the arms of Hitler" any way.

Would the above radio commentator have claimed that "a man's religion and the strength of his conviction are his own personal matter," and "religion should not interfere with politics" if these convictions were used to oppose Hitler and his evil plots against the Jews? Recent historians have attempted to fault the Catholic Church because of its "silence" regarding Nazi atrocities against Jews and other enemies of the Reich.[30] The point in raising this issue is not to debate whether the historians are correct in their assessment of the role Pope Pius XII played in dealing with the Jews but to show that these contemporary critics expected him to speak out, condemn, and confront the Nazi regime *because* he was a religious leader.

Critics of Christian involvement are selective in their assessment of the application of religion to contemporary life, including politics. Our own nation faced a crisis over slavery and Native American resettlement. Would the humanist guardians of neutrality want to propose that religious leaders should have remained silent (neutral) on the slavery issue? I doubt it. Religious views are not neutral when they support a liberal social agenda as they did in the era of the civil rights movement led by the *Rev.* Martin Luther King, Jr. or when in 2003 Governor Bob Riley of Alabama appealed to the Bible to argue that the collection of taxes should be restructured.[31] Paul Weyrich pointed out that Riley's appeal to the Bible to raise taxes "drew nothing but praise from those same sources who condemn the mixing of religion and politics."[32]

Congressman Wilson Lumpkin (1783–1870) attempted to use the neutrality argument to keep Christians from arguing against removing the Cherokee Indians from Georgia in what has become known as the "Trail of Tears":

> "[Lumpkin] decried those Christians who left their proper realm and sought to involve themselves in politics as 'canting fanatics.' He said he had no trouble with 'pure religion' (that is, religion that steered clear of politics), 'but the undefiled religion of the Cross is a separate and distinct thing in its nature from the noisy cant of the pretenders who have cost this Government, since the commencement of the present session of Congress, considerably upwards of $100,000 by their various intermeddlings with the political concerns of the country.'"[33]

Liberals and conservatives alike would be horrified at Lumpkin's claim of religious and moral neutrality if it had been used to overlook the horrors of slavery and ethnic cleansing. But the neutrality argument is still used. In 2003, Democrat presidential candidate John Kerry criticized the Vatican for saying that "Catholic politicians like him have a 'moral duty' to oppose laws granting legal rights to gay couples." He went on to say that "it's important to not have the church instructing politicians. That is an inappropriate crossing of the line in America."[34] Would Kerry agree to the following logic of his position?:

- "It's important not to have the church instructing politicians *about slavery*."
- "It's important not to have the church instructing politicians *about ethnic cleansing*."
- "It's important not to have the church instructing politicians *about civil rights*."

The neutrality argument is used to disenfranchise people who disagree on an issue. Clergymen who support homosexual marriages or legalizing same-sex unions on religious grounds are not told to be neutral.[35] Their opinions and influence are welcomed.

Birds of a Feather. . .

So then, for a Christian to adopt the neutrality myth is to fall into the humanist trap, to believe that religious convictions are reserved for the heart, home, and place of worship, while the affairs of this world are best handled by using reason, experience, and technical expertise devoid of religious assumptions and convictions.

Secular humanists have no objection to the Christian faith, provided its beliefs remain private, confined to our homes and church buildings, and just as long as we do not try to live up to our Christian principles in our business and *public* life. On no account must the Spirit and Word of the Lord Jesus Christ be allowed to enter the voting booth or the market place of ideas where the real decisions of modern life are made, nor must religion interfere with such vital matters as education, politics, labor relations, healthcare, taxes, and foreign policy. These activities are supposed to be "neutral," and they can therefore be withdrawn from sectarian influences so the secular spirit of the community can prevail.[36]

Humanists and, unfortunately, too many Christians believe the world's problems can be solved through technical know-how without any regard for divine guidance. This view teaches that special revelation has little or nothing to say about "secular" things like education, politics, and law. The unbeliever, without Scripture, it is maintained, is capable of developing equitable laws, a sound educational philosophy, and a just political system. This is the myth of neutrality.

"I Know It's True because I Saw it on TV"[37]

Many people believe facts are neutral, that they speak for themselves without any interpretation.[38] These same people are under the impression that newscasters and journalists simply "report the news" devoid of biases, preconceived assumptions, or political agendas.[39] This is hardly the case as James Davison Hunter points out in his book *Culture Wars*:

> In the very act of *selecting* the stories to cover, the books to publish and review, the film and music to air, and the art to exhibit, these institutions effectively define what topics are important and which issues are relevant—worthy of public consideration. Moreover, in the *substance* of the stories covered, books published and reviewed, art exhibited, and so on, the mass media act as a filter through which our perceptions of the world around us take shape. Thus, by virtue of the decisions made by those who control the mass media—seemingly innocuous decisions made day to day and year to year—those who work within these institutions cumulatively wield enormous power.[40]

The fact that a story even gets on a thirty-minute news show should make all of us question the notion of neutrality in reporting. There is no such thing as pure, unfiltered, pristine "just the facts" news. All news carries a bias, whether liberal or conservative. It's the result of "how they see the world."[41] Of course, the way people see the world is the right way to see the world. Anyone who sees the world in a different way is seeing it the wrong way. "Network anchor David Brinkley once admitted, 'News is what I say it is—it's something worth knowing by *my* standards!"[42] William Proctor, a veteran reporter and author who has worked for the New York *Daily News,* explains that the media "gospel is rooted in a kind of secular theology that purports to convey infallible social, moral, and political truth—a truth that the paper [*The New York Times*] fervently promotes with all the zeal of the fieriest proselytizer."[43] Proctor describes the editorial and news-gathering policy at the *Times* as "Manhattan Fundamentalism," "a well-defined but also rather rigid package of viewpoints which the paper disseminates widely to influence political, social, and personal beliefs and behaviors."[44]

Similarly, words used in reporting expose a preference for one worldview over another. "Right-wing conservatives" versus "progressives" is just one example. Those who are anti-homosexual are described as "homophobic," "intolerant," "hateful," and "unloving." Those who are opposed to abortion are "anti-choice" never "pro-life." Frank Schaeffer, before he rejected evangelical Christianity, rightly described the bias game:

> Think of the use of labels to categorize political activity. Some labels are used to neutralize the actions of certain groups; others denote being "one of us," acceptable.
>
> The words "right wing," "fundamentalist," "pro-life," "absolutist," and "deeply religious," are put-downs more than categories. Conversely, think of the unspoken pat on the back and blessing that the following words convey: "moderate," "pluralistic," "liberal," "civil libertarian," "pragmatic," and "enlightened."[45]

Robert Bazell of NBC, interviewed in 1986, said flatly, "Objectivity is a fallacy.... There are different opinions, but you don't have to give them equal weight." Linda Ellerbee wrote that "There is no such thing as objectivity. Any reporter who tells you he's objective is lying to you."[46]

In July of 1990, *The Los Angeles Times* published a series of articles on bias in abortion reporting. David Shaw, a *Times* staff writer, found "that the press often favors abortion rights in its coverage, even though journalists say they make every effort to be fair."[47] Here is what one journalist says about bias and reporting as it relates to abortion:

> "At base, abortion isn't about politics, and it isn't about the law," says reporter Eileen McNamara of the Boston Globe. "It's about philosophy and it's about morality and it's about your world view, and newspapers are ill-equipped to deal with those issues."[48]

Most media elites are ill-equipped to see their partiality because they cannot conceive of a contrary opinion to be either morally or factually right when compared to what they believe is their own objective understanding of the issue. Most honestly believe that the position they take on any topic is not biased or prejudicial but neutral.

Of course, if a person holds a particular view because of certain religious convictions, there is no possible way that he or she could ever be "objective." Colleen Cook, a television industry insider, observed that "There was an unwritten rule that if a reporter was 'religious' he shouldn't let it interfere with the job of being 'objective.'" This led Cook to ask, "Since when does agnosticism qualify one as neutral on an issue?"[49] The so-called neutral reporter, Walter Cronkite concluded, is "someone not bound by doctrine or committed to a point of view in advance."[50] Cronkite might have believed this, but he never practiced it. No one does. It's impossible not to be committed to some value system, some moral way of looking at the world. If not, then why choose to make the tragic death of a prominent retired physician, educator, and philanthropist and eleven members of his family front-page news[51] over that of a criminal who was shot and killed in a gun fight with police? Why do newspapers fail to show pictures of aborted babies in the debate over abortion but seem to have no problem publishing gruesome pictures of emaciated bodies of concentration camp victims, the mass graves of the Kurds ordered killed by Saddam Hussein after the Gulf war in 1991, or film footage of returning service men and women fighting in Iraq and Afghanistan?

John C. Lennox, Professor in Mathematics at the University of Oxford and Fellow in Mathematics and the Philosophy of Science at Green Templeton College, tells us that "no one can escape [bias]—neither author nor reader. We are all biased in the sense that we all have a worldview that consists of our answers, or partial answers, to the questions of the universe and life thrown at us. Our worldviews may not be sharply, or even consciously, formulated, but they are there nonetheless."[52]

Conclusion

Since experience (not to mention the Bible) tells us that there is no neutrality, we must assume that some philosophy will dominate the public policy playing field. For Christians to claim "neutrality" is to give all opposing ideologies a free ride in the development of public policy decision making. "If religious-based values are not dominant, some other beliefs will be."[53] Jesus requires Christians to be "the salt of the earth" and the "light of the world," which means "we must interact with—and influence—public institutions." The Christian's responsibilities in the political order are prayer, obedience, and using "Scriptural principles to shape public policy."[54]

Notes

1. Cornelius Van Til, *Essays on Christian Education* (Nutley, NJ: Presbyterian and Reformed, 1974), 26.

2. Quoted in "Specks, Logs & Marriage," *World* (August 9, 2003), 8.

3. Jannell McGrew, "Riley to Display Plaque," *Montgomery Advertiser* (September 5, 2003).

4. John W. Whitehead, *Grasping for the Wind: The Search for Meaning in the 20th Century* (Grand Rapids, MI: Zondervan, 2001).

5. Mark Kramer, ed., *The Black Book of Communism: Crimes, Terror, Repression* (Cambridge, MA: Harvard University Press, 1997), 4.

6. D. James Kennedy and Jerry Newcombe, *What If Jesus Had Never Been Born?* (Nashville, TN: Thomas Nelson, 1994), 236.

7. Lloyd Billingsley, *The Generation that Knew Not Josef: A Critique of Marxism and the Religious Left* (Portland, OR: Multnomah Press, 1985), 38. "Historian Robert Conquest, in *The Harvest of Sorrow*, his definitive account of Stalin's reign of rural terror, estimated that 14.4 million people, half of them children, perished." (Lewis Lord, "A reign of rural terror, a world away," *U.S. News & World Report* (June 30/July 7, 2003), 4.

8. David Chilton, *The Days of Vengeance: An Exposition of the Book of Revelation* (Horn Lake, MS: Dominion Press, [1987] 2006), 135.

9. Rousas J. Rushdoony, *The Institutes of Biblical Law* (Phillipsburg, NJ: Presbyterian and Reformed, 1973), 465.

10. John Horn and Tina Daunt, "In Roman Polanski case, is it Hollywood vs. Middle America?" (October 1, 2009): http://tinyurl.com/ydu4bpc. See Alan Sears and Craig Osten, *The Homosexual Agenda: Exposing the Principal Threat to Religious Freedom Today* (Nashville: Broadman & Holman, 2003).

11. Vernadette Ramirez Broyles, "Political table must also seat the religious," *The Atlanta Journal-Constitution* (August 13, 2003), A15.

12. Gary DeMar, *Thinking Straight in a Crooked World: A Christian Defense Manual* (Powder Springs, GA: American Vision, 2001).

13. Rheta Grimsley Johnson, "'People' vs. Fundamentalists," *The Marietta Daily Journal* (September 2, 1986), 4A.

14. To counter this argument, see Thomas Sowell, "Classroom Brainwashing," *Inside American Education: The Decline, the Deception, the Dogmas* (New York: Free Press, 1993), 34–69. Also, Charles J. Sykes, *The Hollow Men: Politics and Corruption in Higher Education* (Washington, D.C.: Regnery Gateway, 1990); Charles J. Sykes, *ProfScam: Professors and the Demise of Higher Education* (Washington, D.C.: Regnery Gateway, 1988); Roger Kimball, *Tenured Radicals: How Politics Has Corrupted Our Higher Education* (New York: Harper & Row, 1990).

15. William Kilpatrick, *Why Johnny Can't Tell Right from Wrong: Moral Illiteracy and the Case for Character Education* (New York: Simon & Schuster, 1992), 115.

16. Suzanne Smalley, "'This Could Be Your Kid,'" *Newsweek* (August 18, 2003), 44–47.

17. Joan Connell, "American Children are Becoming Moral Illiterates," *Marietta Daily Journal* (October 11, 1990), 5B.

18. Kay Haugaard, "The Lottery Revisited," *Unriddling Our Times: Reflections on the Gathering Cultural Crisis*, ed. Os Guinness (Grand Rapids, MI: Baker Books, 1999), 138.

19. Haugaard, "The Lottery Revisited," 141.

20. Peter Jones, *Capturing the Pagan Mind: Paul's Blueprint for Thinking and Living in the New Global Culture* (Nashville, TN: Broadman & Holman, 2003), 50.

21. Charles Colson, "From a Moral Majority to a Persecuted Minority," *Christianity Today* (May 14, 1990), 80.

22. Harvey Cox, *The Secular City* (New York: Macmillan, 1965). Quoted in Franky Schaeffer, *A Time for Anger: The Myth of Neutrality* (Westchester, IL: Crossway Books, 1982), 24.

23. Ted Baehr, "Beware the Bigoted Kibitzers," *The Biblical Worldview* (October 2003). You can also find it here: http://tinyurl.com/yjh8yyl

24. For the story behind *The Last Temptation of Christ,* see Michael Medved, *Hollywood Vs. America: Popular Culture and the War on Traditional Values* (Grand Rapids, MI: Zondervan, 1992), 33–49

25. Quoted in Julia Duin, "Mel Gibson looks right for movie on Jesus," *The Washington Times* (July 7, 2003). Also see Gary North, *The War on Mel Gibson: The Media Versus the Passion* (Powder Springs, GA: American Vision, 2004).

26. Heard on WGST, Atlanta, Georgia (September 12, 1986).

27. Richard V. Pierard, "Why Did Protestants Welcome Hitler?," *Fides et Historia* (North Newton, KS: The Conference on Faith and History), X:2 (Spring 1978), 13

28. Pierard, "Why Did Protestants Welcome Hitler?," 14.

29. William L. Shirer, *The Rise and Fall of the Third Reich* (New York: Simon and Schuster, 1960), 236. Emphasis added.

30. John Cornwell, *Hitler's Pope: The Secret History of Pius XII* (New York: Viking Press, 1999).

31. Larry Copeland, "Alabamians defeat $1.2B tax hike," *USA Today* (September 9, 2003).

32. Paul Weyrich, "Politicians, Scripture, and Tax Collectors" (September 17, 2003): www.newsmax.com/archives/articles/2003/9/16/225240/shtml

33. Quoted in John Wilson, "Why Evangelicals *Can't* Opt Out of Political Engagement," *Books & Culture* (July 15, 2002), www.christianitytoday.com/books/features/bccorner/020715.html. See John G. West, Jr, *The Politics of Revelation and Reason: Religion and Civic Life in the New Nation* (Lawrence, KS: University Press of Kansas, 1996).

34. Quoted in "Kerry criticizes Vatican Pressure," *Atlanta Journal-Constitution* (August 2, 2003), D4.

35. Robert P. George, *The Clash of Orthodoxies: Law, Religion, and Morality Crisis* (Wilmington, DE: ISI Books, 2001), 75.

36. E. L. Hebden Taylor, "Religious Neutrality in Politics," *Applied Christianity* (April 1974), 19.

37. From the album *Centerfield*, "I Saw It on T.V." by John Fogerty, 1985.

38. Roy A. Clouser, *The Myth of Religious Neutrality: An Essay on the Hidden Role of Religious Belief in Theories* (Notre Dame, IN: University of Notre Dame Press, 1991), 26–27.

39. In an interview that appeared in the January 23, 1995, issue of *New York Magazine*, Tad Friend wrote that I had said the following about former Georgia governor Lester Maddox: "Maddox is an anachronism, a corpse that just smells bad" ("Does America Hate New York . . . Or Has It Just Stopped Caring?," 32). Here's what I really said: "If Lester Maddox was dead and buried, you northern reporters would go to the cemetery and dig him up just so you could say that you interviewed him." I was trying to make the point that Northern reporters purposely look for well-known stereotypes to slant their stories about the South.

Maddox was a Southern stereotype for many Northerners. He is best known, besides for riding his bicycle backwards, for standing outside his Pickrick Restaurant in 1964 denying blacks entrance (his son and some of his patrons wielded pick handles) in defiance of new federal civil rights legislation. For an account of the incident, see Bob Short, *Everything Is Pickrick: The Life of Lester Maddox* (Macon, GA: Mercer University Press, 1999), chap. 5. To show his disdain for the press, the official portrait of Lester Maddox contains a photograph of his wife, two peaches, and a fish wrapped in a copy of the *Atlanta Constitution*.

40. James Davison Hunter, *Culture Wars: The Struggle to Define America* (New York: Basic Books, 1991), 225.

41. Bernard Goldberg, *Bias: CBS Insider Exposes How the Media Distort the News* (Washington, D.C.: Regnery, 2002), 5.

42. David Brinkley, quoted by Edith Efron, "Why Speech on Television Is Not Really Free," *TV Guide* (April 11, 1964), 7. Quoted in Colleen Cook, *All That Glitters: A News-Person Explores the World of Television* (Chicago: Moody Press, 1992), 32.

43. William Proctor, *The Gospel According to the New York Times: How the World's Most Powerful News Organization Shapes Your Mind and Values* (Nashville, TN: Broadman & Holman, 2000), 11–12

44. Proctor, *The Gospel According to the New York Times*, 31.

45. Franky Schaeffer, *A Time for Anger: The Myth of Neutrality* (Westchester, IL: Crossway Books, 1982), 15. Since writing *A Time for Anger*, Schaeffer has rejected his evangelical background which he describes in his book *Crazy for God: How I Grew Up as One of the Elect, Helped Found the Religious Right, and Lived to Take All (or Almost All) of It Back* (Da Capo Press, 2007). For a critique, see Gary DeMar, "A Review of Frank Schaeffer's 'Crazy for God'" (July 31, 2007): http://www.americanvision.org/article/a-review-of-frank-schaeffers-crazy-for-god-/

46. Dinesh D'Souza, "Mr. Donaldson Goes to Washington," *Policy Review* (Summer 1986), 24–31. Quoted in Marvin Olasky, *Prodigal Press: The Anti-Christian Bias of the American News Media* (Westchester, IL: Crossway Books, 1988), 59.

47. David Shaw, "Abortion Bias Seeps Into News," *The Los Angeles Times*, reprinted from the *Los Angeles Times* (July 1–4, 1990), 1.

48. Shaw, "Abortion Bias Seeps Into News," 27.

49. Cook, *All That Glitters*, 33.

50. Walter Cronkite, quoted in "Cronkite Spears Agnew," *Variety* (November 4, 1970), 28. Quoted in Cook, *All That Glitters*, 34.

51. David Simpson, "Air crash kills 12 in family," *Atlanta Journal-Constitution* (July 21, 2003), A1 and A8.

52. John C. Lennox, *God's Undertaker: Has Science Buried God?* (Oxford, England: Lion Hudson , 2009), 14.

53. Doug Bandow, *Beyond Good Intentions: A Biblical View of Politics* (Westchester, IL: Crossway Books, 1988), 16.

54. Bandow, *Beyond Good Intentions*, 76.

6

"Jesus Was Not A Social Reformer"

Myth, Lie, or Half-Truth?: *We should follow Jesus' example in everything. Since He did not get involved in worldly things like politics, neither should Christians.*

> It is exceedingly strange that any followers of Jesus Christ should ever have needed to ask whether social involvement was their concern, and that controversy should have blown up over the relationship between evangelism and social responsibility. For it is evident that in his public ministry Jesus both 'went about ... teaching ... and preaching' (Matthew 4:23; 9:35 RSV) and 'went about doing good and healing' (Acts 10:38 RSV). In consequence, 'evangelism and social concern have been intimately related to one another throughout the history of the Church....'[1]

Bus driver Chito Sangalang had the look of excruciating pain on his face as the nails were driven into the palms of his hands and feet as he was nailed to a cross. The cross was lifted up for the crowd to see before Sangalang was taken down. In addition to Sangalang, ten others were nailed to wooden crosses that day. One man had taken part in the annual ritual for fourteen years. During the Easter season in the Philippines, crucifixions are carried out following Jesus' example. These penitents could make the case that they are only doing what Jesus did. Of course, few if any follow Jesus' example in every detail! No one dies. And as far as I know, no one has been raised from the dead after three days.

Let's suppose that we follow Jesus' example regarding marriage and children. Jesus never married and, of course, contrary to Dan Brown, author of *The DaVinci Code*, never had children. Should we follow His example? But we know that Jesus blessed the institution of marriage by performing His first miracle at a wedding in Cana (John 2:1–11) and by giving instructions on the marriage relationship. He enjoins couples to remain married based on one of the Bible's earliest commands: "That He who created them from the beginning made them male and female, and said, 'For this cause a man shall leave his father and mother and shall cleave to his wife; and the two shall become one flesh'" (Matt. 19:5–6).

The Roman Catholic Church has manufactured an unbiblical doctrine by making Jesus the example for its unmarried and celibate priests. Once this approach is taken, there is no end to the way the Bible can be misunderstood and misapplied. "The four Gospels show that Jesus was unmarried so that he could be free to be poor and to preach his message. He had nowhere to lay his head. He was a street rabbi. He lived on handouts, and he was even buried in a borrowed grave."[2] Jesus did not remain unmarried so "he could be free to be poor and to preach his message." Rather, Jesus' singleness was related to His unique nature and mission. He was God who became man (John 1:1, 14). Jesus' mission was to save His people from their sins, not to be a model husband and father, although He was a model Son. Having said this, the Bible does use Jesus as an example of a loving husband but in a redemptive context, in terms of self-sacrifice that should be imitated (2 Cor. 11:2; Eph.

5:22–33). Jesus performed His unique redemptive objective and His unconditional love by paying the ultimate price for the redemption of His people—death on a cross.

Being poor, or taking a vow of poverty, is not a requirement for ministry. Someone with a lot of money could take care of his family as well as provide for the spiritual and physical needs of brothers and sisters in Christ (James 2:14–18) in addition to financing mission work around the world. How would a vow of poverty prove advantageous to a missionary enterprise? Many doctors join the mission field because they can afford to leave their practice and not spend valuable time raising financial support.

Jesus never owned a house: "The foxes have holes, and the birds of the air have nests; but the Son of Man has nowhere to lay His head" (Matt. 8:20). Jesus spent time in Peter's home and never told him to sell it (8:14). And yet, Jesus never condemned the ownership of property by rightful owners even though He had no money to pay even the smallest tax (17:24–27). Based on these two examples, following the chapter title's myth, Christians should give all their money away to non-Christians (since, by Jesus' example, Christians cannot possess money) and never own a house.

Again, by following Jesus' example, Christians have the authority to take possession of other people's property because of need. Jesus told His disciples that if anyone asked them why they were taking a donkey and a colt, they were to say, "The Lord has need of them" (21:3). Should we follow Jesus' example and declare common ownership of anything that we claim we need because Jesus did?

A Higher Principle?

Centuries ago the church debated the issue of using Jesus as an example for ministry. The Spiritualists of the fourteenth century, a sect of the Franciscan Order, "contended eagerly for the view that Christ and his apostles had possessed absolutely nothing, either separately or jointly. This proposition had been declared heretical in a trial before an inquisitor."[3] While it's true that Jesus called His apostles to follow Him and leave their work behind (Matt. 4:18–22), this is not much different from young people postponing work to get a college degree or a professor who takes a sabbatical to research a writing project. Paul worked as a tentmaker while in ministry (Acts 18:3). There is no biblical requirement to take a vow of poverty. Contrary to what the Bible actually teaches, St. Francis of Assisi made poverty and celibacy mandatory for all who would join his Order.

> 1. This is the rule and way of life of the Brothers Minor: to observe the holy gospel of our Lord Jesus Christ, living in obedience, without personal belongings and in chastity. . . .
>
> 6. The brothers shall possess nothing, neither a house, nor a place, nor anything. But, as pilgrims and strangers in this world, serving God in poverty and humility, they shall continually seek alms, and not be ashamed, for the Lord made himself poor in this world for us.[4]

Jesus and the other New Testament writers made no such demand on the apostles or the church in general (1 Cor. 7:2–4).[5] We know that "the apostles, and the brothers of the Lord, and Cephas [Peter]" had a right to take along "a believing wife" on their missionary journeys (1 Cor. 9:5). This hardly follows the example of Jesus and the requirement of celibacy for priests in the Roman Catholic Church.

In addition, Paul supports paying those who preach the gospel: "If we sowed spiritual things in you, is it too much if we should reap material things from you?" (1 Cor. 9:11). In none of his discussions about these matters does Paul refer to Jesus as an example to follow when it comes to marital status or economic position. Rather, he turns the attention of his readers to analogies from everyday life and "the Law of Moses" (1 Cor. 9:8–9; cf. Deut. 25:4). Jesus told His disciples that when the scribes and Pharisees sit in the seat of Moses, that is, when they speak true to Moses, do and observe all that they tell you (Matt. 23:2–3). Moses, that is, the Old Testament Law in particular, is authoritative. This is why Paul describes Scripture as being "inspired" or "God-breathed" (2 Tim. 3:16). The entire New Testament is equally authoritative.

Some conclude that while the Old Testament is filled with admonitions for involvement in what are now described as social issues, New Testament believers, because of an obligation to a new and "higher principle," are not to involve themselves in such worldly affairs. The prophets of the Old Testament spoke out boldly against all types of social injustice. How can the "better covenant" of the New Testament be indifferent to social injustice?

Render Unto Caesar

Some argue that Christians should not be involved in politics or social issues because Jesus and the disciples did not vote, rally support for certain social issues, or argue for Christian involvement. There are good reasons for this. Israel was a captive nation under judgment with no voice in Roman governmental affairs. The inscription on the tribute coin given to Jesus (Matt. 22:15–22) read: "'TI[berius] CAESAR DIVI AUG[usti] F[ilius] AUGUSTUS,' or, in translation, 'Tiberius Caesar Augustus, son of the deified Augustus.' The inscription was virtually an ascription of deity to the reigning emperor. . . . The irritating presence of the coin was a constant reminder to the Jews of their subservient condition."[6] The Jews showed their true allegiance and the reason for their foreign domination when they cried out in Pilate's court when their Messiah was presented to them, "We have no king but Caesar" (John 19:15).

The first-century church developed in a time of political oppression. While Christians were treated cordially by the Roman government for a time, it was not too long before persecution reached a fever pitch. It was Nero who blamed the Christians for the burning of Rome. "[T]he Christians were covered with tar and set up in the imperial parks as living torches, while their women were shamelessly exhibited in mythological pantomimes before being devoured by wild bulls."[7] In fact, the Soviet Union borrowed much from Roman domination tactics. Nikita Khrushchev stated that "When Stalin says dance, the wise man dances!"[8] This echoes the voice of the Beast, Nero Caesar,[9] who decrees that only those who are marked with his name can buy or sell (Rev. 13:11–18). Reforms are impossible under such conditions. Christians living in the former Soviet Union had no voice in civil affairs.

> The deepest reason why the early Christians had less to say about the future of earthly society than had the prophets of Israel was not their mistaken foreshortening of its period, but the fact that they had no present voice or vote in the general affairs of that society. St. Paul addressed his epistles to little groups of men and women who were endeavoring to live the true Christian life in the midst of a vast and powerful, but wholly alien and pagan, society and suited what he had to say to their current needs and problems. It is therefore unfair to expect from these epistles a direct answer to the further questions which inevitably suggest themselves to the mind, because they arise out of the circumstances, of those who like ourselves possess both voice and vote and have accordingly as much responsibility as anybody else for the human direction of affairs of the *respublica terrena*.[10]

Israel could not act in civil cases until permission was granted by the provincial government of Rome. The elders of Israel had biblical authority to execute capital offenders but not while they were under the domination of Rome. The Pharisees brought Jesus to Pilate because they were "not permitted to put any one to death," especially by crucifixion (John 18:31).

In time, however, Rome lost its grip on the world, and Christians began replacing the corrupt courts of paganism with a biblical system of justice (1 Cor. 6:1–11). We should be reminded that the rallying cry of the early church was "Jesus is Lord" (Acts 16:31). The

Roman provincial authorities would not have been concerned with what they considered to be a Jewish sect (24:5, 14) as long as these "Christians" (11:26) had maintained that Jesus was *a* lord, subservient to the Roman Emperor and just one god among the many gods already part of the Roman pantheon. Of course, if Christians had "presented Jesus to the Greco-Roman world as 'another' God, their faith would long since have gone the way of Mithraism."[11]

At first, Christianity was perceived as a threat solely to the Jewish leadership. In time, however, Christianity became a threat to Rome because of the implications of the absolute lordship of Jesus Christ: "'These men who have upset the world have come here also;. . . and they all act contrary to the decrees of Caesar, saying that there is another king, Jesus'" (Acts 17:6–7). You cannot serve two masters. If Jesus is indeed Lord and King (Rev. 19:16), then even Caesar would have to bow before Him (Phil. 2:9–11; cf. Matt. 2:1–18). The Emperors saw the consistency in this view.

As citizens of the United States, we do not live under Caesar! This may come as a shock to Christians; but it's true. In principle, we are to render unto Caesar what belongs to Caesar only when we define our "Caesar." We live under the Constitution of the United States at the Federal level in which we have multiple freedoms, including the right, according the First Amendment, "to petition the government for a redress of grievances." The Tenth Amendment to the Constitution informs us that "the powers not delegated to the United States by the Constitution, nor prohibited by it to the states, are reserved to the states respectively, or to the people."

We are also under the constitutional jurisdiction of the state where we live. There may be additional laws at the county, borough, city, or parish level. These are our "Caesars." As citizens, we can vote, express our political opinions, start political parties, support political candidates, campaign and lobby for the enactment of legislation, freedoms that did not exist in first-century Jerusalem or anywhere else in the Roman Empire.

God Has Already Spoken

There is another reason why Jesus and Paul did not lay down a social agenda. Since the New Testament "spoke out of a Jewish background and context," direct allusions to political and economic ideologies "may have been unnecessary. Christians must understand that their faith is rooted in Old Testament Judaism and that the Mosaic Covenant and Law (which contain highly specific political, economic, judicial, and social precepts) can give guidance even today."[12] This is why Paul could write that "*All* Scripture is God-breathed" (2 Tim. 3:16 NIV). Paul had what we call the Old Testament in mind since the New Testament had not been completed and compiled at that time. There was no need for Jesus or Paul to repeat principles related to social activism and concern that had already been laid down in great detail.

A Negative Example

While Jesus is often looked upon as a *positive* example of why Christians should *not* be involved in social issues, the Pharisees are seen as a *negative* example for why Christians should *not* get involved in social issues. The general impression is "the Pharisees were the best people of their day; and yet they were the greatest failures."[13]

The Pharisees were *not* "the best people of their day." The best people were men like Zacharias (Luke 1:6), Simeon (2:25), Joseph (Matt. 1:19), the Good Samaritan (Luke 10:33), and women like Anna (2:36), Mary (1:46–56), and Elizabeth (1:6). Elizabeth and Zacharias "were both righteous in the sight of God, walking blamelessly in all the commandments and requirements of the Lord" (1:6). The commandments of God were neglected by the Pharisees (Mark 7:8). They had become experts "at setting aside the commandment of God in order to keep [their] tradition." (7:9). Jesus told the Pharisees that they had the devil as their father (John 8:44). James B. Jordan sets the record straight on the true character of the scribes and Pharisees:

> We are used to thinking of the scribes and Pharisees as meticulous men who carefully observed the jots and tittles [of God's law]. This is not the portrait found in the Gospels. The scribes and Pharisees that Jesus encountered were grossly, obviously, and flagrantly breaking the Mosaic law, while keeping all kinds of man-made traditions. Jesus' condemnation of them in Matthew 23 certainly makes this clear, as does a famous story in John 8. There we read that the scribes and Pharisees brought to Jesus a woman taken "in the very act" of adultery (John 8:1–11). How did they know where to find her? Where was the man who was caught with her? Apparently he was one of their cronies. Also, when Jesus asked for anyone "without sin" (that is, not guilty of the same crime) to cast the first stone, they all went away, because they were all adulterers.[14]

A persistent belief beleaguers the church because the Pharisees have been portrayed as strict adherents to the law, and Jesus had His greatest theological disputes with the Pharisees, therefore, Jesus was opposed to the law. This is not what the Bible teaches. When the "scribes and the Pharisees . . . seated themselves in the chair of Moses," that is, when the law was properly taught and applied, the people were to do all that they told them (Matt. 23:2–3). At the same time, Jesus admonished the people "not to do according to their deeds" (23:3).[15]

In the same way, Christians today must listen to all of God's Word, not just the outward example of Jesus and certainly not the negative example of the Pharisees. The whole Bible has been given for the whole of life. There are numerous admonitions for reform: from education to caring for the poor; from ensuring just weights and measures to seeing that there is equal justice for all under God's law. The power of the gospel and the work of the Holy Spirit in the life of God's people can be great instruments for reform in the world.

What's a Captive to Do?

How should Christians respond to reform efforts under political regimes where they have no rights, no freedom of religion, speech, press, or assembly? For the most part, prior to the fall of most of Eastern Europe's Communist governments and the former Soviet Union, Christians behind the iron curtain had little say in the way their nation operated. This was true of nearly all citizens. Christians often were specifically signaled out for persecution.[16]

In the former Soviet Union, for example, Christians were forbidden to "set up benefit societies, cooperatives of industrial societies; to offer material aid to [their] members; to organize children's and young persons' groups for prayer and other purposes, or general biblical, literary or handicraft groups for the purpose of work or religious instruction and the like, or to organize groups, circles, or sections; to arrange excursions and kindergartens, open libraries and reading rooms, organize sanatoria or medical aid."[17] There was little possibility for social reform under such repressive regimes.

Prior to these oppressive conditions, the church could have done something and did not. One might even be able to make the case that the Russian church's *lack* of social involvement had a part in the 1917 revolution that led to religious and political oppression and the spread of Communism around the world.

> It is a sad but irrefutable fact that the Russian Orthodox Church at the time of the Bolshevik Revolution was engaged in a fruitless attempt to preserve its religious treasures (chalices, vestments, paintings, icons, etc.) and was therefore unable to relate meaningfully to the tremendous social upheavals then taking place.[18]

Once the old corrupt government fell and the repressive regime of the Marxists came to power, strategies for reform had to be rethought. In a nation under repressive domination, the most immediate need of the Christian community is the production of

Christian literature, family instruction, worship, prayer, and ways to keep their efforts secret, not grand efforts of social reform that have no chance of success. The goal is to wait out the inevitable collapse of the illegitimate political system and be ready to replace it when it falls (2 Tim. 3:7–9).

Once the iron curtain fell, it was learned that Christians were at the forefront of many of the efforts to topple communism and bring about reform from the inside. When they had an opportunity to institute change, Christians took advantage of the window of opportunity in a big way. Rev. Laszlo Tokes, the Hungarian pastor who sparked the Romanian revolution, stated that "Eastern Europe is not just in a political revolution but a religious renaissance." Instead of being executed, Rev. Tokes believed he was saved through "divine intervention."

The reports that reached the western news media recounted "references to 'Jesus,' the 'Christian spirit,' and Czechoslovakia's role as the 'spiritual crossroads of Europe.'"[19] It was not enough for these Christians to be free to worship. They also wanted to participate in every facet of their nation's life. The church in Czechoslovakia did not take a "hands off" approach to social issues once the iron curtain began to crumble. The Christian leadership saw it as their duty to bring effectual change to the broader culture.

Josef Tson followed a similar path in Romania as early as 1947. Tson told a friend that "Communism is an experiment that has failed. It wasn't able to fulfill any of its promises and nobody believes in it any more. Because of this, it will one day collapse on its own. . . . When communism collapses, somebody has to be there to rebuild society! I believe our job as Christian teachers is to train leaders so that they will be ready and capable to rebuild our society on a Christian basis."[20]

Tson started a training program in 1981 for Christian leaders who remained in Romania. The Communist regime eventually fell, and Nicolae Ceusescu and his wife were captured and executed on December 25, 1989. Tson had trained more than a thousand people all over Romania. Today, these people are the leaders in churches, evangelical denominations, and key Christian ministries in the former officially atheistic nation.

Reform efforts can never stop. Christians must be eternally vigilant. On July 1, 2003, Tokes warned the young people of Romania that "'foreign' values and mentalities, such as communism, materialism, imperialism and internationalism, imposed on us before 1989, are surviving in Romania, dressed up in a 'Social Democratic coat.'" His message was the same: "We need to return to the Christian civic system of values."[21]

A Word of Caution

Some have abused Jesus' name and deeds in their attempts to bring about a "better society." Jesus has been portrayed as a social revolutionary, the purveyor of a "liberation theology" which is little more than Karl Marx dressed in religious garb. Ronald H. Nash, a long-time professor of theology and philosophy and a vocal critic of this so-called liberation theology, wrote:

> Liberation theologians have one thing right. Christians ought to be concerned about liberating people from poverty, tyranny and, of course, from sin.
>
> The major problem with many liberation thinkers thus far is their uncritical acceptance of economic, political, and theological ideas that cut them off from beliefs, practices, and institutions that offer people genuine liberation.[22]

Because of the way Christ's redemptive message and work had been minimized by modern-day "liberationists" and previous social gospel advocates,[23] Christians have been reluctant to preach a "social gospel" message in the name of Christ. Who can blame them from abandoning the social dimension of the gospel when social gospel advocate Walter Rauschenbusch wrote, "It is not a matter of getting individuals into heaven but of transforming the life on earth into the harmony of heaven."[24] Even so, why should Christians abandon an area of legitimate biblical concern just because others have perverted Jesus' message, methods, and goals?

Every biblical doctrine has been perverted in some way. Salvation by grace through faith has become "easy believism" for some. A misunderstanding and misapplication of Romans 6:14 that we are "not under law, but under grace" has led to the "carnal Christian" heresy. A belief that Jesus' Second Coming is near has led many Christians to be preoccupied with the next event in eschatological time while ignoring centuries of failed prophetic predictions. As Christians, we do not jettison biblical doctrines because they are misunderstood and misapplied by some. In the same way, we cannot abandon biblical social reform because of a similar abuse. The Bible considers outward reform to be, first, evidence of internal renewal (Matt. 7:15–23), and second, a beacon to those who are in darkness to see the light of the gospel of grace (Matt. 5:13–16; Luke 2:32). Failure to comply with the Bible's admonitions for outward reform hinders an effective proclamation of the gospel. Reform acts as a "light on a hill" for those without the gospel.

> See, I have taught you statutes and judgments just as the LORD my God commanded me, that you should do thus in the land where you are entering to possess it. So keep and do them, for that is your wisdom and your understanding in the sight of the peoples who will hear all these statutes and say, "Surely this great nation is a wise and understanding people." For what great nation is there that has a god so near to it as is the LORD our God whenever we call on Him? Or what great nation is there that has statutes and judgments as righteous as this whole law which I am setting before you today? (Deut. 4:5–8).

The statutes and laws that God has given to His people are the standards of reform. They are the "good works" that those outside of Christ are to "see" (Matt. 5:16).

Is it possible that when the church abandoned its duty to reform society along biblical lines (personal transformation leads to societal transformation) that humanistic, anti-Christian forces replaced the vacuum left by evangelical Christianity? Prior to the rise of theological, social, and political liberalism, James Davison Hunter points out that there was no dichotomy between the gospel as it affected the individual and how it worked its way throughout society:

> As several scholars have noted, the legacy of nineteenth-century Evangelicalism was not only a stalwart commitment to the growth of Christianity (through domestic revivals and evangelisation and through foreign missionary activity) but also, within many quarters, a dedication to concretely address the needs of the socially and economically disadvantaged.... Though the chief priority was always "spreading the gospel," the philanthropic dimension of Christianity was in a way ignored. This was true not only among the Presbyterian Calvinists and the Baptists, who connected this with their postmillennial hope of reforming society in preparation for the return of Christ, but also among the Holiness and Pentecostal denominations and sects in their passion for revival....
>
> * * * * * *
>
> Once again, though the practical, benevolent side of Christianity was always secondary to the supreme purpose of evangelism and personal piety, the two objectives were seen as working hand in hand. Uplifting the sinner and saving his soul fused together in an integrated thrust.[25]

In time, however, the social dimension of the gospel was looked upon with suspicion by those who held to an orthodox Christianity. Liberalism gave up the gospel for "Social Christianity." Conservatives saw the "priority of social service in the mission of the Christian church"[26] as a breech of the faith. Instead of retrieving the gospel, fundamentalists abandoned social service and turned this legitimate area of ministry over to a civil government that is purely secular and has grown by multi-trillion-dollar proportions. J. Edwin Orr comments:

> The United States was being rapidly industrialized, and the Christian Gospel was beginning to influence the situation. Evangelical sentiment was expressed by Mrs. Barnardo thus: 'The State should deal with it, but does not: the Church of Christ must!' Responsibility of the State was recognized.
>
> In the same sequence of logic, once the State has undertaken its responsibilities in the way of education, medicine and the like, there is no longer the same urgency or even reason for missionaries to shoulder the burden. Their very limited funds could be put to better use elsewhere.
>
> In the homelands of Evangelical Christianity, the step-by-step improvement of social conditions, the leavening of the lump by the Christian conscience, was accompanied by a development of social impetus by Society itself, so that it was no longer necessary for Christians to initiate ideas for new social improvements—they simply joined efforts with other enlightened citizens. Their ministry of pioneering was channeled more and more into needier fields abroad. There, where the social conscience was often feeble, they were free to combine their urgent evangelism with urgent social betterment, their hosts accepting the former so long as it was accompanied by the latter.[27]

While the devil's house of social ills was being swept clean by the gospel and social applications of the gospel, turning society over to the State brings to mind the words of Jesus: "When the unclean spirit goes out of man, it passes through waterless places seeking rest, and not finding any, it says, 'I will return to my house from which I came.' And when it comes, it finds it swept and put in order. Then it goes and takes along seven other spirits more evil than itself, and they go and live there; and the last state of that man becomes worse than the first" (Luke 11:24-26). With its long list of social programs, civil government is making the church irrelevant.

The State in the nineteenth century, reflecting some remnant of the Christian worldview having been "swept clean" through a powerful Christian influence, was looked upon as a "Christian partner." But in time, with the State's increasingly secular character, the social facets under its care reflected the State's secular face.

Conclusion

Jesus made it possible for personal and social reform to take place. The transformation of individual lives was to lead necessarily to the transformation of families, occupations, churches, schools, and governments. The history of the gospel of Christ is the history of the transformation of the world.

Notes

1. John Stott, *Human Rights and Human Wrongs: Major Issues for a New Century*, 3rd ed. (Grand Rapids, MI: Baker Books, [1984] 1999), 17.
2. Noel C. Burtenshaw, "Imitation of Jesus Not Mere Celibacy," *The Atlanta Journal-Constitution* (August 26, 1990), C2.
3. Otto Zöckler, "Saint Francis of Assisi and the Franciscan Order," *The New Schaff-Herzog Encyclopedia of Religious Knowledge*, ed. Samuel Macauley Jackson, 15 vols. (Grand Rapids, MI: Baker Book House, 1952), 4:359.
4. "The Rule of Francis," *Eerdmans' Handbook to the History of Christianity*, ed. Tim Dowley (Grand Rapids, MI: Eerdmans, 1977), 266, 267.
5. For a discussion of this difficult passage, see Gordon D. Fee, *The First Epistle to the Corinthians*, NICNT (Grand Rapids, MI: Eerdmans, 1987), 277–280.
6. Merrill C. Tenney, *New Testament Times* (Grand Rapids, MI: Eerdmans, 1965), 152.
7. Ethelbert Stauffer, *Christ and the Caesars*, trans. K. and R. Gregor Smith (Philadelphia, PA: The Westminster Press, 1955), 140.

8. Madsen Pirie, *The Book of the Fallacy* (London: Routledge & Kegan Paul, 1985), 19.

9. Kenneth L. Gentry, Jr., *Before Jerusalem Fell: Dating the Book of Revelation*, rev. ed. (Powder Springs, GA: American Vision, 1998), 193–219 and *The Beast of Revelation*, rev. ed. (Powder Springs, GA: American Vision, 2002).

10. John Baillie, *The Belief in Progress* (New York: Charles Scribner's Sons, 1951), 199.

11. Rodney Stark, *For the Glory of God: How Monotheism Led to Reformations, Science, Witch-Hunts, and the End of Slavery* (Princeton, NJ: Princeton University Press, 2003), 1. For a discussion of Mithraism, see Joel McDurmon, *Manifested in the Flesh: How the Historical Evidence of Jesus Refutes Modern Mystics and Skeptics* (Powder Springs, GA: American Vision, 2007) and *Zeitgeist the Movie Exposed: Is Jesus an Astrological Myth?* (Powder Springs, GA: American Vision, 2009).

12. Larry Poston, "The Adult Gospel," *Christianity Today* (August 20, 1990), 25.

13. George W. Lasher, "Regeneration—Conversion—Reformation," *The Fundamentals: A Testimony to the Truth*, eds. R. A. Torrey, A. C. Dixon, et al., 4 vols. (Grand Rapids, MI: Baker Book House, [1917] 1988), 3:140.

14. James B. Jordan, *Through New Eyes: Developing a Biblical View of the World* (Brentwood, TN: Wolgemuth & Hyatt, 1988), 267.

15. John MacArthur makes the mistake of equating morality or good works in the name of Christ with the "moralism" of the Pharisees. He writes: "Jesus went head to head with the most superficially moral people in His world, the most religious people in His world, the Pharisees and the scribes. And He used his most scathing, His most searing, His most severe invectives on the religious right of His day. In Matthew 23, Jesus addressed the religious leaders of His time, the moral people, the people who were the fastidious keepers of the law of God and human tradition." ("The Deadly Dangers of Moralism," a message delivered at Grace Community Church in Sun Valley, California some time in 2002. This partial transcription is taken from tape GC 80–257).

16. Mikhail Khorev, *Letters from a Soviet Prison Camp* (Grand Rapids, MI: Baker Book House, 1989).

17. "Concerning religious societies," Resolution of the Central Committee, 8 April 1929, para. 17. Cited in Evgeny Barabanov, "The Schism Between the Church and the World," *From Under the Rubble*, ed. Alexander Solzhenitsyn (Boston, MA: Little, Brown and Company, 1975), 180.

18. Donald G. Bloesch, *Crumbling Foundations: Death and Rebirth in an Age of Upheaval* (Grand Rapids, MI: Zondervan, 1984), 30.

19. Barbara Reynolds, "Religion is greatest story ever missed," *USA Today* (March 16, 1990), 13A.

20. Josef Tson, "The Cornerstone at the Crossroads," *Wheaton Alumni* (August/September 1991).

21. Nora Georgescu, "UDMR [Democratic Hungarian Union of Romania] radicals raise a profile again" (July 1, 2003), (www.nineoclock.ro/index.php?issue=2718&show=politics).

22. Ronald H. Nash, "Evangelical Response to Liberation Theology," *Family Protection Scoreboard*, a special issue on "Liberation Theology: Will It Liberate or

Enslave People?" published by National Citizens Action Network (1989), 25. For further study of liberation theology, see Gerard Berghoef and Lester DeKoster, *Liberation Theology: The Church's Future Shock* (Grand rapids, MI: Christian's Library Press, 1984); Ronald H. Nash, ed., *On Liberation Theology* (Milford, MI: Mott Media, 1984); Emilio A. Nuñez C., *Liberation Theology*, trans. Paul E. Sywulka (Chicago: Moody Press, 1985); Edmund W. Robb and Julia Robb, *The Betrayal of the Church: Apostasy and Renewal in the Mainline Denominations* (Westchester, IL: Crossway Books, 1986).

23. Charles Howard Hopkins, *The Rise of the Social Gospel in American Protestantism: 1865–1915* (New Haven, CT: Yale University Press, 1940) and Robert T. Handy, ed., *The Social Gospel in America* (New York: Oxford University Press, 1966). Also see Richard M. Gamble, *The War for Righteousness: Progressive Christianity, the Great War, and the Rise of the Messianic Nation* (Wilmington, DE: ISI Books, 2009).

24. Walter Rauschenbusch, *Christianity and the Social Crisis* (New York: Macmillan, 1907), 65.

25. James Davison Hunter, *Evangelicalism: The Coming Generation* (Chicago, IL: University of Chicago Press, 1987), 40, 41.

26. Hunter, *Evangelicalism*, 41.

27. J. Edwin Orr, *The Fervent Prayer: The Worldwide Impact of the Great Awakening of 1858* (Chicago, IL: Moody Press, 1974), 181.

7

"The Church Should Not Be Involved In 'Social Issues'"

Myth, Lie, or Half-Truth?: *The church's mission is solely spiritual. God has not called His people to reform the world but only to save souls out of the world.*

> It is not the judgments of the courts, but rather the moral judgments of the masses of men and women which constitute the chief defense of life and property. It is public opinion that moulds our laws and institutions; and one of the greatest forces for moulding this opinion has been the church with its Bible. In fact, Christianity is today the most deep-seated and powerful influence in its formation. Thus it is that Christian principles, by slow degrees, are helping toward divine justice as the fundamental basis of all human law.[1]

"To the pulpit, the *PURITAN PULPIT*, we owe the moral force which won our Independence,"[2] John Wingate Thornton writes. Ministers of the gospel confronted the issues of their day by appealing to the people in terms of the Bible. The annual "Election Sermon" still "bears witness that our fathers ever began their civil year and its responsibilities with an appeal to Heaven, and recognized *Christian morality as the only basis of good laws.*"[3] In addition, the clergy were often consulted by the civil authorities in the colonies, "and not infrequently the suggestions from the pulpit, on election days and other special occasions, were enacted into laws. The statute-book, the reflex of the age, shows this influence. *The State was developed out of the Church.*"[4] The American pulpit "gave birth to America," Alexis de Tocqueville observed long ago. This truth is substantiated by a study of the historical record as Ellis Sandoz shows in *Political Sermons of the American Founding*:

> On the eve of the revolution, in his last-ditch attempt to stave off impending catastrophe, Edmund Burke reminded the House of Commons of the inseparable alliance between liberty and religion among Englishmen in America. Mercy Otis Warren noted in her 1805 history of the American Revolution: "It must be acknowledged, that the religious and moral character of Americans yet stands on a higher grade of excellence and purity, than that of most other nations." Of the Americans on the eve of the Revolution Carl Bridenbaugh has exclaimed, "who can deny that for them the very core of existence was their relation to God?"[5]

There were some ministers, however, who refrained from appealing to the Bible as a guide to social reform. Rev. Nathaniel Ward (*c.* 1578–1652), pastor at Ipswich, Massachusetts, in his election sermon of June 1641, grounded "his propositions much upon the Old Roman and Grecian governments." John Winthrop (1588–1649), first governor of Massachusetts, described this as "an error." There was good reason for Winthrop's objection: Why should the church appeal to "heathen commonwealths" when it is the heathen principles that have made it necessary for the church to be involved in reform efforts? Winthrop believed that "religion and the word of God make men wiser than their neighbors," thus, "*we* may better *form rules of government for ourselves*" than to adopt the failed principles of the past, what he called, "the bare authority of the wisdom, justice, etc., of those heathen commonwealths."[6] It was the heathen past that had to be swept clean if the people of God were to become the model of Christian charity that Winthrop spoke about aboard the flagship *Arbella* in 1630. Such a task is no less true in our own day.

What follows is a brief study of the emphasis of Christian reform efforts throughout the church's history. While the church has not been perfect in these struggles, there is no doubt that the existing social structure, what is often described as "Christian civilization,"[7] has been the result of Christian energy to bring the "whole purpose of God" (Acts 20:27) to bear on the whole of life.

Reform through the Ages

The first-century church had to live within the confines of the existing laws of the Roman Empire. The Apostle Paul had to confront the Roman institution of slavery when he had led a runaway slave, Onesimus, to Jesus Christ (Phil. 10). Should Paul have called for the abolition of slavery by petitioning the Roman government? Should the apostle have encouraged Onesimus to lead a rebellion against the Roman slave holders and ultimately against the Roman government? Should Paul have remained silent on the issue, claiming that it was not the responsibility of the church to involve itself in social reform?

As we've already noted, the church was in no position to petition the Roman government to do much of anything, let alone release millions of slaves that were vital to the Roman way of life. There was little that Israel could do, even when faced with the murder of infants (Matt. 2:16).

> No formal protest is recorded as having been registered with the king, and no action violating accepted civic law is

> reported. It may have been that the action was taken too rapidly to allow organized protest. But it seems more likely that any protest of citizenry would have been quickly suppressed by the Roman state.[8]

The Roman State was indifferent to the slaughter of infants and the institution of slavery. Of course, this does not mean the church should remain silent when the odds are stacked against it. A law can be opposed without a revolution taking place.

The historian Edward Gibbon estimates that there were more than sixty million slaves throughout the Roman Empire. Other writers place the estimates even higher. Tacitus, a Roman historian of the first century, writes that the "city of Rome was in constant fear of an uprising of the slaves. When a measure was proposed in the senate to have all slaves dress alike to distinguish them from freemen, the suggestion was promptly killed by the argument that to do so would reveal to the slaves their great numerical strength and endanger the peace of the city by a possible revolt."[9]

No Legal Standing

Jews had few civil rights as compared to Roman citizens (Acts 22:22–29), and slaves had none at all. Roman law gave masters nearly absolute power to sell, exchange, seize for debt, or kill a slave at will. "Slaves had no legal standing in the courts, no legal parentage, no right to hold property, and no civil rights. When compelled to testify in the courts their depositions were legal only when taken under torture."[10] Slaves were treated worse than cattle. If a slave killed his master, all of the slaves in his household could be put to death. Tacitus relates an incident where the revolt of one slave over his master resulted in the death of about six hundred household slaves.

> In ancient times slavery was widespread. Especially among the Greeks it was common practice to reduce

> captives and often criminals and debtors to the state of bondage. On the island of Delos sometimes as many as ten thousand slaves were sold in a single day. Among the Romans the lot of the slave seems to have been more cruel than among the Greeks. The slave was not considered to have any rights. The law offered him no protection.[11]

Paul did not remain silent on the slavery issue. He worked for lasting reform by dealing with Christian brethren who would in the future impact the Roman government and the institution of slavery directly. In time, slavery would be abolished without revolution. Revolution rarely, if ever, brings lasting reform. Once the cycle of revolution begins, there is little that can be done to stop it.

Legal Emancipation

As a runaway slave, Onesimus would have had little chance of survival in the Roman world. He would have lacked the necessary "papers" to travel and work. Paul instructs him to return to his master, Philemon. Paul understood that social reform must flow from personal reform. The advocation of revolution to bring about reformation is an unbiblical idea. Philemon had to be convinced that slavery was wrong before an appreciable change could take lasting effect. Many other Christians had to be equally convinced that slavery was wrong before it could be abolished. By going back to his master, Onesimus could be legally emancipated and thus enjoy the same rights as other free men without civil repercussions.

It is evident from other New Testament passages that slavery, as it was practiced by the Greeks and Romans, was abhorrent to God. Kidnappers—"slave-dealers"—are denounced along with murderers and sodomites (1 Tim. 1:9–10). The Old Testament view of slavery is quite different from that practiced by Greece, Rome, and in the United States prior to the 1860s. Biblical slavery was designed for a convicted thief who was unable to make restitution for his crime (Ex. 22:1–3). Bad debts were often paid through a form of indentured servitude (Deut. 15), a practice that the United States Constitution retained even after the abolition of chattel slavery: "Neither slavery nor involuntary servitude, *except as a punishment for crime whereof the party shall have been duly convicted*, shall exist within the United States, or any place subject to their jurisdiction" (Amendment XIII, Section 1).

Although other types of slavery existed in Israel, none of them resembled the Roman institution.[12] For the Hebrew indentured servant, the seventh year was the year of emancipation (Ex. 21:1–2). If the jubilee year arrived before the seventh year then it was in that year that freedom was granted (Lev. 25:39–41). Cruelty was never permitted (Ex. 21:26–27). Slavery as "man stealing," the type of slavery practiced in Greece, Rome, England, Africa, and the United States, would not have been permitted under biblical law: "And he who kidnaps [lit., *steals*] a man, whether he sells him or he is found in his possession, shall surely be put to death" (21:16).

As far as we know, Philemon was not a slave trader. He owned at least one slave like countless other Roman citizens, although we do not know the reason for Onesimus's servitude. Onesimus could have been an indentured servant who was repaying a debt. In any case, Paul was taking the first steps in setting forth a doctrine of social reform regarding a practice that was common and accepted in the Roman world. He was far ahead of his time by working with Christians who were slave owners to develop an equitable and non-revolutionary arrangement for their emancipation.

Jesus Sets the Pattern

Jesus had established the precedent for the abolition of slavery when He declared the "*fulfillment of the provisions of the jubilee year* (Luke 4:16–21)."[13]

> Christianity did not inaugurate a violent crusade against slavery. To have commanded and attempted the

> immediate overthrow of slavery in the Roman Empire would probably have wrought great havoc, brought greater burdens and suffering upon the unfortunate slaves, plunged masters and slaves into protracted war, and turned Europe and Asia into fields of blood.[14]

The apostle Paul built on the theological foundation for emancipation laid down by Jesus when he wrote that in Jesus "there is neither slave nor free man" (Gal. 3:28). Emancipation would have to come through reconciliation in Jesus Christ where the slave could be regarded as a brother. This was Paul's admonition to Philemon, that he would receive Onesimus back to him "no longer as a slave, but more than a slave, a beloved brother" (Phil. 16).

The message of freedom made its way slowly through the church and empire. In time, however, Rome would be judged by God for trafficking in slaves. Those "kings of the earth who committed acts of immorality" (Rev. 18:9) would come under the judgment of God (18:10) because of their buying and selling "slaves and human lives" (18:13).

The sad fact is that it took centuries before the church became the reforming institution that Jesus and Paul set out for it to be. It's true that "multitudes of slaves were received into the Christian brotherhood," and "under the reign of Hadrian, 117–138, the law forbade the arbitrary killing of a slave and granted the right of trial to establish innocence or guilt." In addition, "under Constantine, 312–337, and the succeeding emperors further legislation relieved their conditions. . . . Further legislation to improve conditions of the slaves was enacted under Justinian, 527–567. All privileges accorded to citizens were granted to emancipated slaves."[15]

Laws protecting freemen slowly were applied to the slave community. "Under the influence of Christianity much favorable legislation was secured, many burdens lightened, many abuses righted, and more humane treatment secured."[16] Nearly 1800 years passed before full emancipation of slaves was championed by the church, although there were pockets of reform efforts before total emancipation was realized.

The English Abolition Movement

Generally, the Christian community in England supported slavery. An example of this blindness can be seen in the career of John Newton (1725–1807). Newton was an infamous slave trader. The church knows him best as the author of such well-know hymns as "Amazing Grace" and "Glorious Things of Thee Are Spoken." Newton's opposition to slavery did not develop until *after* he became a Christian, and even while Newton was a Christian, he was also a captain of a slave ship. "Newton penned the beloved hymn 'How Sweet the Name of Jesus Sounds in a Believer's Ear' during the leisure time afforded by a voyage from Africa to the West Indies."[17]

In time, however, Newton confessed "shame" for "the misery and mischief to which [he had], formerly, been an accessory." He eventually denounced his former occupation with the publication of *Thoughts Upon the African Slave Trade* (1788), "a stinging attack upon slavery that makes scenes from Alex Haley's *Roots* seem mild by comparison."[18] Newton believed, prior to his denunciation of the slave trade, that he could be a good Christian and still participate in a great evil. "By 1788 Newton considered it 'criminal' to remain silent and not inveigh with evangelical fervor against the entire slave system. This conviction did not arise automatically upon his conversion, but from ethical deliberations that [William] Wilberforce set in motion."[19]

England's abolition movement was almost entirely led by the evangelical wing of the church. At the pleading of Lady Middleton and Bishop Porteus, James Ramsay wrote a long *Essay on the Treatment and Conversion of Slaves in the British Sugar Colonies* (1784). Ramsay was "convinced that men will not respond to lessons of eternal redemption from those who enslave them on earth, or about heaven when kept in hell. . . . He proposed steps to total

Emancipation, and suggested that free labour would yield more profit to plantation owners."[20]

William Wilberforce, upon being struck with the oppression inherent in the slave trade, wrote in his diary, "Almighty God has set before me two great objectives: The abolition of the slave trade and the reformation of manners."[21] Wilberforce began his mission in 1787. His efforts were ridiculed and lampooned in popular cartoons. "The attitude in the House of Lords was summed up by the member who declared flatly, 'All abolitionists are Jacobins.'"[22] Such an accusation is the modern equivalent of calling someone an anarchist, Bolshevik, Marxist, socialist, or revolutionary. A bill outlawing slavery finally passed in 1807. Had the British government "not been in the hands of Christians there seems little reason to have expected it to mount its massive, expensive, and voluntary campaign against slavery."[23]

American Abolition at Great Cost

The past practice of slavery in the United States continues to affect those who were enslaved against their will. Although emancipation has come, it took a long and arduous road. Keep in mind that it wasn't until the 1860s that slavery was constitutionally abolished. John Eliot, "the apostle to the Indians," protested in 1675 against the treatment of captives in King Philip's War. Most of the male captives (including those who voluntarily surrendered) were enslaved and traded to the West Indies for black slaves. Eliot argued that sending the Indians away hindered their conversion to the blessings of Christianity. Eliot was one of the earliest Christians to challenge the slave trade. "This usage of them," Eliot said of the Indian captives, "is worse than death."[24]

The silence, and in many cases the support of slavery, by much of the evangelical wing of the church in the United States, especially in the South, brought about emancipation at great cost. The task of "liberating" slaves was left to radicals and revolutionaries.

America is still paying a heavy price for the unrighteous way blacks were treated and the way they were emancipated. If modern anti-reformists had their way, the institution of slavery would still be with us. They would be preaching to the church to remain silent on the issue since, in their way of thinking, the church should not be involved in social issues.

The Bible as the "Magna Carta" of the Poor and Oppressed

As we have seen, the church has been in the forefront of establishing political freedom as in the antislavery crusade in England. In addition, there is a long tradition of the establishment of schools and hospitals around the globe. Medical and educational missionary work has its origins in the evangelical struggle for reform. Great efforts of social reform followed the preaching of the gospel. "Historians have attributed to [John] Wesley's influence rather than to any other the fact that Britain was spared the horrors of a bloody revolution like France's."[25] His philosophy of social reform was derived from the Bible.

Caring for the Poor and Infirm

The New Testament church was involved in all types of reform efforts, with widows and orphans receiving special care. "The English philosopher Sir Francis Bacon (1561–1626) declared that 'there never was found, in any age of the world, either religion or law that did so highly exalt the public good as the Bible.'"[26] Scripture set forth policies to care for the poor, widows, orphans, and strangers (Deut. 14:28–29). Land owners were obligated to set aside a portion of their harvested fields for the less fortunate (Lev. 19:9) for purposes of gleaning (23:22). The remaining sheaves were to be left for the poor (Deut. 24:19), while the crops that grew of themselves were to remain unharvested in the seventh year as a way of helping the poor (Ex. 23:10–11).[27] "In his *Controverted Questions* (1892),

Thomas Huxley paid a remarkable tribute to the advanced social thinking that motivated this type of legislation in the Pentateuch":

> The Bible has been the Magna Carta of the poor and of the oppressed; down to modern times no State has had a constitution in which the interests of the people are so largely taken into account, in which the duties so much more than the privileges of rulers are insisted upon, as that drawn up for Israel in Deuteronomy and Leviticus; nowhere is the fundamental truth that the welfare of the State, in the long run, depends on the uprightness of the citizen so strongly laid down.[28]

The Old Testament commands for social reform in helping the poor, especially the widow and orphan, were not lost on the New Testament writers. Relief efforts were immediately taken up by the early church to care for the "widows" who "were being overlooked in the daily serving of food" (Acts 6:1; cf. 1 Tim. 5:8–10). When it was learned that there would be "a great famine all over the world," the disciples, "in the proportion that any of [them] had means, each of them determined to send a contribution for the relief of the brethren living in Judea" (Acts 11:28–29).

The church continued the biblical tradition of reform efforts as it grew in number and influence. The relief of the poor was always high on the reform list. Caring for the infirm fell to the church as well. "Take, for example, the way Christians tried to help afflicted fellow Christians and pagans alike during the mid-third century plague. Dionysius, bishop of Alexandria, described his flock's activities as 'visiting the sick without a thought as to the danger, assiduously ministering to them, tending them in Christ.'"[29] Cotton Mather (1663–1728) had an abiding interest in medical matters. "When a small pox epidemic threatened Boston he proposed to the local physicians that they practice the method [of inoculation] and save the town."[30]

It is no accident that many hospitals carry the names of churches: Lutheran General, Christ, Mercy Hospital, Presbyterian-St. Luke's, Swedish Covenant, and dozens more. Jews, Roman Catholics, and Eastern Orthodox believers have a prestigious tradition of social reform in the area of medical care. Mather, in his *Essays to Do Good* (1710), "proposed that men and women, acting either as individuals or as members of voluntary associations, should engage in 'a perpetual endeavor to do good in the world.'"[31]

Caring for the Dispossessed

As Christians gained influence and positions of authority, reform efforts expanded. Abortion, infanticide, and the abandonment of children were common practices in Roman society. Many parents considered children a burden. If they did not leave them to die from exposure, they would leave them in public places provided for such a purpose. "Occasionally benevolent persons might rescue such children. Sometimes witches would take them and use their bodies for incantations. Some of them died from exposure, while the majority were taken and reared by lewd persons and finally sold as slaves or prostitutes."[32] The reform efforts of Christians changed all of this.

> The Church councils, Christian emperors, and lawmakers sought by declarations and legislation to combat the crime. As early as 323 the Council of Nice decreed that hospitals should be established in the chief cities and towns, and exhorted that these hospitals should make provision to take care of abandoned children.
>
> Houses of Mercy were provided by the Church for these foundlings. A marble vessel was placed at each church to receive exposed infants. These children were sometimes adopted by members. Those not cared for by some private family were taken under the charge of the Church.[33]

The evils of abortion and infanticide were also an accepted part of Roman society. Some laws prohibiting the practices were instituted by the pagan emperors, but the measures were rarely if ever enforced. Laws banning abortion and infanticide came into being because it was Christianity that sought to establish the dignity and value of all human beings, even the unborn. It has only been since the early 1970s that this Christian tradition of reform regarding the protection of the unborn has been overturned. Our nation, including many churches, have accepted infanticide, euthanasia, and "mercy killing" (suicide). These were uncommon procedures before the vibrant Christian tradition of social reform was shaken by the legalization of abortion in 1973 and the move in other formerly Christian nations to legalize euthanasia.

"Just Preach the Gospel"

A number of Christian leaders profess that the church's job is only "to preach the gospel." This seems to be the emphasis of Cal Thomas and Ed Dobson in their book *Blinded by Might*. Dobson, former board member of the Moral Majority and a personal assistant to Jerry Falwell, writes that he has "avoided all political activity" as the pastor of a Baptist church in Grand Rapids, Michigan. While his personal beliefs about the moral direction of the nation have not changed, what has changed is that he now believes "that the way to transform our nation has little to do with politics and everything to do with offering people the gospel."[34] And once these people embrace the gospel, then what do they do? Can they vote? Does it matter how they vote? Is politics morally neutral?

Aren't there implications to the gospel message? Jesus and the New Testament writers certainly thought so. Jesus said that you will know a converted person by the fruit his profession produces (Matt. 7:15–23). A "profession of faith" does not validate a person's conversion. James tells us that faith without works is dead (James 2:14–26). "This is pure and undefiled religion in the sight of our

God and Father, to visit orphans and widows in their distress, and to keep oneself unstained by the world" (1:27). Should Christians stay out of politics if laws are passed that hurt orphans and widows? Homosexuals are pushing to have laws changed to allow "gay couples" to adopt children. Many of these adoptees are orphans.

Maybe the advocates of a "just preach the gospel" message have a limited understanding of the comprehensive transforming effects of the gospel. Paul told the Ephesian elders that he did not shrink from declaring to them the "whole purpose of God" (Acts 20:27). Paul's letters to the churches will show that he spent as much time on Christian behavior after conversion as he did on correct doctrine. He wrote about the "renewing of the mind" (Rom. 12:2) which can be applied to education and politics. Paul also discusses such "secular" issues as "contributing to the needs of the saints" (our duty to the church) (12:13) and the ministry of civil government, including paying taxes "to whom tax is due" (our duty to the State) (13:7). Politics is one area where many Christians want to draw the line.

> It is hoped that but a few will think the subject of [civil government] an improper one to be discussed on in the pulpit, under a notion that this is *preaching politics*, instead of Christ. However, to remove all prejudices of this sort, I beg it may be remembered that "all Scripture is profitable for doctrine, for reproof, for correction, for instruction in righteousness" [2 Tim. 3:16]. Why, then, should not those parts of Scripture which relate to *civil government* be examined and explained from the desk, as well as others. Obedience to the civil magistrate is a Christian duty; and if so, why should not the nature, grounds, and extent of it be considered in a Christian assembly? Besides, if it be said that it is out of character for a Christian minister to meddle with such a subject, this censure will at last fall upon the holy apostles. They write upon it in their epistles to Christian churches; and

> surely it cannot be deemed either criminal or impertinent to attempt an explanation of their doctrine.[35]

Jonathan Mayhew's point is well taken. If the writers of Scripture, as instruments of God's will (2 Tim. 3:16–17), did not think it improper to discuss political issues, then how can ministers who claim allegiance to an inspired and infallible Bible fail to address politics and every other issue discussed in Scripture? The entire created order is open to discovery, study, and discussion.

Paul repeats the commandments prohibiting adultery, murder, and theft (Rom. 13:9) and sums up his specific exhortation on the law with the general command to "love your neighbor as yourself" (13:9). These instructions came after Paul informs the Roman Christians that the civil magistrate is a "minister of God" (13:4) who is to make a determination between good and evil behavior (13:3). What standard should the magistrate (God's civil *minister*) use to make these judgments?

These commandments have multiple social applications. Certainly the civil magistrate is to find it his duty to love his neighbor by not burdening him with excessive taxation and bureaucratic entanglements to frustrate his God-endowed freedoms to earn a living and provide for his family. No doubt the magistrate is to work for a civil order that results in a "tranquil and quiet life in all godliness and dignity" (1 Tim. 2:2) for the people of God. In the first-century, all that these Christians could do was appeal to God with "entreaties and prayers, petitions and thanksgivings" since they had no freedom to petition the Roman Empire with their political wishes (1 Tim. 2:1).

It seems by all of this that Paul went beyond what many might think is "just preaching the gospel." You can find similar emphases in all the New Testament letters as well as in the ministry of Jesus. Redemption from sin, the new birth, is the first step in what it means to be a "new creature" in Christ (2 Cor. 5:17). These first steps are described by the writer to the Hebrews as "elementary principles of the oracles of God" (Heb. 5:12), the milk stage of growth (1 Peter 2:2). The time must come when the student matures to become a teacher (Heb. 5:12). The goal is to grow in Christ: "For every one who partakes of milk is not accustomed to the word of righteousness, for he is a babe. But solid food is for the mature, who because of practice have their senses trained to discern good and evil" (5:13–14). The "only-preach-the-gospel" mentality stunts the growth of the new convert. The writer to the Hebrews is adamant about development in the faith, so much so that he offers the following admonition to his readers: "Therefore leaving the elementary teaching about the Christ, let us press on to maturity, not laying again a foundation of repentance from dead works and of faith in God" (6:1).

Revivalism and Social Reform

Ernest Fremont Tittle claimed "that 'Evangelical religion' could never hope to produce a humane social order."[36] This assertion is impossible to prove when one looks carefully at the historical evidence. Charles Finney, best known as a revivalist preacher, saw an obvious relationship between evangelism and social reform. John Stott writes about Finney's views:

> Social involvement was both the child of evangelical religion and the twin sister of evangelism. This is clearly seen in Charles G. Finney, who is best known as the lawyer turned evangelist and author of *Lectures on Revivals of Religion* (1835). Through his preaching of the gospel large numbers were brought to faith in Christ. What is not so well known is that he was concerned for "reforms" as well as "revivals." He was convinced . . . that the gospel "releases a mighty impulse toward social reform" and that the church's neglect of social reform grieved the Holy Spirit and hindered revival. It is astonishing to read Finney's statement in his twenty-third lecture on revival that "the great business of the church is to reform the world . . . .

> The Church of Christ was originally organised to be a body of reformers. The very profession of Christianity implies the profession and virtually an oath to do all that can be done for the universal reformation of the world."[37]

These are remarkable words considering the general evangelical and fundamentalist attitude toward social reform in our day. Most Christians have no idea that a theology of reform was developed by men who are known only as "soul winners." But when we dig a bit deeper into Finney's thought, we soon learn that he too met resistance in his advocation of reform efforts. He was amazed that the church treated "the different branches of reform either with indifference, or with direct opposition." Finney described opposition to reform efforts as "monstrous" and "God-dishonoring."[38] In spite of opposition, however, reforms were realized. Our nation is living off the moral capital of a distant generation of believers who made the gospel real in their time.

Conclusion

Christianity once saved the world from barbarism by redeeming the pagan civilization of Rome, a decrepit and dying culture. The barbarians are once again loose in the land and pounding on the gate, not because the barbarians are so formidable but because of the lack of a commitment to social reform by the church. The splendor of these early reform efforts form the backdrop for evangelical works of social reform that swept through our nation in its formative years. These great Christian pioneers have left the church with a great legacy. We dare not squander their efforts by preaching a gospel that has no regard for man and this world.

Notes

1. P. Marion Simms, *The Bible in America: Versions that Have Played Their Part in the Making of the Republic* (New York: Wilson-Crickson, 1936), 294–295.
2. John Wingate Thornton, *The Pulpit of the American Revolution or, The Political Sermons of the Period of 1776 with a Historical Introduction, Notes,*

and Illustrations (New York: Burt Franklin, [1860] 1970), xxxviii. Emphasis in original.

3. Cited in Thornton, *The Pulpit of the American Revolution*, xxiii. Emphasis in original.

4. Thornton, *The Pulpit of the American Revolution*, xxii-xxiii. Emphasis in original.

5. Ellis Sandoz, *Political Sermons of the American Founding* (Indianapolis: Liberty*Press*, 1991), xiv.

6. Thornton, *The Pulpit of the American Revolution*, xxv.

7. "'The Battle of Britain,' said Mr. Churchill on the 18th of June 1940, 'is about to begin. Upon this battle depends the survival of Christian civilization.'" (John Baillie, *What is Christian Civilization?* [London: Humphrey Milford/Oxford University Press, 1945], 5).

8. O. Palmer Robertson, "Reflections on New Testament Testimony Concerning Civil Disobedience," *Journal of the Evangelical Theological Society* 33:3 (September 1990), 332.

9. Charles David Eldridge, *Christianity's Contributions to Civilization* (Nashville, TN: Cokesbury Press, 1928), 21.

10. Eldridge, *Christianity's Contributions to Civilization*, 21.

11. William Hendriksen, *Exposition of Colossians and Philemon* (Grand Rapids, MI: Baker Book House, 1964), 233.

12. Gary North, *Tools of Dominion: The Case Laws of Exodus* (Tyler, TX: Institute for Christian Economics, 1990), 111–206, 209–47 and James B. Jordan, *The Law of the Covenant: An Exposition of Exodus 21–23* (Tyler, TX: Institute for Christian Economics, 1984), 75–92; James B. Jordan, *Slavery in Biblical Perspective* (Niceville, FL: Biblical Horizons, 1980).

13. North, *Tools of Dominion*, 125.

14. Eldridge, *Christianity's Contributions to Civilization*, 25.

15. Eldridge, *Christianity's Contributions to Civilization*, 26–28.

16. Eldridge, *Christianity's Contributions to Civilization*, 28.

17. John D. Woodbridge, Mark A. Knoll, and Nathan O. Hatch, *The Gospel in America: Themes in the Story of America's Evangelicals* (Grand Rapids, MI: Zondervan, 1979), 233.

18. Woodbridge, Knoll, and Hatch, *The Gospel in America*, 233.

19. Woodbridge, Knoll, and Hatch, *The Gospel in America*, 234.

20. John Pollock, *Wilberforce* (Belleville, MI: Lion Publishing, [1977] 1986), 51.

21. Quoted in Charles Colson, *Kingdoms in Conflict* (Grand Rapids, MI: Zondervan, 1987), 100.

22. Colson, *Kingdoms in Conflict*, 104.

23. Otto J. Scott, *The Secret Six: John Brown and the Abolitionist Movement* (New York: Times Books, 1979), 85.

24. Lester B. Scherer, *Slavery and the Churches in Early America, 1619–1817* (Grand Rapids, MI: Eerdmans, 1975), 39.

25. John Stott, *Human Rights and Human Wrongs: Major Issues for a New Century* (Grand Rapids, MI: Baker Books, [1984] 1999), 17–18. See J. Wesley

Bready, *England: Before and After Wesley—The Evangelical Revival and Social Reform* (London: Hodder and Stoughton Limited, 1939).

26. Quoted in Gabriel Sivan, *The Bible and Civilization* (New York: Quadrangle/The New York Times Book Co., 1973), 77

27. For a history and theology of caring for the poor and homeless, see George Grant, *Bringing in the Sheaves: Replacing Government Welfare with Biblical Charity,* rev. ed. (Windsor, NY: The Reformer Library, 1995) and *The Dispossessed: Homelessness in America* (Westchester, IL: Crossway Books, 1986).

28. Quoted in Sivan, *The Bible and Civilization*, 77.

29. "Medicine's Religious Roots," *Christianity Today* (September 10, 1990), 34.

30. Gordon W. Jones, "Introduction" to Cotton Mather, *The Angel of Bethesda: An Essay Upon the Common Maladies of Mankind* (Barre, MA: American Antiquarian Society, [1724] 1972), xv.

31. Robert H. Bremner, *American Philanthropy* (Chicago, IL: University of Chicago Press, [1960] 1982), 12.

32. Eldridge, *Christianity's Contributions to Civilization*, 33.

33. Eldridge, *Christianity's Contributions to Civilization*, 34.

34. Cal Thomas and Ed Dobson, *Blinded By Might: Can the Religious Right Save America?* (Grand Rapids, MI: Zondervan, 1999), 21.

35. Jonathan Mayhew, *A Discourse Concerning Unlimited Submission and Non-Resistance to the Higher Powers* (January 30, 1749) in Thornton, *The Pulpit of the American Revolution*, 47–48.

36. Norris Magnuson, *Salvation in the Slums: Evangelical Social Work, 1865–1920* (Grand Rapids, MI: Baker Book House, [1977] 1990), xiii.

37. Stott, *Human Rights and Human Wrongs*, 20.

38. Finney, quoted from "Letters on Revivals—No. 23," *The Oberlin Evangelist* (n.d.) in Donald Dayton, *Discovering an Evangelical Heritage* (Peabody, MA: Hendrickson Publishers, [1976] 1988), 20. Dayton writes that "Letters on Revivals—No. 23" is left out of modern editions of these letters. He calls it an "egregious example of censorship" (19).

PART THREE

Christians and Politics

8

"Politics is Dirty"

Myth, Lie, or Half-Truth?: *Like so much in life, politics is a dirty business. The best way to avoid being infected is to avoid any type of participation.*

Some, unfortunately, think that politics is a dirty word and a corrupt game that public officials play. In reality, it is the very fabric of the democratic system of government that we cherish so much. While it is made up of people like us who have problems and often yield to self-interests and lesser motives, it is still the strength of our society.[1]

Your husband hears your five-week old baby crying. You know the problem. She has a dirty diaper. You know what needs to be done. Her diaper needs changing. You're tired. The baby's been cranky all day, and you need a rest, even if it's only a short one. Your ever-loving husband is in his workshop. "Honey," you call out to him, "would you be a dear and check on Julie?" He returns with baby in tow and passes her off to you and says, "Her diaper's dirty. I can't change it."

Sounds ridiculous, doesn't it? Dad was sent to change what was dirty, a natural and necessary thing. If his response is so foolish, why is it that when we get into an area like politics, some can justify their inaction by making a similar claim?: "Politics is dirty! I can't get involved." If you view politics as something dirty (impacted by immoral people), then look at it in terms of a slogan on a bumper sticker: "Politicians are like diapers. They need to be changed often."

Civil Government Is Established by God

Civil government is established by God, therefore, it is a legitimate area of activity for Christians (Matt. 22:21; Rom. 13:1; 1 Tim. 2:1–4; 1 Peter 2:13–17). There was a need for civil government when man sinned and became a threat to other men (Gen. 4:23). Politics is the process of electing the best men to office to protect law-abiding citizens against the lawless (Ex. 18; Deut. 1:15; cf. 1 Tim. 3:1–7). Soon after the flood, God formalized civil government by, as Martin Luther wrote, sharing "his power with man" and granting "him power over life and death among men" (Gen. 9:4–6).[2] To speak out against the principle of political involvement is to call God's wisdom into question and to allow despots to rule.

Civil Government Is One Government Among Many

The political sphere is a created government like family government and church (ecclesiastical) government. "God has instituted civil government just as He has set up the church and the family. To say we want nothing to do with civil government is to say that God's institution is not important."[3] We are created in the image of God. God is the Governor over all creation, and He has called us to be delegated and limited governors under His one, all-embracing, and unlimited government (cf. Isa. 9:6–7): self-governors, family governors, church governors, and civil governors. The civil or political sphere is an area of legitimate governmental activity that has a designated jurisdiction (*juris*=law + *diction*=speak: to "speak the law") and a set of prescribed laws for its operation. It has its dirty elements when evil men practice evil schemes by not following the law. "So is business, law, labor, education, sports, and just about every other activity you can imagine. It's part of the human condition known as sin."[4]

> The burden of proof is on the one who thinks that the politics of running a government is any more dirty or dishonest than the politics of running a bank, labor union, trucking company, college, or even a church. Because of its life in a goldfish bowl, the governmental process may actually be a bit cleaner and more honest than the process of running most other social institutions.[5]

Christians should be involved in politics *because* it's dirty. "Dirty" is not the same as *inherently* sinful. Because we live in a fallen world, all things are tainted by sin. To claim that where there is sin there cannot be Christian involvement is to deny involvement in everything! God expects Christians to clean up their own lives after their conversion (Acts 26:20). The clean-up process should extend to the family. Remember, children are to obey their parents in the Lord (Eph. 6:1). This means sinful attitudes and actions must be substituted with godly attitudes and actions. Husbands are to love their wives (5:25), and wives are to be subject to their husbands (5:22). Certainly the church has the responsibility to get its house in order (1 Peter 4:17). Most of the New Testament epistles were written to churches, some of which had serious moral problems (1 Cor. 5:1–8).

This clean-up process does not come naturally. It's a matter of cleaning "out the old leaven" (1 Cor. 5:7): "Let us behave properly as in the day, not in carousing and drunkenness, not in sexual promiscuity and sensuality, not in strife and jealously. But put on the Lord Jesus Christ, and make no provision for the flesh in regard to its lusts" (Rom. 13:13–14). These sinful attitudes and actions are present in all of us, and they manifest themselves in self-government, family government, church government, and civil government. Paul's admonition applies to every area where sinful man acts, and he acts everywhere.

People Make Politics What It Is

It's been said that clothes make the man. In biblical terms we can state that the character of the people will determine what type of political system a nation gets. Our nation was founded on the belief that religious man undergirds a society. "In the last resort, our civilization is what we think and believe. The externals matter, but they cannot stand if the inner convictions which originally produced them have vanished."[6] Dirty politics is the reflection of sinful men and women—politicians and voters included. "Or, to put it another way, we are getting what we deserve. We are reaping what we have sown."

> So when a sleazy candidate gets elected, or when your local newspaper or TV station seems to favor the abortionists, or when a jury in Cincinnati says an abominable set of photographs isn't legally obscene—when any of those things happen, don't leap to the conclusion that someone did a number on us. Consider instead the sober likelihood that the sleazy politician really represents the values of the people who voted, that most subscribers to the paper and those who watch TV really don't care about—or even prefer—abortion, and that precious few jurors are willing to sit in judgment on anything.[7]

Politics is only as good as the people who make it their calling and those who put them into office either by voting or refusing to vote. The maintenance of good government is dependent on good people. Of course, this is true of everything—from the local grocery store to the family restaurant down the street. George Washington gave this advice to the nation in his Farewell Address:

> Of all the dispositions and habits which lead to political prosperity, religion and morality are indispensable supports.

No governing document can create freedom, national stability, or security by using compulsion to induce compliance to a set of ideals. The best political intentions are no match for the will of the people. In purely human terms, people are the determiners of the goodness of a nation's political system. John Adams wrote: "Our Constitution was made only for a moral and religious people. It is wholly inadequate to the government of any other."[8] When self government under God and His law is abandoned for self-serving opportunism and lawlessness, we should expect a decline in the health of the nation. Politics will indeed become dirty and infect all of us with its poison.

Dirty Business

Why is politics left out of the clean-up process when politics plays such a significant part in our lives? Who else has the means to clean it up? If Christians do not, who will? Generally speaking, Christians have stayed out of politics, making its corruption even more pronounced. The answer is not to consign politics to even more corruption by ignoring its potential as an area for redemption and restoration. Mark O. Hatfield, former United States Senator from the state of Oregon, relates the following on the question of corruption and politics:

> I have often been asked: "How can you be a Christian and be in politics?" There is inherent in this question the popular idea that politics is dirty and that no honest person would get himself involved. Have you ever heard a doctor or a lawyer asked that question? Yet certainly there are as many cases of professional or ethical misconduct in their occupations as among politicians.[9]

Sports is a dirty business. Ben Johnson of Canada was suspended after his world-record-breaking performance at the 1988 Olympic Games in the 100 meters because it was learned that he used performance-enhancing drugs. Pete Rose, holder of the all-time hit record and former player and manager for the Cincinnati Reds, was banned from baseball because he gambled on the sport. Mark McGuire, the first baseball player to hit 70 home runs in a season, was accused of taking performance-enhancing supplements. Barry Bonds, who surpassed McGuire's record with 73 home runs and Hank Aaron's home run total record with 762 in 2007, was also accused of taking performance-enhancing drugs. The 2001 Little League World series was tainted when it was learned that Danny Almonte was 14 instead of 12. There are now frequent reports of parents and players fighting at youth sports games.[10] In 2003, Kobe Bryant, a guard for the Los Angeles Lakers, admitted he had committed adultery and was charged with raping a nineteen-year-old woman.

How many parents will remove their children from participating in sports because of the dirt? The International Olympic Committee has been working hard to clean up those sports where steroids are the drug of choice for athletic enhancement, especially in track and field and weightlifting. These officials recognize that there is dirt, but they have not abandoned sports because of it. Roberto Alomar spit in the face of an umpire because he didn't like a call. A parent of a young hockey player killed another parent after a hockey match. Instead of abandoning sports because of these horrible events, parents and officials are working to clean up youth sports by requiring parents to take classes on how to behave and sign "good conduct codes." The problem is with people who bring the "dirt" (sin) with them to the game, not with sports themselves.

The Bible and Political Involvement

The Bible never condemns political involvement. John the Baptist does not rebuke Herod for his political position, but only for his sinful actions as a ruler (Matt. 14:4; Mark 6:18). John does not tell the soldiers he encounters to resign their commissions. He only exhorts them to act ethically (Luke 3:14). Jesus does not quarrel with Pontius Pilate over whether he should rule; He only reminds Pilate *why* he rules and, implicitly, by what standard he ought to rule (John 19:11). Again, clean politics is the emphasis. Paul calls rulers God's "ministers," servants in the political sphere (Rom. 13:4). These rulers are to promote the good. Paul appeals to Caesar, the seat of Roman *political* power, in order to gain a hearing for the cause of the gospel (Acts 25:11). Why turn to the civil magistrate for civil protection if the civil government (politics) is inherently evil? How could Paul ask support for the purity of the gospel from something that was inherently "dirty"?

"A Presbyterian Conflict"

The desire to retreat from political concerns is mostly a recent phenomenon. John Witherspoon, a minister in the Presbyterian church and the President of Princeton College, was one of the signers of the Declaration of Independence. In 1775 "the new provincial congress of New Jersey . . . was opened with prayer by John Witherspoon. . . . A combatant of skepticism and the narrow philosophy of the materialists, he was deputed by Somerset county to take part in applying his noble theories to the construction of a civil government."[11] Witherspoon, to make his case for political involvement, preached a fast-day sermon at Princeton that encouraged his Christian students to take hope in the providence of God despite the present circumstances and to acknowledge that God had been protecting the colonies in their struggle for freedom. Witherspoon "united the gospel ministry with the labours of the patriot."[12] Apologizing for the political but necessary nature of his discourse, he did not shrink from his ministerial responsibility as it pertained to civil issues:

> You are all my witnesses, that this is the first time of my introducing any political subject into the pulpit. At this season, however, it is not only lawful but necessary, and I

> willingly embrace the opportunity of declaring my opinion without hesitation, that the cause in which America is now in arms, is the cause of justice, liberty, and of human nature.

Unlike what many ministers believe today, "It was a distinguished feature in the American revolution that religious feeling was closely connected with political action."[13] A great number of historians contend that the thirteen colonies would never have broken away from Great Britain had it not been for Christians, especially those holding to a Presbyterian form of government. An ardent colonial supporter of King George III wrote home: "I fix all the blame for these extraordinary proceedings upon the Presbyterians. They have been the chief and principal instruments in all these flaming measures. They always do and ever will act against government from the restless and turbulent anti-monarchial spirit which has always distinguished them everywhere."[14] The Presbyterians, because of their doctrines of multiple civil jurisdictions and the right of lesser magistrates (colonial governments) to impose themselves through representatives chosen by the people between the greater magistrate (English Parliament) and the people, supported independence from British rule because of a broken legal agreement. "Ministers sat on Revolutionary committees and thousands of Presbyterians hastened to join the Revolutionary forces, where they proved the most steadfast of Washington's soldiers."[15]

The framers of the Constitution, "with no more than five exceptions (and perhaps no more than three), . . . were orthodox members of one of the established Christian communions: approximately twenty-nine Anglicans, sixteen to eighteen Calvinists, two Methodists, two Lutherans, two Roman Catholics, one lapsed Quaker and sometime-Anglican, and one open Deist—Dr. [Benjamin] Franklin, who attended every kind of Christian worship, called for public prayer, and contributed to all denominations."[16] It was Franklin who said the following to the delegates of the Constitutional Convention:

> All of us who were engaged in the struggle [in the war for independence] must have observed frequent instances of a superintending Providence in our favor. To that kind Providence we owe this happy opportunity of consulting in peace on the means of establishing our future national felicity. And have we now forgotten that powerful Friend? Or do we imagine we no longer need His assistance? I have lived . . . a long time, and the longer I live, the more convincing proofs I see of this truth—that God Governs in the affairs of men. And if a sparrow cannot fall to the ground without His notice,[17] is it probable that an empire can rise without His aid? We have been assured . . . in the Sacred Writings, that "except the Lord build the house, they labor in vain that build it."[18] I firmly believe this; and I also believe that without His concurring aid we shall succeed in this political building no better than the builders of Babel.

Franklin was not known as orthodox in his religious beliefs,[19] but there is no doubt that he understood what made nations great. It wasn't geography, natural resources, or monetary prosperity. The reason most colonial Christians got involved in politics was because it was dirty. The "dirt" was affecting their lives, property, and sacred honor. The church had come under the State's jurisdiction to the detriment of the church. Christians rallied to involve themselves in the political process to keep the church free from political oppression.

Politics Will Not Save Us

After concluding that politics is an area for Christian ministry, it should be made clear that there can be a danger in seeing politics as doing too much. The people in Gideon's day saw politics as *the* solution to their immediate problems (Judges 8:22–23), when, in fact, *they* were the problem, every man doing what was right in his own eyes (17:6). They reasoned that if they only had a powerful king to rule over them, their problems would be solved. So they thought. Gideon rejected their overtures to make him their savior-king. "The LORD shall rule over you," was Gideon's response (8:23). Gideon was not asserting that politics was evil but that men cannot save us even if they are ordained by God.

Later, Abimelech wanted to turn the people back to the political faith (9:1–6). Jotham, the only surviving son of Gideon, warns the people of the inherent dangers in such a move (9:7–15). While there is the offer of shade (political salvation and security), it is an illusion that brings with it a shocking and destructive tyranny (9:15). The choice of politics as a substitute for the gospel brought with it further oppression. Instead of crying out to God in repentance, the people abandoned personal holiness and opted for a new definition of what ought to be. The corrupted family (Judges 14–16) and priesthood (1 Sam. 2:12–17, 22–36) led the people to turn to the State for salvation (1 Sam. 8). In the process, they rejected God from being king over them (8:7).

Christians ought to call politics into question when it promises salvation, but not because it's an illegitimate sphere of Christian activity. This is the mistake John MacArthur makes in his book *Why Government Can't Save You.*[20] He outlines what he believes is "an alternative to political activism." In doing so, he creates an either/or option for Christians: It's either evangelism or political activism. Evangelism and politics do different things; this does not mean that one is necessary and the other indifferent. Let's position his argument in these ways:

- It's either evangelism *or* changing the tax structure to put more money in the hands of consumers.
- It's either evangelism *or* working to overturn laws supporting slavery and racial discrimination.
- It's either evangelism *or* working to change laws that allow a woman to kill her preborn baby.

- It's either evangelism *or* stopping laws legalizing homosexual marriages.

Why can't we engage in evangelism *and* political activism? Will people who come to Christ automatically know what the Bible says about these issues? Isn't part of the discipleship process teaching new Christians the whole purpose of God? MacArthur asserts that "believers are certainly not prohibited from being directly involved in government as civil servants, as some notable examples in the Old and New Testaments illustrate. Joseph and Daniel in Babylon are two excellent models of servants God used in top governmental positions to further His kingdom."[21] He lists other examples: The centurion's servant (Matt. 8:5–13), Zacchaeus the tax collector (Luke 19:1–10), Cornelius the centurion (Acts 10), and the Roman proconsul Sergius Paulus (Acts 13:4–12).

MacArthur writes that "the issue is one of priority."[22] Who will disagree? If his book had dealt with the relationship between evangelism and political action, then his thesis would have been more in line with what the Bible teaches. He takes issue with an author who states, "The Christian life begins with spiritual transformation. . . . But then we are meant to proceed to the restoration of all God's creation." This includes private and public virtue, education, law, science and medicine, literature, art, and music. MacArthur objects. He does not see these things as "a biblical mandate." In fact, he believes that such thinking is "unbiblical and dangerous."[23] By taking this position, MacArthur has written off thousands of years of Christian influence and cultural reformation. According to historian Rodney Stark, "In contrast with the dominant religious and philosophical doctrines in the non-Christian world, Christians developed science because they *believed* it *could* be done, and *should* be done."[24]

MacArthur is under the false impression that Christians who get involved in "political activism" are claiming that such activity will bring about the reformation of society. This is far from the truth.

Politics is one biblical sphere of God's delegated temporal governments; family and church governments are two others. Politics (civil government) has a major impact on our lives. It's the Christian's duty to be involved, if only to keep the State from imposing its will over us and oppressing the church and family.

Civil government (the realm of political activity) was never meant to save any more than the family or church. Family, church, and civil government are God-ordained governmental jurisdictions. While we are to redeem politics (actually, politicians) , we are never to view this government as the solution to our nation's problems. The purpose of involvement in politics is more than the replacement of non-Christians with Christians. There are numerous things that civil government ought not to do. A civil government based on a biblical view of the State would mean a drastic reduction in its size and power and a return of jurisdiction to individuals, private enterprise, families, churches, and local civil governments.

Maintaining the Status Quo

There are similar dangers that often fester in the church. It's sad and frightening to think that much of the church is purposely immobilized as the culture decays. There were German Christians who spoke out against the Nazi ideology and its threats to the nation, but not much interest was generated in the early days of the Third Reich. William Shirer makes this striking point:

> I should have realized that a people who had so lightly given up their political, cultural and economic freedoms were not, except for a relatively few, going to die or even risk imprisonment to preserve freedom of worship. What really aroused the Germans in the 1930's were the glittering successes of Hitler in providing jobs, creating prosperity, restoring Germany's military might, and moving from one triumph to another in his foreign policy. . . .[25]

The danger from within the church is just as serious as the danger from without. In many cases, the danger from within is more sinister because it bears the voice, mark, and presumed authority of the church (Acts 20:30).[26] The church must not be tricked into believing that our problems can be solved solely or even mainly through political means. Getting a Christian President will not do it. Stacking Congress and the Supreme Court with Christians will not do it. These are all good things, but they are not enough. Those who hold these powerful offices must understand the purpose and limits of civil government. Civilizations are built when all of life is influenced by the leavening effects of the gospel resulting in changed lives and changed lifestyles.

Too often we are quick to turn to politics because as individuals, families, and churches, we generally have failed to be faithful in areas of immediate responsibility. Our efforts must be directed at the top and bottom. Individual lives, families, and churches must be reformed, and at the same time, reforms must come from the centers of political influence. You can't change just one thing.

Christians must be careful not to use the power and authority of civil government as a political hammer.[27] Let's suppose Christians do change the political system through peaceful, non-revolutionary democratic action.[28] Should they continue to increase the size and scope of civil government, raise taxes for "good" programs, push for prayer in public schools, shore up the Social Security system, and use the power of the Supreme Court to pass "Christian laws"? Or should Christians work to decrease the power of civil government at the federal and state levels, lower the tax burden for all citizens, push for personal responsibility in financial matters, get civil government at all levels out of the education business, and rein in the power of the Supreme Court by putting it in balance with the other branches of government? A great deal of wisdom is needed in knowing how to govern.

Conclusion

The first chapter of Genesis ends with this evaluation of creation: "And God saw all that He had made, and behold, it was very good" (1:31). The "tree of the knowledge of good and evil" was not evil. Even as Adam and Eve ate the fruit, the fruit itself was not evil. The Garden where they committed their sin was not evil. The *decision* to disobey God was evil. What they *did* with God's good creation was morally wrong. Sin is what people do with things. The Apostle Paul demonstrates that the avoidance of "things" does not make a person holy:

> If you have died with Christ to the elementary principles of the world, why, as if you were living in the world, do you submit yourself to decrees, such as, "Do not handle, do not taste, do not touch!" (which all refer to things destined to perish with the using)—in accordance with the commandments and teachings of men? These are matters which have, to be sure, the appearance of wisdom in self-made religion and self-abasement and severe treatment of the body, but are of no value against fleshly indulgence. (Col. 2:20–23).

While things might offer temptations (sex, money, and power), there is no inherent sinfulness in created things. In another place, the apostle addresses a similar issue: "For everything created by God is good, and nothing is to be rejected, if it is received with gratitude; for it is sanctified by means of the word of God and prayer" (1 Tim. 4:4–5). While these passages do not *directly* mention civil government, they do set forth a series of principles that can be applied even to the realm of politics, especially since civil government is God's minister. Civil government, because it is a *government* like families and churches are governments, is a realm where Christians have an *obligation* to be involved; it is a duty.

Notes

1. Joseph M. Stowell, "Can God Bless Politics?," *Moody Monthly* (September 1990), 4.

2. Quoted in Robert Duncan Culver, *Toward a Biblical View of Civil Government* (Chicago, IL: Moody Press, 1974), 72.

3. Robert L. Thoburn, *The Christian and Politics* (Tyler, TX: Thoburn Press, 1985), 17.

4. John Eidsmoe, *God and Caesar: Christian Faith and Political Action* (Westchester, IL: Crossway Books, 1984), 56.

5. Daniel R. Grant, *The Christian and Politics* (Nashville, TN: Broadman Press, 1968), 12.

6. Paul Johnson, *The Enemies of Society* (New York: Atheneum, 1977), 117.

7. Joel Belz, "Evidence Mounts: We Are Still a Small Minority," *World* (October 13, 1990), 3.

8. J. Howe, "The Changing Political Thought of John Adams." Quoted in Wayne House, ed., *Restoring the Constitution: 1787–1987* (Dallas, TX: Probe Books, 1987), 10.

9. Mark O. Hatfield, "How Can a Christian be in Politics?," *Protest and Politics: Christianity and Contemporary Affairs* (Greenwood, SC: The Attic Press, 1968), 7.

10. Jennifer Brett, "Parents conduct turns kids' sports into brawl games," *Atlanta Journal-Constitution* (June 29, 2003), C1.

11. George Bancroft, *History of the United States from the Discovery of the American Continent*, 10 vols. (Boston, MA: Little, Brown & Company, 1860), 8:442.

12. *Biography of the Signers to the Declaration of Independence*, rev. ed. 5 vols. (Philadelphia: William Brown and Charles Peters, 1828), 2:206.

13. *Biography of the Signers to the Declaration of Independence*, 2:205.

14. Quoted in Loraine Boettner, *The Reformed Doctrine of Predestination* (Nutley, NJ: Presbyterian and Reformed, [1932] 1969), 383.

15. John T. McNeill, *The History and Character of Calvinism* (New York: Oxford University Press, 1954), 348.

16. M. E. Bradford, *A Worthy Company* (Westchester, IL: Crossway Books, 1988), viii.

17. Matthew 10:29.

18. Psalm 127:1.

19. On Franklin's religious views, see Walter Isaacson, *Benjamin Franklin: An American Life* (New York: Simon & Schuster, 2003), 32–33, 86–88, 107–113, 451, 467–468. Also see Gary DeMar, *The Case for America's Christian Heritage* (Powder Springs, GA: American Vision, 2009).

20. John F. MacArthur, Jr., *Why Government Can't Save You: An Alternative to Political Activism* (Nashville: Word, 2000).

21. MacArthur, *Why Government Can't Save You*, 8–9.

22. MacArthur, *Why Government Can't Save You*, 9.

23. John MacArthur, Letter (August 15, 2000), sent to "Grace to You" supporters.

24. Rodney Stark, *For the Glory of God: How Monotheism Led to Reformations, Science, Witch-Hunts, and the End of Slavery* (Princeton, NJ: Princeton University Press, 2003), 147.

25. William Shirer, *The Nightmare Years, 1930–1940* (Boston, MA: Little, Brown and Co., 1984), 156.

26. This is most evident when the Episcopal Church ordained a practicing homosexual as bishop. See Cathy Lynn Grossman, "Episcopalians elect female leader," *USA Today* (June 19, 2006), 1A. The Bible's clear teaching on the sinfulness of homosexuality is overruled by the decree of the church. See Claudia Wallis, "A House Divided," *Time* (August 18, 2003), 50–51. Katherine Jefferts Schori was elected as the presiding bishop of the Episcopal Church USA in 2006. She supports same-sex marriage.

27. David W. Hall, *Savior or Servant?: Putting Government in Its Place* (Oak Ridge, TN: The Kuyper Institute, 1996).

28. Harry Van Dyke, *Groen Van Prinsterer's Lectures on Unbelief and Revolution* (Jordan Station, Ontario, Canada: Wedge Publishing Foundation, 1989).

9

"Religion and Politics Do Not Mix"

Myth, Lie, or Half-Truth?: *The best way to run a government is to keep it completely free from any type of religious principles or ideals. A secular government is the best type of government.*

> 1. God only—and never any creature—is possessed of sovereign rights, in the destiny of nations, because God alone created them, maintains them by his almighty power, and rules them by his ordinances. 2. Sin has, in the realm of politics, broken down the direct government of God, and therefore the exercise of authority, for the purpose of government, has subsequently been invested in men as a mechanical remedy. And 3. In whatever form this authority may reveal itself, man never possesses power over his fellow-man in any other way than by an authority which descends upon him from the majesty of God.[1]

Early in the nineteenth century, a blasphemer in New York thought that religion and politics did not mix. "Nonsense, ruled Justice James Kent, for the people need religion and morality 'to bind society together.' He then added: 'The people of this state, in common with the people of this country, profess the general doctrines of Christianity as the rule of their faith and practice.' The decision in this case, the justice concluded, rested upon the incontrovertible fact that 'we are a Christian people.'"[2]

While more Christians are steadily being convinced that the Bible has something to say about *some* social issues, like family and education where an immediate and personal moral impact is felt, there are others who still have trouble with a biblical view of economics, law, morality, and, the subject of this chapter, politics. Like oil and water, religion and politics are said not to mix. When the Bible does address political issues, the argument is made that it only does so in the context of a necessary and unavoidable evil. In this view, politics is more than dirty, it's downright diabolic.

The claim is not being made that civil government (the political or legislative process) should be used to change or reform men and women (though the fear of punishment has an effect on people who might consider committing a crime). The purpose of God's law as it relates to the civil magistrate is to punish and restrain evil, to protect human life and property, and to provide justice for all people. Only God can regenerate the heart. An individual cannot be made good by keeping the law. The law is a tutor to lead us to Christ (Gal. 3:24) and a standard by which we know if we are conforming to the moral will of God (Rom. 13:8–10; 1 Tim. 1:8–11). People who follow the law make good citizens. Those who despise the law are a terror to others. English philosopher Thomas Hobbes (1588–1679) asks, "For what reason do men [arm themselves], and have locks and keys to fasten their doors, if they be not naturally in a state of war?"[3]

A Restraint on Evil

The objection from Christians that religion and politics do not mix can be answered in at least four ways. First, it's true that the Bible's primary concern is not politics. Of course, the same could be said about the family and church not being the Bible's primary concern. And yet, there are few Christians who would maintain that Christians should not be involved in developing biblical models for the family and church.

Second, because there is sin in the world, God has created temporal ways of dealing with it. In family government, God has designated mothers and fathers as rulers (governors) to admonish and discipline their children because children tend to disobey their parents (Eph. 6:1–3). The "rod of correction" is one instrument of discipline (Prov. 13:24). In the church, depending on the ecclesiastical governmental structure, bishops (Episcopalian), elders (Presbyterian), and deacons (Congregational) have ecclesiastical authority in their respective churches and/or denominations. The reason for church government, including its laws and discipline, is the reality of sin even among Christians (e.g., 1 Cor. 5–6). Paul outlines ways for churches, as ecclesiastical governments with real and necessary authority, to handle disputes among members (1 Cor. 6:1–11).[4]

Third, *civil* government has been given authority to maintain order in society, to punish evildoers, and to promote the good (Gen. 9:5–6; Rom. 13:1–6; 1 Pet. 2:13–14). Essentially, civil governments have jurisdiction over what people do of a criminal nature (theft, rape, murder, etc.). As Thomas Jefferson put it, "the legislative powers of government reach actions only."[5] But what actions deserve punishment? Left to itself, history has shown us that civil governments can be notoriously unjust and tyrannical. Genocide has been committed against racial and ethnic groups with the full approval of civil governments. With no moral reference point outside the State, civil governments are not bound by ethical constraints. For example, "In 1933, it was officially declared in Germany that the final authority as to the principles of the State and the law is the National Socialistic German Workers' Party; that no other political party could be formed; and that the Fuehrer should make its laws."[6]

Fourth, politics, because it deals with civil government, is not a necessary evil; it's necessary because of evil (Gen. 4:4–15, 23–24; 9:5–7). The sword is the State's God-ordained instrument of "wrath." This is why the "law is not made for a righteous man, but for those who are lawless and rebellious, for the ungodly and sinners, for the unholy and profane, for those who kill their fathers or mothers, for murderers and immoral men and homosexuals and kidnappers and liars and perjurers" (1 Tim. 1:9–10). Since civil government has the power of the sword, it is incumbent upon Christians to get involved in politics to ensure that political officials use it wisely and with restraint.

Secularism has become the official State religion of many nations. Social theorist Herbert Schlossberg observes: "Western society, in turning away from the Christian faith, has turned to other things. This process is commonly called *secularization*, but that conveys only the negative aspect. The word connotes the turning away from the worship of God while ignoring the fact that something is being turned *to* in its place."[7] Some ideology, always religious in nature, will fill the vacuum left by the exodus of the Christian faith.

The mixing of religion and politics is unavoidable. To prohibit one religion only opens the door for the entrance of another. There is no neutrality. Secularism is just as religious as Christianity and inherently dangerous since it has no built-in restraints. Those who "helped undermine the fabric of traditional Christian Europe" created the "frightful void that communism, socialism and later national socialism would fill." As the anti-Nazi writer Ernest Junger wrote, "Deserted altars are inhabited by demons."[8]

The Challenge of Pluralism

One of the newest challenges to the Christian worldview as it relates to politics is "pluralism." In theory, pluralism espouses an egalitarian religious and ethical theory based on the premise that exclusive religious beliefs (e.g., monotheism) have no place in the discussion of political issues. "Pluralism is the cultural belief that there are many right ways to live and believe. There are no absolutes, so there's nothing to be dogmatic about. Find whatever works for you.... Pluralism reduces convictions to convenient opinions and makes dogmatism an outdated approach to life and experience."[9]

Some advocates of pluralism recognize that religious values have a role to play both socially and politically, just like religion has a role to play in every aspect of life. For them, however, Christianity cannot be the *only* standard. Under this view of pluralism all religious and non-religious views are considered equal in establishing social and political norms. There can be no sure word from God. "Unfortunately, Christians who have been seduced by pluralism no longer say, 'Thus saith the Lord...' or, 'The Bible says....' Instead, we say, 'It seems to me...' or, 'It's not for me, but I'm glad it works for you.' Yet the psalmist claims that the laws of God are *right* (Psalm 19:8). Scripture is clear that there is a right and wrong and that we will personally be held accountable."[10]

Pluralism seems attractive because it eliminates the need to do battle over religious first principles. The hope is to find common ethical principles that all people can agree on. This is the argument of David Rensberger, professor of New Testament at the Interdenominational Theological Center in Atlanta, Georgia. He claims that groups like the ACLU would not object to having certain laws hanging on a courthouse wall so long as they are "tenets of a universal ethical code." He argues that "all societies demand respect for elders and for marital unions, and forbid murder and theft—however they may define those concepts."[11] And that's the problem! Cultures that believe in human sacrifice and cannibalism would not agree that they were violating the prohibition against murder found in the sixth commandment. Societies that still practice slavery would not agree that they were committing a crime or even a sin by stealing men and women (Ex. 21:16), a clear violation of the eighth commandment. What about abortion? Prior to 1973, abortion was considered a crime, a violation of the sixth commandment. This previous criminal procedure is now a constitutional right. Professor Rensberger has turned law into moral Silly Putty.

Polygamy on Trial

In the eighteenth century, the courts agreed that it was necessary for the State to enforce the biblical requirement of monogamy over against polygamy (many wives). They justified their ruling *because* of moral absolutes found in Christianity. If we follow the argument of Professor Rensberger, polygamy should be acceptable *because* it has a long history of consent among many nations. The courts, up to this point in time, have taken a different position. In the nineteenth century, the Supreme Court, in several decisions, upheld the seventh commandment. The justices ruled that polygamy "is contrary to the spirit of Christianity and of the civilization which Christianity has produced in the Western world."[12] In *Davis v. Beason* (1890), the Court came to a similar conclusion based on biblical law:

> Bigamy and polygamy are crimes by the laws of all civilized and Christian countries. They are crimes by the laws of the United States, and they are crimes by the laws of Idaho. They tend to destroy the purity of the marriage relation, to disturb the peace of families, to degrade woman, and to debase man. Few crimes are more pernicious to the best interests of society, and receive more general or more deserved punishment. To extend exemption from punishment for such crimes would be to shock the moral judgment of the community. To call their advocacy a tenet of religion is to offend the common sense of mankind.

Pluralism, if consistent, changes the way laws are made. Without any way to account for making laws other than by way of judicial or legislative fiat, anything goes with no reference point for judgment. What's legal today could, on the judgment of five of nine

Supreme Court justices, be illegal tomorrow. This is hardly what our Founders established:

> Under the doctrine of pure pluralism—to which many secularists say they subscribe—all lifestyles are permitted. Thus, in the end, cannibalism, human sacrifice, group suicide, the Manson Family, polygamy, and kiddie porn would have to be allowed. "Who are we to say what is right and what is wrong?" is the common refrain. Clearly, society cannot long survive if this principle is pushed to its logical conclusion and everyone is free to write his own laws. Thus, we subscribe to pluralism within certain limits. We allow a wide range of behavior, even though we don't always approve of it. But we do not permit all behavior. We do not even allow all so-called "victimless" behavior—such as prostitution, drug addiction, drunkenness, and the like. The reason we don't is that our laws presuppose certain truths. Pure freedom of conscience, then, can never really be tolerated. Government neutrality on matters of religion and morals is a modern myth. We can never escape the question: Whose faith, whose values, whose God undergirds the civil laws of a nation?[13]

If it can be shown that the prohibition against polygamy is primarily religious, then under pluralism, a case could be made for allowing the practice *because* it has a religious foundation. This has already been done for homosexuality. There has been an almost universal prohibition of homosexuality, condemned by both Church and State for thousands of years. "When the first great book on the English Legal system was written—Blackstone's *Commentaries on the Laws of England*—its author referred to sodomy as 'the infamous crime against nature, committed either with man or beast . . . the very mention of which is a disgrace to human nature.'"[14]

Down the Slippery Slope

As in England and the rest of Europe, sodomy was illegal in the thirteen American colonies. Nothing changed with the drafting of the Constitution in 1787. No supposed absolute "right to privacy" was put in the Constitution that legalized the practice. These early Christian politicians, lawyers, and statesmen saw no problem in mixing religion with politics in the case of sodomy. In 2003, the Supreme Court, in a 5 to 4 decision, struck down all anti-sodomy laws, thereby establishing itself as America's new authoritarian religion.

For a time, pluralism makes all opinions equal. An anti-sodomy position is just as legitimate as a pro-sodomy position, therefore, it would be illegitimate to impose an anti-sodomy position on those who want to practice sodomy. Same-sex and unmarried couples would receive the same rights as legally married couples under the doctrine of pluralism. Homosexuals in the United States are pushing the inevitable logic of the court's pro-homosexual ruling to include homosexual marriage. If there is no fixed standard based on the absolutes of the Bible, then such a position is reasonable. Will polygamy be next? What logic can be used to outlaw the practice?

This same logic extends to the abortion issue. Doctors who protect the unborn and work to save premature babies born through heroic measures and advanced technology are no more ethical and deserving of praise than doctors who perform abortions or who deliberately snuff out the life of a terminally ill patient. A consistent pluralism doctrine means that any reference to religion as a basis for an action is at first muted and then eventually nullified. Judges who hold pro-life opinions on abortion are routinely denied the right to serve on various courts *because* they are pro-life. "Opponents to Senate confirmation of Alabama Attorney General William Pryor (a devout Catholic) assert his 'deeply held moral beliefs' disqualify him from service on the 11th U.S. Circuit

Court of Appeals. . . . Christians who ground their political opposition to legalized 'gay marriage' in Scripture are marginalized as 'intolerant' and their arguments deemed illegitimate for public consumption."[15]

Pluralism denies the Bible's view that "righteousness exalts a nation" (Prov. 14:34), since righteousness cannot be defined in terms of any single religion or based on the collective religious will. The Bible could never be applied to political issues under the pluralism doctrine. If it was determined, for example, that a Christian judge based his ruling *against* any capital crime on his understanding of the Bible, he would most likely be overruled by a higher court. Am I exaggerating?:

> U.S. District Court Judge Charles A. Moye removed the sentence of death Feb. 16 [1989] from Brandon Jones, who was convicted in 1979 of murder. Judge Moye ruled that the jury "had a duty to apply the law of the state of Georgia . . . not its own interpretation of the precepts of the Bible." The jury asked for the Bible during its consideration of a penalty for the crime, not while assessing guilt.[16]

The man was convicted of murder. The Bible says that murder is wrong. What if those serving on the jury had used their understanding of the Bible when they came to the decision that the defendant was guilty of murder based on their beliefs about the Bible? Would the accused have been set free or retried?

Additional examples might help to dispel the perceived "advantages" and perceived "objectivity" of pluralism. Under pluralism, in principle, all religions are equal. It follows that the precepts espoused by each religion would also be equal. In the eyes of the State, there would be no fundamental difference between churches that worship God and those that worship Satan. Is this possible in a country that has been described by the Supreme Court in 1892 as "a Christian nation"?[17] Rhode Island, where religious pluralism got its start, sanctioned Our Lady of the Roses Wiccan Church by granting it tax-exempt status. This "church" is a coven of witches and satanists![18]

Florida no longer requires Notaries to affirm "so help me God" on their written oath of office. Most presidents since George Washington have taken their oath of office with a hand on a Bible. Washington's Bible was opened to two passages illustrating Genesis 49:13–15 on the left page and the text of Genesis 49:13–50:8 on the right. Ronald Reagan took the oath of office on the King James Bible used by his mother, Nellie Reagan, opened to 2 Chronicles 7:14.[19] The tradition has been continued down to this day. Presidents end their oath with "so help me God."

When judges appear before the Supreme Court, they must take the following oath: "Do you solemnly swear that as an attorney and as a counselor of the court you will conduct yourself uprightly, and according to law, and that you will support the Constitution of the United States, **so help you God?**" As an attorney takes this oath, his hand is resting on a Bible that has been in possession of the Court since 1808.[20]

The Rev. Gerard LaCerra, chancellor of the Archdiocese of Miami, understands the implications of the action that removes "so help me God" from the oath of office: "What are we supposed to base our commitments on if something like this is removed? The State?"[21] In time, pluralism leads to the messianic State which establishes its own brand of exclusive religion—itself!

The ACLU sued a North Carolina judge because he started each court session with prayer, a brief plea to God for justice. These are the "offending" words:

> O Lord, our God, our Father in Heaven, we pray this morning that you will place your divine guiding hand on this courtroom and that with your mighty outstretched arm you will protect the innocent, give justice to those who have been harmed, and mercy to us all. Let truth be

heard and wisdom be reflected in the light of your presence here with us today. Amen.

A United States District Judge ruled that the judge's "prayer in the courtroom is contrary to the law of the land,"[22] that is, the Constitution. Based on historical evidence, this is impossible to maintain since prayer, including national days of prayer and thanksgiving, have been a part of America's founding. There is nothing unconstitutional about a judge praying in a courtroom. The Bible is still used in many courts to swear in witnesses, with the witnesses acknowledging with "So help me God." Congressional chaplains are constitutional: "The legislature by majority vote invites a clergyman to give a prayer; neither the inviting nor the giving nor the hearing of the prayer is making a law. On this basis alone . . . the saying of prayers, per se, in the legislative halls at the opening session is not prohibited by the First and Fourteenth Amendments."[23]

If there is no God, there is no law of any kind. How can a judge render a just decision if there is no fixed standard of justice? Why should a witness tell the truth?[24] Since the courts have consistently voted to uphold Darwinian evolution as the explanation for the origin of life,[25] how can there ever be a fixed ethical absolute beyond the decision of judges? And what makes the decisions of judges just?[26]

The Messianic State

Christians who believe that pluralism is the answer to political controversies have not made a sincere effort to study its implications. History is filled with examples of the State assuming the role of god once all religions are either made equal or made illegal. The State must find a way to legitimize its authority to rule, or it will be constantly overthrown by the people. When the civil magistrate and the people reject the view that the ruler's authority comes from God (Rom. 13:1)—thus making him responsible to rule in terms of God's law and making the citizenry responsible to obey as well—he makes himself a god and establishes his own laws. Thus, to oppose the king is to oppose god or the gods. Prior to *Magna Carta* (1215), kings viewed their decrees as a "divine right"[27] with no imposed limitations.

In ancient Greece, the Athenian citizen, "while free to worship his private gods, was under a duty to participate in the worship of Zeus and Apollo in the legally prescribed manner. Neglect to do so disqualified one from holding the office of magistrate."[28] This is the doctrine of pluralism in action: the citizenry can hold to private religious beliefs while the State governs in terms of a deity of its own design. In time, even private religious beliefs and practices are no longer tolerated.

Pre-Christian Rome had a similar system. Augustus revived the older deities to solidify his position and authority as emperor. The motivation was political. "In short, it was but another illustration of the use of religion as an engine to further state policy."[29] Augustus went further than his predecessors by "setting his great uncle Julius Caesar among the gods, and commanded that the worship of the Divine Julius should not be less than the worship of Apollo, Jupiter, and the other gods. Augustus thus initiated what has been called the real religion of pre-Christian Rome—the worship of the head of the state. At his death Augustus too joined the ranks of the gods, as did other emperors after him."[30] Like Greece, Rome tolerated private religious beliefs and practices "as long as they did not intervene in the political arena, where the state religion enjoyed a monopoly."[31] In time, however, religious toleration ceased. Refusal to worship Caesar was a manifestation of disloyalty that was often met with cruel retribution, although refusal to worship Jupiter was still tolerated. The emperor was a god who was a cut above the traditional gods, Jupiter included.

With the entrance of Judaism and Christianity to the Roman social and political scene with their declaration of the *shema*—"Hear, O Israel! The LORD is our God, the LORD is one! (Deut. 6:4; cf. Mark 12:29)—an immediate conflict arose. In time, just to be a Christian was an offense against Rome and the gods, especially the emperor who, during the reign of Domitian (A.D. 81–96), was addressed "as *dominus et deus*, 'my Lord and God.'"[32] The Christians could avoid persecution, but at great cost: "Any accused person who denied Christ and gave satisfactory proof that he abjured his errors, by adoring the gods and the emperor's image and cursing Christ, was to be immediately acquitted."[33] So much for the benefits of pluralism. Pluralists hold to the following doctrine: All beliefs are acceptable except for any belief that says not all beliefs are acceptable.

Rome Revisited

You would be wrong if you thought that the deification of the State is solely an attribute of the ancient world. France resurrected the idea in grand but bloody style. While the Christian religion would be totally separated from French politics, this did not mean that religion itself would be banished. The vacuum was filled with a new god. The French "proclaimed the goddess of Reason in Notre-Dame Cathedral in Paris and in other churches in France. . . . In Paris, the goddess was personified by an actress, Demoiselle Candeille, carried shoulder-high into the cathedral by men dressed in Roman costumes."[34]

The French revolutionaries were so opposed to mixing any part of Christianity with politics, that they overturned the entire social order. Their supposed "religious neutrality" created a state of "anti-religion," an implicit atheism. Seeing where atheism was taking the country, the "cult of the Supreme Being" was established as a deistic civil religion controlled by the newly installed political establishment. To separate the Christian religion from the new revolutionary republic, the standard Gregorian calendar was reconfigured[35] to reflect a more "reasonable," non-religious approach to keeping time:

> It is noteworthy that the two greatest atheistic regimes in history—the revolutionary governments of France in 1792 and Russia in 1929—tried to change the traditional

> week, hoping thereby to destroy Christianity. The French set up a ten-day week and the Soviets a five-day week, and both were rigidly enforced, but each lasted only a few years.[36]

While America's Constitution declares that it was "DONE in the Year of our Lord" 1787, the revolutionary French calendar began with a new year one.

Following the French revolutionary trend, the traditional way of dating scholarly papers and books is beginning to change among intellectuals and liberal theologians. B.C. (Before Christ) and A.D. (*Anno Domini*: Year of our Lord) are being rejected in favor of B.C.E. (Before Common Era) and C.E. (Common Era). "One apostate Christian theologian argues that the demise of Christianity is so obvious that 'some future generation may well be moved to discard the Christian calendar entirely, and rename the year A.D. 2000 as 1 G.E., the first year of the global era.' . . . Just as B.C./A.D. are ceding to B.C.E./C.E., Christmas is giving way to 'Winter Break,' and Easter to 'Spring Break.' Instead of marking our calendar in relation to the events of the Christmas story, we now celebrate, as pagans have done, the predictable cycle of the year and nature's circle of life."[37]

These ideological changes have a long history in the rejection of God from the universe. The French Revolution consolidated power into a new nationalism that enticed some "to speak of the 'goddess France.' It meant that those who fought for France were no longer simply doing a job for which they were paid, but were patriots rendering due obeisance to a deity. For them, to do their duty was to do their *sacred* duty, language that has remained part of the liturgy of patriotism to the present, even in officially atheistic countries like the Soviet Union."[38]

The March of God on Earth

One would be hard pressed to find modern politicians who would claim that the State is divine, but more often than not actions speak louder than words. For modern secularists, the political sphere is no less divine than the city-states of Greece and Rome and the deified nationalism of eighteenth-century France, Stalinist Russia, or Nazi Germany. For numerous modern-day politicians, the State is a saving institution instead of a ministry designed and instituted by God for the maintenance of justice. In too many cases, today's State plays the role of benefactor (savior) instead of its biblical role as an administrator of civil justice. The words adorning one of the pediments of the Supreme Court reads: "Justice the Guardian of Liberty." Rejecting this role for itself, "The idol state uses the language of compassion because its intention is a messianic one. It finds the masses harassed and helpless, like sheep without a shepherd, needing a savior."[39] The messianic State promises to set up heaven on earth through coercion and the consolidation of power in the hands of a few. The result is a loss of freedom for the many. It does this in the name of its religion. This is an old story:

> Now [Herod] was very angry with the people of Tyre and Sidon; and with one accord they came to him, having won over Blastus the king's chamberlain, they were asking for peace, *because their country was fed by the king's country*. And on an appointed day Herod, having put on his royal apparel, took his seat on the rostrum and began delivering an address to them. And the people kept crying out, "The voice of a god and not of a man!" And immediately an angel of the Lord struck him because he did not give God the glory, and he was eaten by worms and died (Acts 12:20–23).

As this passage shows, God does not tolerate pluralism. From what we have seen, we can conclude that it is impossible to separate religion from politics. Herod fed the people and demanded worship from the people, and the people were quick to respond favorably.

Some religion, even if it is atheism or paganism, will always be mixed with politics. To exclude Christianity merely opens the door to some other religion.

A Closer Look at the Bible

Human government is derivative of God's government. The realm of politics obtains its authority from God (Rom. 13:1). While God's power is unlimited, all earthly power, politics included, is limited: "The Most High God is ruler over the realm of mankind, and He sets over it whomever He wishes" (Dan. 5:21). Historically, the church reflected on these truths and began to assess its rulers in terms of biblical norms. "During the eighth and ninth centuries the Christian church effected nothing short of a revolution in the forms of Western politics. Put briefly, there developed an idea of the pervasive religious and moral responsibility of the ruler."[40] The ruler was neither divine nor exempt from heaven's rule. The Christian religion specified the ruler's duties and limitations.

To separate Christianity from politics is only to align it with any number of anti-religious concepts. As Abraham Kuyper, former Prime Minister of the Netherlands has written, "no political scheme has ever become dominant which was not founded in a specific religious or anti-religious conception."[41] In time, anti-religious fervor becomes a religion itself.

Rulers as Ministers of God

Scripture tells us that civil rulers are put in positions of authority for our good (Rom. 13:4). The civil magistrate is a "minister of God." The word "minister" is the same Greek word that is translated "deacon" and "servant" elsewhere in Scripture. There are a number of rulers today who still retain the title of "minister," reflecting the biblical language of civil responsibility. The highest civil official in Japan and England is given the title of "Prime Minister." Such a title has religious connotations: "By me [Wisdom] kings reign, and rulers decree justice. By me princes rule, and nobles, all who judge rightly" (Prov. 8:15–16). The truly just ruler will acknowledge that justice is derived by following God's wisdom. "Both Charles the Bald, his grandson, and Alfred in England, compared themselves to Solomon, ruling in accordance with divine wisdom, and Alfred as a lawgiver saw himself in a succession of lawgivers beginning with Moses."[42]

Rulers as Ministers under God's Authority

Rulers are to serve God "with reverence" (Psalm 2:11). It is God who "will cut off the spirit of princes; He is feared by the kings of the earth" (76:12). A time will come when all "the nations will fear the name of the LORD, and all the kings of the earth Thy glory" (102:15). The New Testament has not nullified the role of God's authority over rulers since Jesus "is the image of the invisible God, the firstborn of all creation. For by Him all things were created, both in the heavens and on earth, whether visible and invisible, *whether thrones or dominions or rulers or authorities—all things have been created by Him and for Him*" (Col. 1:15–16). Jesus "*has put* [past tense] *all things* [this would include politics] in subjection under His feet" (1 Cor. 15:27). The rulers of this world are required to understand God's wisdom. Their lack of understanding led Rome and Israel to crucify "the Lord of glory" (1 Cor. 2:8).

Rulers as Ministers of Righteousness

Jethro instructed Moses to teach the rulers and the people "the statutes and the laws," and to "make known to them the way in which they are to walk, and the work they are to do" (Ex. 18:20; cf. Deut. 17:18–20; Psalm 2:10–12; 2 Sam. 23:3–4). Noah, an agent of the civil magistrate under the authority of God (cf. Rom. 13:1), is given authority to execute murderers (Gen. 9:6–7); Joseph is made ruler in Egypt (41:38–49); Moses was the civil ruler in Israel and, because of Jethro's counsel, appointed lesser magistrates to perform civil duties (Ex. 18:13–27); "case laws" are listed for the government of family, church, *and* civil government (Ex. 21–23); God instructs both priests, judges, and kings to follow the law of God (Deut. 17:14–20); the book of Judges is filled with examples of rulers operating in the civil sphere: Othniel (Judges 3:9), Ehud (3:15), Shamgar (3:31), Deborah/Barak (4:4, 6), Gideon (6:11), Jephthah (11:1), and Samson (14:1). In Hebrews, these civil magistrates are commended:

> And what more shall I say? For time will fail me if I tell of Gideon, Barak, Samson, Jephthah, of David and Samuel and the prophets *who by faith conquered kingdoms, [and] performed acts of righteousness. . .*" (Heb. 13:32–33).

Their *civil* deeds were acts of faith. The political realm is ministerial. It demands faith and allegiance to God as the sole Governor of the world (Isa. 9:6–7). The books of Samuel, Kings, and Chronicles tell of the rise and fall of kings and kingdoms, with individual kings singled out for their faithfulness (e.g., 2 Chron. 25:2; 26:4; 27:2). Daniel served as one of Darius' three commissioners (Dan. 6). Nehemiah was appointed "governor" in Israel (Neh. 5:14).

The New Testament is not without examples of political involvement, although to a lesser extent. Keep in mind that Israel was a captive nation at the time of Jesus' earthly ministry. The civil rulers of Israel (elders of the people) could not even implement their own law in their own country (John 18:31), but not because of any theological restriction set forth in Scripture. Given the opportunity, the Jewish State would have been fully operative.

John the Baptist did not tell the Roman soldiers to abandon their positions within the State. Jesus and the Apostle Paul had the utmost respect for civil rulers. In fact, Jesus spoke more harshly against the religious leaders of His day and only used one derogatory remark against a civil official, calling Herod "that fox," probably having reference to his being controlled by a woman. Paul commended "the city treasurer" Erastus (Rom. 16:23). Prayers are to "be made on behalf of all men, for kings and all who are in authority. . ." (1 Tim. 2:1–2). Should these prayers be made so rulers should *not* be influenced by religious values? Religion—the Christian religion—has a legitimate role to play in politics. Who better to rule, a tyrant who despises the things of God or a Christian who understands that as a governor he is ultimately under God's government and civil government is limited in its jurisdictional authority and power?:

> That God is vitally concerned with political affairs is quite easy to demonstrate: it is God who ordained governments in the first place (Rom. 13:1; Rom. 2:21). He is the One who establishes particular kings (Prov. 16:12; Psa. 119:46, 47; 82:1, 2). Therefore, He commands our obedience to rulers (Rom. 13:1–3). Rulers are commanded to rule on His terms (Psa. 2:10ff.). Even in the New Testament activity of political import is discoverable. Jesus urged payment of taxes to *de facto* governments (Matt. 22:15–22). In response to reminders of King Herod's political threats against Him, Jesus publicly rebuked the king by calling him a vixen (Luke 13:32). He taught that a judge is unjust if he does not fear God (Luke 18:2, 6). John the Baptist openly criticized King Herod (Luke 3:19, 20). Peter refused to obey authorities who commanded him to cease preaching (Acts 5:29). The Apostle John referred to the Roman Empire as "the beast" (Rev. 13).[43]

Conclusion

Politics, then, is people acting and making decisions about civil relationships based upon a set of first principles that have a religious foundation. To deny that this area of decision-making is to be affected by religion is to deny the lordship of Jesus Christ over a particular area of life. The Bible and the historical record of the church show that religion and politics have had a healthy relationship.

Notes

1. Abraham Kuyper, *Lectures on Calvinism* (Grand Rapids, MI: Eerdmans, [1931] 1970), 85.

2. *Reynolds v. Ruggles* (1811), cited in Edwin S. Gaustad, *Faith of Our Fathers: Religion and the New Nation* (New York: Harper & Row, 1987), 117.

3. Quoted in Baron De Montesquieu, *The Spirit of Laws*, trans. Thomas Nugent, 2 vols. (London: G. Bell and Sons, Ltd., 1914), 1:4

4. Horace L. Fenton, Jr., *When Christians Clash: How to Prevent and Resolve the Pain of Conflict* (Downers Grove, IL: InterVarsity Press, 1987); Lynn R. Buzzard and Thomas S. Brandon, Jr., *Church Discipline and the Courts* (Wheaton, IL: Tyndale, 1987); Lynn R. Buzzard and Laurence Eck, *Tell It to the Church: Reconciling Out of Court* (Elgin, IL: David C. Cook, 1982).

5. Thomas Jefferson, Letter to the Danbury Baptists, 1802. See Daniel L. Dreisbach, *Thomas Jefferson and the Wall of Separation Between Church and State* (New York: New York University Press, 2002), chap. 3.

6. William L. Burdick, *The Bench and Bar of Other Lands* (Brooklyn: Metropolitan Law Book Co., 1939), 422.

7. Herbert Schlossberg, *Idols for Destruction: The Conflict of Christian Faith and American Culture* (Wheaton, IL: Crossway Books, [1983] 1993), 6.

8. Quoted in Erik von Kuehnelt-Leddihn, *Leftism Revisited: From de Sade and Marx to Hitler and Pol Pot* (Washington, D.C.: Regnery Gateway, 1990), 279.

9. Joseph M. Stowell, *The Dawn's Early Light: Daring to Challenge the Deepening Darkness* (Chicago, IL: Moody Press, 1990), 52–53.

10. Stowell, *The Dawn's Early Light*, 53.

11. David Rensberger, "Commandments force-fed," *Atlanta Journal-Constitution* (October 3, 2003), A19.

12. *The United States v. Late Corporation of the Church of Jesus Christ of Latter Day Saints* (1890).

13. Benjamin Hart, *Faith and Freedom: The Christian Roots of American Liberty* (Dallas TX: Lewis and Stanley Publishers, 1988), 357.

14. Quoted in William Dannemeyer, *Shadow in the Land: Homosexuality in America* (San Francisco, CA: Ignatius Press, 1989), 57.

15. Verdadette Ramirez Broyles, "Political table must also seat the religious," *Atlanta Journal-Constitution* (August 13, 2003), A15. Also see Bob Dart, "Pryor clears judicial panel," *Atlanta Journal-Constitution* (July 24, 2003), B1, B4.

16. "Georgia Judge Overturns Death Sentence Because Jury Consulted Bible," *ALL News: The Official Newsletter of the Pro-Life Movement* (April 7, 1989), 7. As the following case demonstrates, the Bible has been used to illustrate a point of law in Georgia's legal code:

> Iron pins are a common and useful means of identifying property corners and they and other similar monuments serve a useful purpose. The installation and maintenance of permanent monuments identifying land corners even preserves the good order of society itself. From earliest times the law not only authorized but protected landmarks.

Interference with landmarks of another was a violation of the Mosaic law. See Deuteronomy 19:14; 27:17; Job 24:2; Proverbs 22:28; 23:10. (256 Ga. 54, *International Paper Realty Company v. Bethune.* No. 43092. Supreme Court of Georgia, June 10, 1986).

17. *Church of the Holy Trinity v. The United States* (143 United States 457), 1892. See David J. Brewer, *The United States: A Christian Nation* (Powder Springs, GA: American Vision, [1905] 1996).

18. *Chronicles* (November 1989), 7–8.

19. *New York Times* (January 12, 1981).

20. Fred J. Maroon, *The Supreme Court of the United States* (New York: Thomasson-Grant & Lickle, 1996).

21. "'God' Removed from Notaries' Oath," *The Kansas City Star* (February 18, 1990), 2A.

22. "Judges Prayer Banned," *Marietta Daily Journal* (October 20, 1990), 4A.

23. *Chambers v. Marsh*, 463 U.S. 783 (1982), 675 F. 2d 228. See James P. Moore, Jr., *One Nation Under God: The History of Prayer in America* (New York: Doubleday, 2005).

24. Under the Federal Judiciary Act of 1789, no witness could testify who "did not believe that there is a God who rewards truth and avenges falsehood." This requirement was not changed until 1906. The general consensus of the time held that an atheist could not be trusted as a witness: "The Court of Common Pleas of Chester County (New York) . . . rejected a witness who declared his disbelief in the existence of God. The presiding judge remarked, that he had not before been aware that there was a man living who did not believe in the existence of God; that this belief constituted the sanction of all testimony in a court of justice; and that he knew of no cause in a Christian country where a witness had been permitted to testify without such belief." (The New York *Spectator* [August 23, 1831], quoted in Alexis de Tocqueville, *Democracy in America,* 2 vols. New York: Alfred A. Knopf, [(1834, 1840) 1960], 1:306).

25. Francis J. Beckwith and Gregory Koukl, *Relativism: Feet Firmly Planted in Mid-Air* (Grand Rapids, MI: Baker Books, 1998), 156–164.

26. Arthur Allen Leff, "Unspeakable Ethics, Unnatural Law," *Duke Law Journal,* 1979:6 (December 1979), 1229–1249.

27. M. Stanton Evans, *The Theme is Freedom: Religion, Politics, and the American Tradition* (Washington, D.C.: Regnery, 1994), chap. 9.

28. Leo Pfeffer, *Church, State, and Freedom* (Boston, MA: Beacon Press, 1953), 9.

29. Pfeffer, *Church, State, and Freedom,* 9–10.

30. Pfeffer, *Church, State, and Freedom,* 10.

31. Pfeffer, *Church, State, and Freedom,* 10.

32. Schlossberg, *Idols for Destruction,* 185.

33. Pfeffer, *Church, State, and Freedom,* 11.

34. Francis A. Schaeffer, *How Should We Then Live?* in *The Complete Works of Francis A. Schaeffer: A Christian Worldview,* 5 vols. (Westchester, IL: Crossway Books, 1982), 5:149.

35. Denise Dersin, ed., *What Life Was Like During the Age of Reason* (Richmond, VA: Time-Life Books, 1999), 106–107 and Douglas Amrine, *Did You*

Know?: New Insights into a World that is Full of Astonishing Facts and Astounding Stories (New York: Reader's Digest Association, Inc., 1990), 269.

36. Henry M. Morris, *The Long War Against God: The History and Impact of the Creation/Evolution Conflict* (Grand Rapids, MI: Baker Book House, 1989), 311.

37. Peter Jones, *Capturing the Pagan Mind: Paul's Blueprint for Thinking and Living in the New Global Culture* (Nashville, TN: Broadman & Holman, 2003), 1, 163–164.

38. Schlossberg, *Idols for Destruction*, 178.

39. Schlossberg, *Idols for Destruction*, 185.

40. Henry Mayr-Harting, "The West: The Age of Conversion (700–1050)," *The Oxford Illustrated History of Christianity*, ed. John McManners (New York: Oxford University Press, 1990), 101.

41. Kuyper, *Lectures on Calvinism*, 78.

42. Mayr-Harting, "The West: The Age of Conversion (700–1050)," 102.

43. Kenneth L. Gentry, Jr., "The Greatness of the Great Commission," in *The Journal of Christian Reconstruction*, Symposium on Evangelism, ed. Gary North 3:2 (Winter 1981), 45. For an expansion of this theme, see Gentry's *The Greatness of the Great Commission: The Christian Enterprise in a Fallen World*, rev. ed. (Tyler, TX: Institute for Christian Economics, [1990] 1993).

10

"The Christian's Citizenship is in Heaven"

Myth, Lie, or Half-Truth?: *Because the Christian's true home is in heaven, any talk about earthly responsibility as it relates to citizenship is misdirected.*

> In the modern world, then, each Christian is a citizen of two nations: An earthly nation like France, England, or the U.S.A., and the heavenly nation (Eph 2:6; not of this world, John 18:36), the church. Though we belong entirely to Christ, we do not on that account renounce our citizenship in the earthly nations, any more than we leave our earthly families. Indeed, we seek to be good citizens, for those earthly nations themselves, and their rulers, received their authority from God (Rom 13:1–7).[1]

I will protect the German people,' Hitler shouted. 'You take care of the church. You pastors should worry about getting people to heaven and leave this world to me.'"[2] Adolf Hitler's angry response was directed at Martin Niemöller, a decorated World War I submarine commander, an uncompromising nationalist, and a minister of the gospel. Niemöller had written *From U-Boat to Pulpit* in 1933, showing that "the fourteen years of the [Weimar] Republic had been 'years of darkness.' In a final word inserted at the end of the book he added that Hitler's triumph at last brought light to Germany."[3] He soon learned that the flickering light of the Reich was an incendiary bomb that would destroy the hopes and freedoms of the German people. That light would be used to ignite gas ovens in the extermination of millions of Jews and other "undesirables." By 1935, "Niemöller had become completely disillusioned."[4]

Niemöller became a public critic of Hitler and his policies, "protesting against the anti-Christian tendencies of the regime, denouncing the government's anti-Semitism and demanding an end to the state's interference in the churches."[5] Not everyone followed Niemöller's lead. Numerous pastors swore a personal oath of allegiance and obedience to Adolf Hitler. Other pastors were sent to concentration camps for their defiance. Niemöller was imprisoned for his defiance.

Why did many in the church comply with Hitler's policies? Hitler understood the theology of the churches of his day. Hermann Rauschning, a Hitler confidant, relates what he heard Hitler say about the clergy:

> "The Protestants haven't the faintest conception of a church," I heard Hitler saying. "You can do anything you like to them—they will submit. They're used to cares and worries. . . . They are insignificant little people, submissive as dogs, and they sweat with embarrassment when you talk to them."[6]

For many church-going Germans, their heavenly citizenship obligated them blindly to accept the prevailing civil requirements of citizenship and to remain silent no matter what atrocities might be committed. "In no country except with the exception of Czarist Russia did the clergy become by tradition so completely servile to the political authority of the State."[7] Niemöller tried in vain to awaken the church against Hitler's plans: "'We have no more thought of using our own powers to escape the arm of the authorities than had the Apostles of old. No more are we ready to keep silent at man's behest when God commands us to speak. For it is, and must remain, the case that we must obey God rather than man.'"[8] A Christian's heavenly citizenship, Niemöller concluded, must have an impact in the world in which he lives.

What Does it Mean to be an "Alien"?

Pastor and author John Piper uses Hebrews 13:14, 1 Peter 2:11, and Philippians 3:20 in an attempt to dispel the idea that Christians can have a lasting impact on this world. He writes that Christians "exert influence as happy, brokenhearted outsiders"[9] who should only count on having limited and temporal success this side of heaven. The above passages have nothing to do with the success of Christian involvement in the world. The writer to the Hebrews (13:14) is contrasting the soon-to-be judged city of Jerusalem (Matt. 24:1–34) with that of "the city which has foundations, whose architect and builder is God" (Heb. 11:10). Earlier in Hebrews we read, "But you have come to Mount Zion and to the city of the living God, the heavenly Jerusalem. . ." (12:22; cf. Gal. 4:26). This new city, the heavenly Jerusalem, is a present reality while we are in this world. It's the reality of Jesus' redemptive work that makes our work possible in the here and now. The comments of F. F. Bruce help to put these verses into proper theological context:

> The people of God are still a pilgrim people, treading the "highways to Zion," but by virtue of his sure promise they have already arrived there in spirit. Our author may retain the symbolism of "up there" when he speaks of God, but he makes it clear that his people need not climb the heavenly steeps [heights] to seek him, for he is immediately accessible to each believing heart, making his dwelling in the fellowship of the faithful.[10]

Peter's description of Christians in the first century "as aliens and strangers" (1 Pet. 2:11) is a reference to their alienation from old covenant Judaism. Those in Christ are the true people of God, "a chosen race, a royal priesthood, a holy nation, a people for God's own possession" (1 Pet. 2:9). Before Christ, they "were not a people" (1 Pet. 2:10).

Piper is wrong when he writes that "American culture does not belong to Christians, neither in reality nor in biblical theology. It never has. The present tailspin toward Sodom is not a fall from Christian ownership, 'the whole world lies in the power of the evil one' (1 John 5:19). . . . God's rightful ownership will be manifest in due time."[11] "World," in this context, does not mean the earth but only those who are outside of Christ, otherwise John would be saying that our families and even the church are under the dominion of Satan. Peter describes the "world" at the time of Noah's flood as being "destroyed, being flooded with water" (2 Pet. 3:6). But what was actually destroyed? "The 'world' that was destroyed," Paul Marshall writes, "was not the 'world' of the creation itself but the 'world' of sinful people. The sinful world—the conspiracy of evil against God—was destroyed. But Noah and his family and the animals and the birds were rescued in order to begin life again."[12]

"God's rightful ownership" has been from the beginning. God is "a great King over all the earth" (Ps. 47:2). Jesus reinforces this truth when He tells His disciples, "All authority has been given to Me in heaven *and on earth*" (Matt. 28:18). The true outsiders are the usurpers who claim that this world is their world. Following Piper's view, Christians are immigrants, or at best second-class citizens, in a world created for rebels but owned by God and redeemed by Jesus. This makes no sense.

Multiple Citizenships

Richard Land and Louis Moore write, "We Christians are citizens of two realms—the earthly and spiritual. Such dual citizenship includes rights and responsibilities in both spheres."[13] Some want to argue that the Christian's heavenly citizenship by definition nullifies any earthly citizenship responsibility. The Apostle Paul saw no contradiction in claiming his Roman citizenship (Acts 16:37–39; 22:22–29) and maintaining that he was also a citizen of heaven (Phil. 3:20). There is no contradiction in Peter's words when he commands us to submit ourselves "to every human institution, whether to a king as the one in authority, or to governors as sent by him for the punishment of evildoers and the praise of those who do right" (1 Peter 2:13–14) and his words to the officers of the temple when he and the apostles said, "We must obey God rather than men" (Acts 5:29).

The Christian has multiple civil citizenships: city, county, state, and nation. Being a citizen of any one of these does not nullify the citizenships of the others. For example, the Apostle Paul was a Roman citizen (Acts 22:27–29) of the city of Tarsus in the region of Cilicia (21:39) and a resident of Jerusalem in the district of Judea (22:3). Had Israel not been subjected to the sovereignty of Rome's political dominance, Paul could have exercised his tribal citizenship as a resident of the "tribe of Benjamin" (Phil. 3:5).

In a similar way, a United States citizen has a national, state, county, and city citizenship, none of which usurps the validity of the others. In some states borough governments (e.g., Pennsylvania, New Jersey, New York, Minnesota) and parish governments (e.g., Louisiana) operate. Each of the multiple civil authorities holds real power and sovereignty. Their civil authority can be used to curtail the power of another legitimate but power-hungry government or an illegitimate governing power claiming jurisdiction through coercion.

Through multiple civil citizenships citizens have legitimate access to the seats of power where influence can be exerted on a local level. Abolition of these many civil distinctions leads to despotism and tyranny. Adolph Hitler was able to consolidate his power by eliminating "the separate powers of the historic states" and subjecting them "to the central authority of the Reich, which was in his hands. . . .

'Popular assemblies' of the states were abolished, the sovereign powers of the states were transferred to the Reich, all state governments were placed under the Reich government and the state governors put under the administration of the Reich Minister of the Interior."[14] With indifference to political concerns by most Christians, Hitler easily consolidated political power.

One of the tenets of Marxism as outlined in the *Communist Manifesto* was the "gradual abolition of the distinction between town and country, by a more equable distribution of the population over the country." Our American constitutional framers designed a decentralized civil government which also decentralized power and authority. Our forefathers feared the type of government that gave rise to Nazism and Communism.

Why Bother?

In his book *The Ten Commandments*, Hermann Rauschning describes Hitler's master plan of a complete reordering of this world along purely humanistic lines. At an intimate gathering in Berlin shortly after the National Socialists came to power, the author heard Hitler discuss his true intentions as they related to "the ethical foundation of life." Rauschning "wrote down the conversation as well and faithfully as" his memory allowed, and in 1937 passed parts of it to the future Pope Pius XII, Protestant clergymen, and published other parts in his book *The Voice of Destruction*.[15] What was the response by these leaders?: "skepticism, disagreement, and even confusion."

Writing as an eyewitness to the events unfolding before him, Rauschning offered a warning that few people wanted to hear. "It concerns all of us," he wrote. "It deals with the deliberately planned battle against the dignified, immortal foundation of human society; the message from Mount Sinai. Let us name it clearly and simply: Hitler's Battle Against the Ten Commandments."[16]

Hitler and his malleable henchmen hated God's law. They knew that it was the only thing that stood between them and their new world order. Hitler described God as "that Asiatic tyrant." True freedom, as Hitler saw it, is freedom *from* God's law. Rauschning recounts the following ravings by Hitler while spending the evening with him and other Nazi party loyalists at the Reich Chancery:

> The day will come when I shall hold up against these commandments the tables of a new law. And history will recognize our movement as the great battle for humanity's liberation, a liberation from the curse of Mount Sinai, from the dark stammerings of nomads who could no more trust their own sound instincts, who could understand the divine only in the form of a tyrant who orders one to do the very things one doesn't like. This is what we are fighting against: the masochistic spirit of self-torment, the curse of so-called morals, idolized to protect the weak from the strong in the face of the immortal law of battle, the great law of divine nature. Against the so-called ten commandments, against them we are fighting.[17]

If our only citizenship is in heaven, why bother fighting Hitler's anti-Christian methods? Who cares if God's law is not being honored? Heaven is our home. Unfortunately, many Germans felt the same way in the 1930s and paid a hefty price for their indifference.

Some Christians might object to this emphasis on law. "The Christian faith is about grace and mercy. . . . Why should we be concerned about the Ten Commandments? . . . We're not under law; we're under grace." Civil government is a ministry of law. That's its God-ordained job: "For rulers are not a cause of fear for good behavior, but for evil; . . . for it is a minister of God, an avenger who brings wrath upon the one who practices evil" (Rom. 13:3, 4). How does the civil magistrate know what's good and evil? If there is no objective law, then he is a law unto himself, and we are in trouble. God's law restrains the civil magistrate in the same way it restrains all of us. The law is God's published boundary marker of behavior.

Paul does not dismiss the law for believers: "Owe nothing to anyone except to love one another; for he who loves his neighbor has fulfilled the law" (13:8). And how does one love his neighbor? By not committing adultery (seventh commandment), by not murdering (sixth commandment), by not stealing (eighth commandment), and by not coveting (tenth commandment) (13:9). Paul defines love in terms of the law, specifically the law of the Ten Commandments.

Consider what's happened in America since God and His law have been pushed out of the moral universe. Tens of millions of preborn babies have been killed; sodomy has been made a civil right; and God's name has been turned into a curse word. The secularists are quite content to allow Christians to have their personal Jesus, they just don't want His law. They would support the notion of many misguided Christians who claim that their heavenly citizenship makes them disinterested citizens of this world.

Ultimate Citizenship

Ultimately, the Christian is a citizen of God's kingdom. In Philippians 3:20, Paul mentions this aspect of citizenship: "For our citizenship is in heaven, from which also we eagerly await for a Savior, the Lord Jesus Christ." This idea corresponds to Jesus informing Nicodemus that he must be "born again" [lit., *born from above*] (John 3:5; cf. 14:1–3). In effect, he must become a *redemptive* citizen of heaven. An individual's heavenly "citizenship" does not cancel his earthly citizenship and corresponding civil obligations.

The Christian has an obligation to follow the law of God as it applies to all locales. God's law is the standard whereby all the above mentioned citizenships must operate. Our heavenly citizenship involves comprehensive law keeping. Jesus said, "If you love Me, you will keep My commandments" (John 14:15). Jesus does not restrict the locale of law keeping; therefore, we can conclude that the keeping of His commandments includes every citizenship without exception: county, state, and national.

When Scripture speaks about obeying the civil magistrate (Rom. 13:1–7; 1 Peter 2:13–17), citizens must obey. When civil laws conflict with the laws of heaven, the Christian's first obligation is to his heavenly citizenship (Acts 5:29). While the Christian lives on earth, he remains responsible to various ecclesiastical and civil governments, but he looks for the day when his heavenly citizenship will be fully realized:

> All these [Old Testament believers] died in faith, without receiving the promises, but having seen them and having welcomed them from a distance, and having confessed that they were strangers and exiles on the earth. . . . But as it is, they desire a better country, that is a heavenly one (Heb. 11:13, 16; cf. 1 Peter 2:11).

The church is spoken of as a citizenship: "So then you are no longer strangers and aliens, but you are fellow-citizens with the saints, and are of God's household" (Eph. 2:19). The Christian's heavenly citizenship *automatically* places him in an ecclesiastical body where a law-order should operate (Matt. 16:13–19; 18:15–20; 1 Cor. 6:1–11).

Paul's Example

The Apostle Paul saw no inconsistency in taking advantage of his Roman citizenship (Acts 16:37–39; 22:22–29; 25:12) while maintaining that he was also a citizen of heaven (Phil. 3:20). Paul did not deny his Roman citizenship and claim heavenly citizenship when he was taken to be "examined by scourging" (Acts 22:24). "And when they stretched him out with thongs, Paul said to the centurion who was standing by, 'Is it lawful for you to scourge a man who is a Roman and uncondemned?'" (22:25). Why didn't Paul just "take it," content in the fact that he was a citizen of heaven? Instead, he used the privileges of Roman citizenship to his advantage. While some had purchased their citizenship with large sums of money, Paul "was actually born a citizen" (22:28) and did not apologize for it.

Nowhere do we find Paul repudiating the privileges that came with being a Roman citizen. We should keep in mind that the Caesars considered themselves to be gods. To be actively involved in the realm of politics does not mean that politics has to be free of all pagan thought. Paul proclaimed an unadulterated message to these pagan rulers hoping to persuade them of their religious folly. On several occasions Paul used all of the privileges of his Roman citizenship to his advantage by appealing, not to heaven but to "Caesar," the seat of Roman civil authority (Acts 25:11). Of course, he was using Caesar as a way to advance the gospel to bring others into a heavenly citizenship.

The Sovereignty of Satan

Related to the citizenship issue is the status of Satan in the world. If Satan is sovereign over this world, as so many claim, then it stands to reason that Christians, whose citizenship is elsewhere, cannot participate in a world controlled by the devil. Although, as we've seen above, Paul had no trouble dealing with pagan emperors who thought of themselves as gods. Some Christians will go so far as to declare that "secular government" is "the province of the sovereignty of Satan."[18] This belief is based, in part, on the temptation narratives of Matthew and Luke where Satan offers the kingdoms of the world to Jesus. Satan, showing Jesus "all the kingdoms of the world, and their glory," makes the following promise: "All these things will I give You, if you fall down and worship me" (Matt. 4:9), "for it has been handed over to me, and I give it to whomever I wish" (Luke 4:6). According to this theory, Satan was and is in control of political power structures.

Robert Duncan Culver, a supporter of this view, writes: "It is noteworthy that Jesus did not dispute the claim of dominion over the kingdoms of the world (*kosmos*). His answer was an implicit acknowledgment of the legitimacy of Satan's claim. Under the providence of God it is his to give, or else there was no temptation. In such a case Jesus might have laughed at Satan rather than to have answered with sober quotations of relevant Scripture."[19]

There are several problems with this interpretation. First, we know that Satan is a liar (Gen. 3:4–5). Jesus calls him "a liar, and the father of lies" (John 8:44). Second, does the truth have to be told before a temptation can be real? Why should we expect the truth from someone who is tempting us to do evil? Let's suppose a politician is offered a million dollars if he votes a certain way on some upcoming legislation. The politician agrees and takes the money. As soon as he does, an FBI agent appears, reads him his rights, and then arrests him for accepting a bribe. The money is taken from the politician and put back in the possession of the Justice Department that set up the sting operation. The man who offered the politician the money did not own the money. In fact, the entire operation was a lie. The crime was in the willingness to accept the bribe to influence legislation.

Third, Jesus' sin would have been to accept Satan's offer similar to the way Adam and Eve disobeyed God and ate of the fruit. Did Satan own the tree? Was it his to give? Not at all. Jesus already possessed the kingdoms of the world since He is the creator of all things: "All things came into being by Him; and apart from Him nothing came into being that has come into being" (John 1:3; cf. 1:10).

Fourth, notice that on the first two temptations, Satan questions whether Jesus is the Son of God: "*If* you are the Son of God. . ." (Matt. 4:3, 6). Jesus did not correct the devil by insisting that He was the Son of God. Jesus simply quoted what His and every man's duty is: "Fear God and keep His commandments, because this applies to every person. Because God will bring every act to judgment, everything which is hidden, whether it is good or evil" (Eccl. 12:13–14).

Fifth, we know that before and after the death and resurrection of Jesus, Satan's authority was severely limited: "Now judgment is upon this world; now the ruler of this world shall be cast out" (John 12:31). Satan's status in the world has changed significantly. Jesus said to His disciples, "I was watching Satan fall from heaven like lightning" (Luke 10:18). Jesus is the "King of kings and Lord of lords" (Rev. 19:16). If Satan possessed all the kingdoms of the earth prior to the crucifixion (a debatable point), he certainly doesn't have them now since "all authority" has been given to Jesus "in heaven and on earth" (Matt. 28:18).

Are the "Powers" Evil?

Some go even further in their evaluation of political power by claiming that power is evil in and of itself, especially when it is institutionalized in the realm of politics. The claim is made that Christians cannot get involved in politics because the very nature of government is Satanic. Supposedly, Jesus made this very clear in John 19:11 when He stated that Pilate's power was given to him "from above," that is from rebellious angels. Jacques Ellul in *The Subversion of Christianity* wants to maintain that "'from above' does not denote either God or the emperor but the *exousia* [authority] of political power, which is a rebel *exousia* [authority], an angel in revolt against God."[20] Is this possible? Jesus tells Nicodemus that he must be born "from above" (John 3:3). The same Greek word is used in both places. The authorities "which exist are established by God" (Rom. 13:1); civil government is God-ordained. This does not mean that those in power acknowledge God's sovereignty over them (cf. Dan. 4). Neither does it mean that Christians should not get involved in the political process. Not to be involved in *some* capacity is to deny God as the One who establishes the powers that be.

Christians would agree that the *abuse* of power is evil, as is the abuse of wealth, sex, and freedom. But is power evil in and of itself? While it's true that God has chosen the weak things of the world to confound the strong; it is equally true that God has invested authority and limited power in governmental institutions like family, church, and civil government.

It's the *love* of money that's the root of all kinds of evil, not money itself. Money is God's good gift to man. God created the land of Havilah with gold, and Scripture tells us that "the gold of that land is good" (Gen. 2:12). But money, like power, can be corrupted. Men in positions of authority often abuse power. Nebuchadnezzar, king of Babylon, is a perfect example of the legitimacy and the abuse of power. God judged the king for his claim of absolute and autonomous sovereignty and power.

> The king reflected and said, "Is this not Babylon the great which I myself have built as a royal residence by the might of my power and for the glory of my majesty?" While the word was in the king's mouth, a voice came from heaven saying, "King Nebuchadnezzar, to you is declared: sovereignty has been removed from you, and you will be driven away from mankind, and your dwelling place will be with the beasts of the field." (Dan. 4:30—32a).

In time, however, God restored the king's sovereignty, and "surpassing greatness was added" to him (4:37). How could God restore the king if these powers are evil?

The Present Status of the Devil

Like all creatures, the devil has certain limitations. Even under the Old Covenant, Satan had to be granted permission by God before he could act (Job 1:6–12; 2:1–7). Satan's limitations have been multiplied since the crucifixion, resurrection, and ascension of Jesus.

The Bible shows us that if we "resist the devil he will flee from" us (James 4:7). The only power that Satan has over the Christian is the power we give him and the power granted to him by God (2 Cor. 12:7–12). Scripture tells us that Satan is defeated, disarmed, and spoiled (Col. 2:15; Rev. 12:7; Mark 3:27). He has "fallen" (Luke 10:18) and was "thrown down" (Rev. 12:9). He was "crushed" under the feet of the early Christians, and by implication, under the feet of all Christians throughout the ages (Rom. 16:20). He has lost "authority" over Christians (Col. 1:13). He has been "judged" (John

16:11). He cannot "touch" a Christian (1 John 5:18). His works have been destroyed (1 John 3:8). He has "nothing" (John 14:30). He must "flee" when "resisted" (James 4:7). He is "bound" (Mark 3:27; Luke 11:20). Finally, the gates of hell "shall not overpower" the advancing church of the Lord Jesus Christ (Matt. 16:18). Surely Satan is alive, but he is not well on planet earth.

Satan as the "God of this World"

So then, what does Paul mean when he describes Satan as the "god of this world [*age*]"?[21] (2 Cor. 4:4). (The more accurate translation is *age* rather than "world" since the Greek word *kosmos,* the usual word for "world," is not used.) Supposedly, this verse teaches that Satan has all power and authority in this dispensation and in the locale of planet earth: God is the God of heaven and of the age to come, and Satan is the god of earth and this present evil age. This dualistic view of the universe may be part of Greek pagan philosophy, but it has no place in biblical theology. While it's true that the devil is said to be the "god of this age," we know that God is "the King of the ages" (1 Tim. 1:17). Jesus is in possession of "all authority," in both *heaven* and *earth* (Matt. 28:18–20).

> The modern Dispensationalist goes so far as to say that Satan is in control of this present world. He overlooks the obvious fact that the only three passages of Scripture which denominate Satan "the prince of this world" assert that Christ by His death defeated Satan as prince of the world. With a view to His impending death Jesus said: "Now shall the prince of this world be cast out" [John 12:31]; "the prince of this world cometh, and he hath nothing in me" [John 14:30]; "the prince of this world is judged" [John 16:11].[22]

In addition, we know that Satan's power has not increased since Job's day. He is still a permission-seeking creature (Luke 22:31). This is especially true under the new and better covenant inaugurated by Jesus Christ. Gods do not have to ask permission. As the above verses make clear, Satan is a second-class creature who has been cast out and judged: "The ruler of this world *shall be* cast out" (John 12:31); "the ruler of this world *has been* judged" (16:11).

What, then, does the apostle mean when he describes Satan as "the god of this age"? First, we must never allow one passage to finalize our understanding of a particular doctrine. Scripture must be compared with Scripture. There are no contradictions. Therefore, we can't have God as "the King of the ages" and Satan as "the god of this age." We can't say that Satan has been judged and cast out and still maintain that he is the god of this world similar to the way Jehovah is God of this world.

What *theological* point is Paul trying to make? Jesus tells the Pharisees that the devil is their father (John 8:44). We know that Satan is not their biological father. Rather, he is their *spiritual* father in that they rejected their true Father and His Son, Jesus Christ. They chose Barabbas, "son (*bar*) of *a* father (*abba*), a bastard, over Jesus (Matt. 27:17–20), Son of *the* Father, the true Son:

> Physically these Jews, to be sure, are children of Abraham; but spiritually and morally—and *that* was the issue—they are the children of the devil.[23]

Jesus is describing the devil as one who gives birth to a worldview, a worldview that includes lying and murder. In this sense, Satan is the unbeliever's *spiritual* father. In the same way, Satan is a god to those who cling to the fading glory of the Old Covenant which is a "ministry of death" (2 Cor. 3:7). This is the age over which he is a god, an age that "has no glory on account of the glory that surpasses it" (2 Cor. 3:10). That glory is the finished work of Jesus Christ that has surpassed the administration of the blood of bulls and goats. The unbelieving Jews of Jesus' day were still clinging to the temple and the sacrifices when the true "Lamb of God," who had come to take "away the sins of the world," had been in their midst (John 1:29). They had crucified God's Lamb who was in fact the "Lord of glory."

Second, the devil is *chosen* as a god by "those who are perishing," and he must blind them before they will follow him: "The god of this world *has blinded the minds of the unbelieving,* that they *might not see the light of the gospel* of the glory of Christ, who is the image of God" (2 Cor. 4:4). This passage teaches that unbelievers are *fooled* into believing that "the old covenant," where the "veil remains unlifted," is the way to life (2 Cor. 3:14). Satan is the god of the "ministry of death." The "god of this age" keeps them in bondage, "but whenever a man turns to the Lord, the veil is taken away" (2 Cor. 3:16), and he no longer perceives Satan as a god. Liberty from the ministry of death only comes where the Spirit of the Lord is: "Now the Lord is the Spirit; and where the Spirit of the Lord is, there is liberty" (2 Cor. 3:17). But Satan has blinded the eyes of the unbelieving so they cannot see the lifted veil. They are still trusting in the shadows of the Old Covenant.

Third, like idols in general, the devil is "by nature" not a god (Gal. 4:8; cf. Deut. 32:17; Psalm 96:5; Isa. 44:9–20; 1 Cor. 8:4; 10:20). In Philippians 3:19, Paul tells us that those who are "enemies of the cross of Christ" worship "their appetite": "For many walk, of whom I often told you, and now tell you even weeping, that they are enemies of the cross of Christ, whose end is destruction, *whose god is their appetite, and whose glory is in their shame, who set their minds on earthly things.*" The appetite is not a god, but it can be chosen as a god. Satan is not a god, but he can be set up as an idol similar to the way the children of Israel set up the golden calf (Ex. 32:1–10; cf. Isa. 44:9–28).

Fourth, the only way Satan can pass himself off as a god is to blind his victims. Keep in mind that Jesus described the devil as "a liar, and the father of lies" (John 8:44). Though Satan masquerades as a god and "disguises himself as an angel of light" (2 Cor. 11:14), this does make him a god or an angel of light:

> Satan wishes, albeit vainly, to set himself up as God, and sinners, in rebelling against the true God, subject themselves to him who is the author of their rebellion. The unregenerate serve Satan as though he were their God. They do not thereby, however, escape from the dominion of the one true God. On the contrary, they bring themselves under His righteous judgment; for Satan is a creature and not a God to be served (cf. Rom. 1:18, 25). Just as there is one gospel in the world and every pretended alternative to it is a false no-gospel, so there is only one God of the universe and every other "deity" whom men worship and serve is a false no-god.[24]

When all the evidence is in, we learn that Satan is the god of an age that was passing away. He is the god of choice for those who reject the finished redemptive work of Jesus Christ. "This age" and "this world" are used "in an *ethical* sense," denoting "the *immoral realm of disobedience* rather than the all-inclusive, extensive scope of creation," representing "the life of man apart from God and bound to sinful impulses," a world "ethically separated from God."[25] Martin Luther put it well:

> And though this world, with devils filled, should threaten to undo us.
> We will not fear, for God hath willed His truth to triumph through us.
> The prince of darkness grim, we tremble not for him;
> His rage we can endure, for lo! his doom is sure.
> One little word shall fell him.[26]

Calling Satan the "god of this age" is more a reflection of the condition of "this age" than the real status of the devil. Chrysostom commented that "Scripture frequently uses the term *god*, not in regard of the dignity that is so designated, but of the weakness of those in subjection to it; as when he calls mammon lord and belly god: but the belly is neither therefore God nor mammon Lord, save only of those who bow themselves to them."[27]

Conclusion

When the church *makes* Satan the "god of this age," it has fallen for one of the devil's schemes—giving him a lot more credit and power than he deserves or possesses. He is quite satisfied in having anyone believe one of his lies. Believing in this type of half-truth leads many Christians to deny any stake in this world and the responsibilities that go with an earthly citizenship. Christians are citizens of both heaven and earth because Jesus is Lord of both heaven and earth.

Notes

1. John M. Frame, "Toward a Theology of the State," *Westminster Theological Journal* 51:2 (Fall 1989), 221.
2. Quoted in Charles Colson, *Kingdoms in Conflict* (Grand Rapids, MI: Zondervan, 1987), 140.
3. William L. Shirer, *The Nightmare Years: 1930–1940* (Boston, MA: Little, Brown and Company, 1984), 152.
4. Shirer, *The Nightmare Years*, 152.
5. Shirer, *The Nightmare Years*, 153.
6. Hermann Rauschning, *The Voice of Destruction* (New York: G. P. Putnam's Sons, 1940), 54.
7. William L. Shirer, *The Rise and Fall of the Third Reich* (New York: Simon and Schuster, 1960), 236.
8. Quoted in Shirer, *The Nightmare Years*, 154.
9. John Piper, "Brokenhearted Joy," *World* (December 13, 2003), 51. This article was first published as "Taking the Swagger out of Christian Cultural Influence," *New Horizons* (November 2003), 21.
10. F. F. Bruce, *The Epistle to the Hebrews* (NICNT), rev. ed. (Grand Rapids, MI: Eerdmans, 1990), 357.
11. Piper, "Brokenhearted Joy," 51.
12. Paul Marshall, *Heaven Is Not My Home: Living in the Now of God's Creation* (Nashville, TN: Word Publishing, 1998), 237.
13. Richard D. Land and Louis A. Moore, "Preface," *Christian Citizens: The Rights and Responsibilities of Dual Citizenship* (Nashville, TN: Broadman & Holman, 1994), v.
14. Shirer, *Rise and Fall of the Third Reich*, 200.
15. Hermann Rauschning, *The Voice of Destruction* (New York: G. P. Putnam's

Sons, 1940). In England, it was published in 1939 under the title *Hitler Speaks.*

16. Hermann Rauschning, "Preface," *The Ten Commandments: Ten Short Novels of Hitler's War Against the Moral Code,* ed. Armin L. Robinson (New York: Simon and Schuster, 1943), x.

17. Rauschning, *The Ten Commandments,* xiii.

18. John Howard Yoder, *The Politics of Jesus* (Grand Rapids, MI: Eerdmans, 1972), 195.

19. Robert Duncan Culver, *Toward a Biblical View of Civil Government* (Chicago, IL: Moody Press, 1974), 49–50.

20. Jacques Ellul, *The Subversion of Christianity, The Subversion of Power* (Grand Rapids, MI: Eerdmans, 1986), 115.

21. The Greek word in this passage is *aion,* most often translated as "age." There are other New Testament passages where Satan is described as being "the ruler of the world" (John 14:30). "Age" and "world" seem to be used synonymously in many contexts.

22. R. B. Kuiper, "The Word of God Versus the Totalitarian State," *Westminster Theological Journal* XI (November 1948). Quoted in Gary North, ed., *The Journal of Christian Reconstruction,* Symposium on Politics 5:1 (Summer 1978), 170.

23. William Hendriksen, *Exposition of the Gospel According to John,* 2 vols. (Grand Rapids, MI: Baker Book House, 1953–1954), 2:60.

24. Philip E. Hughes, *Commentary on the Second Epistle of the Corinthians,* (NICNT) (Grand Rapids, MI: Eerdmans, 1962), 127.

25. Greg L. Bahnsen, "The Person, Work, and Present Status of Satan," *The Journal of Christian Reconstruction,* Symposium on Satanism, ed. Gary North 1:2 (Winter, 1974), 22.

26. Martin Luther, "A Mighty Fortress is Our God," third verse.

27. Quoted in Hughes, *Commentary on the Second Epistle of the Corinthians,* 128.

Jesus was not "of the world" in the sense that He did not derive His authority, His power, His standards of conduct from this world. In the same sense, Christians are not of the world. Therefore Christians are to be separated from the world morally. We are not to live by its standards or seek its power for kingdom work. In another sense, however, we are not to go "out of the world" (1 Cor. 5:9-10). Instead, we are to transform it as we bring the redeeming message of the gospel to all nations, and as we obediently implement Christ's spiritual dominion over the earth. Just as Jesus came from heaven to earth, so also the kingdom flows from heaven to earth. This is why we pray, "Thy will be done on *earth* as it is in heaven." [illegible] good commentary on this position. "I do not ask Thee to take them out of the world, but to keep them from [illegible]."

[illegible] Perspective

Pontius Pilate's question about kingship and kingdoms concerned political power [illegible]

[illegible]

11

"There's a Separation Between Church and State"

Myth, Lie, or Half-Truth?: *Christians can be involved politically, but biblical moral values or religious references have no place in American politics.*

> Probably at the time of the adoption of the Constitution, and of the Amendment to it now under consideration, the general if not the universal sentiment in America was, that Christianity ought to receive encouragement from the state, so far as was not incompatible with the private rights of conscience and the freedom of religious worship. An attempt to level all religions, and to make it a matter of state policy to hold all in utter indifference, would have created universal disapprobation, if not universal indignation.[1]

In the Capitol Building, a room is set aside to be used exclusively for the private prayer and meditation of Members of Congress. The central feature of the room is a stained-glass window showing George Washington kneeling in prayer. Behind the life-size image of Washington a prayer is etched in the glass that is taken from Psalm 16:1 and reads, "Preserve me, O God, for in Thee do I put my trust." The two lower corners of the window show the Bible and an open book and a candle, signifying the light from God's law: "Thy Word is a lamp unto my feet and a light unto my path" (Psalm 119:105). Is this a violation of the First Amendment?

A Religionless America?

In a 2003 decision, a Federal District Court stated the following in its ruling against Alabama Supreme Court Chief Justice Roy Moore and the Ten Commandments monument he placed in the State Supreme Court Building in Montgomery, Alabama:

> If we adopt [Judge Moore's] position, the chief justice would be free to adorn the walls of the Alabama Supreme Court's courtroom with sectarian religious murals and decidedly religious quotations painted above the bench.[2]

In fact, this is exactly what we do find in state and federal Supreme Court buildings. For example, a mural of Moses holding the two tables of the law is on the courtroom ceiling of the Supreme Court Chamber in Pittsburgh, Pennsylvania. Then there is the Supreme Court of Pennsylvania that contains large murals depicting Moses and the Ten Commandments ("Hebrew Idea of Revealed Law"), Jesus teaching the Beatitudes ("Christian Idea of Revealed Law"), and Jesus Christ and Disarmament ("International Law") painted by Violet Oakley and commissioned by the state of Pennsylvania and dedicated in 1927. At the dedication ceremony of the Oakley murals, George Wharton Pepper, former United States Senator, jurist, and professor of law, offered the following comments:

> It is in this room that the Supreme Court of Pennsylvania will sit to determine and interpret each of these rules of life as the Commonwealth of Pennsylvania can take account of. As the Judges discharge their solemn duty, I have no doubt that their delicate task will be more wisely performed because of the witness of the walls.[3]

Pepper's words indicate that the murals are more than historical representations of abstract ancient moral law. They are viewed as "rules of life." He went on to say: "When citizens coming into the open court perceive that they are really entering a sacred place it may be that they, too, will be dominated by the sense of order and will yield themselves to the spell which the artist's genius is able to lay upon them."[4] In another mural, Oakley describes the meaning of "Divine Law" as the "Alpha and Omega," the first and the last, "of the law," a phrase taken from the Bible (Rev. 1:8, 11; 21:6; 22:13).[5]

If the federal courts are to be consistent in their rulings, they must remove the words "In God We Trust" from the House and Senate chambers as well as from our nation's currency; the inscription from Leviticus 25:10 from the Liberty Bell; the words from Micah 6:8 that are found on the walls of the Library of Congress; the Psalmist's words that adorn the lawmaker's library; the plaque in the Dirksen Office Building that has the words "IN GOD WE TRUST" in bronze relief; the words on the Jefferson Memorial that read, "God who gave us life gave us liberty"; "Creator," "God," and "Providence" from the Declaration of Independence; "in the year of our Lord" from the United States Constitution; "Almighty God," "piety toward God," "faith in God," "Christian heart," to "spread civilization and Christianity," and "dedicate this nation before God" that appear on the bronze entablature at Mount Rushmore;[6] and other specific religious/Christian declarations found on government buildings in our nation's capital.[7] To remove these religious references would prove what critics of the Christian foundation of America are trying to destroy.

The Ten Commandments on Trial

Many Americans might be surprised to learn that the Supreme Court building has a number of depictions of the Ten Commandments and other lawgivers prominently displayed,[8] some of which are carved in stone, adorning entry ways and visible in the chamber where the justices sit:

- A seated Moses is shown holding the two tablets of the law as the central figure of the east pediment on the exterior of the Supreme Court building.[9]

- An image of the two tables of the Ten Commandments is engraved on the frame of the bronze gates separating the courtroom from the aisle.[10]

- A marble frieze in the Chamber itself shows Moses holding a copy of the tablets on which the Ten Commandments are written.[11]

- Two allegorical figures, representing "The Power of Government" and "The Majesty of Government," stand beside a carved flat-faced tablet with two rows of Roman numerals, I–V and VI–X, an obvious rendering of the Ten Commandments.[12]

- Carved into the bottom panel of the oak doors separating the courtroom from the hallway of the Supreme Court building is a rendering of the Ten Commandments.

As Chief Justice Warren Burger noted in his majority opinion of *Lynch v. Donnelly* (1984), the Supreme Court Chamber in which cases related to religion are heard "is decorated with a notable and permanent—not seasonal—symbol of religion: Moses with the Ten Commandments."[13] State courtrooms and government buildings across our land have housed similar displays for decades without any legal challenge or violation of the First Amendment to the Constitution. "In fact, the Ten Commandments are more easily found in America's government buildings than in her religious buildings, thus demonstrating the understanding by generations of Americans from coast to coast that the Ten Commandments formed the basis of America's civil laws."[14] In addition to what can be seen in the Supreme Court building, there are other noticeable displays of the Ten Commandments and other biblical references:

- A full-scale model of *The Interpretation of Law* showing Moses holding the tablets of the law is on the same floor as the Attorney General's office.[15]
- A statue of Moses holding the Ten Commandments is prominently displayed in the rotunda of the Library of Congress.
- The "Liberty of Worship" statue, which is outside the Ronald Reagan Building, is shown resting on a tablet engraved with ten Roman numerals representing the Ten Commandments.
- A bronze representation of the Ten Commandments in the form of a medallion is embedded in the floor of the National Archives.

The Constitution itself recognizes one of the most religiously specific of the Ten Commandments. In Article I, section 7 of the Constitution, Sunday is set aside as a day of rest for the President, a direct reference to the fourth commandment: "If any Bill shall not be returned by the President within ten Days (Sundays excepted) after it shall have been presented to him, the Same shall be a Law in like Manner as if he had signed it, unless Congress by their Adjournment prevent its return, in which Case it shall not be a Law."

The statute books of all fifty states include prohibitions against blasphemy (third), dishonoring parents (fifth), murder (sixth), adultery (seventh), theft (eighth), and perjury (ninth). The state of Georgia, like many other states, still retains legislation regarding Sunday (fourth).[16] The phrase "Almighty God" is found in numerous state constitutions, a recognition of the first commandment.

In the Georgia General Assembly Unannotated code the following instructions are given to the state's archivist: "Encourage the study of historical documents including but not limited to those which reflect our National Motto, the Declaration of Independence, **the Ten Commandments**, the Constitution of the United States, and such other nationally recognized documents which contributed to the history of the State of Georgia" (45–13–41).

The fact that the United States Constitution ends with "in the year of our Lord" certainly refutes the claim of strict separationists that our Framers desired to separate all aspects of religion from government. Every state constitution recognizes God,[17] and there is no indication that these references refer to anyone other than the God of the Bible. Did Congress violate the First Amendment when it declared 1983 to be "The Year of the Bible" in the following statement?:

> The Bible, the Word of God, has made a unique contribution in shaping the United States as a distinctive and blessed nation. . . . [D]eeply held religious convictions springing from the Holy Scriptures led to the early settlement of our Nation. . . . Biblical teaching inspired concepts of civil government that are contained in our Declaration of Independence and the Constitution of the United States.[18]

The last sentence is interesting: "Biblical teaching inspired concepts of civil government contained in . . . the Constitution." Are we to conclude that the Constitution is unconstitutional? Notice that there is no mention of the Code of Hammurabi, the Koran, the writings of Solon, or the precepts of Confucius.

The Biblical Model Of Church and State

One way to keep Christians out of the public arena, especially in the realm of politics, is to claim that there is a separation between

Church and State. The argument is based on the assumption that in biblical times Church and State were merged, and in modern times the First Amendment separates the two institutions. Supposedly, under biblical law, priests ruled over elders, judges, and kings. If this is the case, so the argument goes, the Bible cannot be used in our modern pluralistic society where the Constitution forbids the State to be ruled by ecclesiastical officers. Of course, as we will see, Church and State were not merged in the Bible, and the Constitution does not mention a Church-State separation because the institutions were already jurisdictionally separate in the colonial era. Max I. Dimont, writing in *Jews, God, and History*, sets the historical record straight:

> In the Mosaic Code the civil authority was independent of the priesthood. Though it is true that the priesthood had the right to settle cases not specifically covered by Mosaic law (Deuteronomy 17:8–12), that did not place it above the civil government. The priesthood was charged with the responsibility of keeping this government within the framework of Mosaic law, just as the United States Supreme Court is not above the federal government but is, nevertheless, charged with the responsibility of keeping it within the framework of the Constitution.[19]

The Bible teaches that there are multiple jurisdictions with specified functions and limits of authority and power: family, Church, and State.[20] Each of these governments has its own jurisdictional boundaries. In Israel, the torah (law) was viewed as the authority for all three governments. While the standard of law was the same, not all laws could be applied in the same way under each jurisdiction. For example, a father could discipline his own child for an infraction, but he could not discipline another family's child, excommunicate a church member, or impose and carry out the death penalty on a criminal who committed a capital crime. While the State has the authority to try and execute convicted murderers and impose other civil penalties, individuals, families, and churches do not.

An elder in a church, in conjunction with other elders in his church, has ecclesiastical jurisdiction within his own ecclesiastical body to discipline any member according to the guidelines laid down in Matthew 18 and to participate in proceedings to reconcile differences between fellow-believers (1 Cor. 6:1–11). He cannot go to another church, however, and exercise discipline there, although he may be asked to sit in a judicial capacity, but only under the direction of the government of the church where the proceedings are administered. Neither can he enter the jurisdiction of civil government as a representative of the church and use the power of the State to impose ecclesiastical laws upon the general citizenry.

None of this means that an individual church member cannot use the Bible to determine whether a candidate running for political office is fit for that office. The Constitution does state that no religious test can be given to someone seeking public office at the Federal level (Art. 6, sec. 3). This article refers to *governments* supplying the test, most probably designed to keep denominational distinctives from being imposed uniformly by the national government.[21] Some scholars claim that since the Constitution requires an "oath or affirmation," and "an oath imposes a sacred obligation," therefore "an oath requirement could be characterized as a 'religious test.' Nineteenth-century church historian Philip Schaff wrote, 'in recognizing and requiring an official oath' for both state and federal officeholders, 'the Constitution recognizes the Supreme Being, to whom the oath is a solemn appeal.'"[22] It seems that George Washington, a constitutional participant and our nation's first president, understood the oath in this way since he took it with his hand on the Bible and stated "so help me God." Some of the constitutional delegates pointed out the religious nature of an oath.[23] None of this means that individual voters cannot develop their own private test and vote accordingly.

Examples of Jurisdictional Separation

These principles have a long history, going back to the Old Testament. Moses became the chief judicial officer in Israel, assisted by numerous lesser *civil* magistrates (Ex. 18:17–26). Aaron, Moses' brother, became the chief *ecclesiastical* officer as High Priest, assisted by numerous lesser priests (29:1–9; Lev. 8). Moses did not carry out the duties of a priest, and Aaron did not perform civil tasks.

In the days of the Judges, Othniel, Ehud, Shamgar, Gideon and Samson served as civil officers (Judges 1–13), while the sons of Micah, Phineas, Eli, and the Levites served in an ecclesiastical capacity (Judges 17; 20:28; 1 Sam. 1–8).

During the period of the monarchy, King Saul served as a civil official while Ahimelech ministered as the chief ecclesiastical leader in the nation (1 Sam. 10 and 21). David was king while Abiathar carried out the duties of a priest (1 Chron. 15:11). David's son Solomon ruled as a civil officer while Zadok pursued ecclesiastical obligations (1 Kings 1:45). King Joash and Jehoiada the priest (2 Kings 11) and King Josiah and the priest Hilkiah (2 Kings 22:4) maintained jurisdictional separation. Even after the return from exile, Church and State as parallel institutions operated with Governor Nehemiah (Neh. 7) and Priest Ezra (Neh. 8).

Jurisdictional Cooperation

In biblical terms, there was never such a separation between Church and State that the State was free from following the guidelines of Scripture for its civil duties (Deut. 17:15–20). Both priest and king were required to sit before the law to be instructed. The priest was to follow guidelines pertaining to ecclesiastical affairs, while the king would glean from Scripture those directives designed for his civil office. If a case was too difficult for the civil ruler to decide, the Bible gives the following instruction: "You shall come to the Levitical priest or the judge who is in office in those days, and you shall inquire of them, and they will declare to you the verdict in the case" (17:9). Notice the use of "the Levitical priest or the judge." Both were required to be experts in the law. The judges did not follow a different standard in adjudicating legal issues. The Levites were to assist the civil ruler as much as the judges, but the Levites were not called on to rule in place of the king.

King David did not dismiss the exhortation of the prophet Nathan after being confronted for his sins of adultery and murder. Although David at first did not know that the rebuke was levelled against him, he did not act as if it was unusual for someone in Nathan's position to seek the counsel of the king and even to offer the king advice. David accepted Nathan's rebuke. He did not tell Nathan that there is a "separation between Church and State": "Then David said to Nathan, 'I have sinned against the LORD'" (2 Sam. 12:13). Modern-day separationists are closer to the way Herod responded when John the Baptist rebuked him for his adultery (Mark 6:14–29).

Crossing the Boundaries

There is always the danger of jurisdictional usurpation, when, say, civil government removes the jurisdictional boundaries and enters the domain of the Church. The Bible cites a number of examples of how the king sought to overrule the authority and jurisdiction of the Church. King Saul assumed the duties of the priests when he offered sacrifices. He stepped out of bounds from his kingly duties (1 Sam. 15:9–15, 22). In another place, Saul killed the godly priest Ahimelech because he would not fulfill the king's *political* goals (1 Sam. 22:6–23). King Jeroboam established his State religion in Bethel and Dan. Non-Levites of the worst character were appointed to serve as priests (1 Kings 12:26–31).

King Uzziah is said to have been "proud" (2 Chron. 26:16). His pride led him to go beyond his legitimate civil jurisdiction. While he was "chief of State," being the king in Judah, he was not a priest. King Uzziah could not assume the role of a priest and perform in the most basic ecclesiastical duties. He had no jurisdictional authority to serve in the Temple, the Old Testament equivalent of the New Testament Church. Uzziah ignored God's law and "acted corruptly, and he was unfaithful to the LORD his God, for he entered the temple of the LORD to burn incense on the altar of incense" (2 Chron. 26:16).

God is serious about jurisdictional separation. The king was struck with the most feared disease in all Israel: leprosy! "And king Uzziah was a leper to the day of his death; and he lived in a separate house, being a leper, for he was cut off from the house of the LORD" (v. 21). He lost access to the Temple, was isolated from the general population, and lost his kingdom to his son, Jotham, who "was over the king's house judging the people of the land" (v. 21).

Azariah the priest was not passive in this incident. He knew the limitations of the king's power. He, along with "eighty priests of the LORD" (v. 17), took action against the king. They "opposed Uzziah the king" (v. 18), making it clear that "it is not for you, Uzziah, to burn incense to the LORD, but for the priests, the sons of Aaron who are consecrated to burn incense" (v. 18). The priests commanded Uzziah to "get out of the sanctuary" (v. 18).

These "ecclesiastical officials" are called "valiant men" (v. 17) because they acted with great risk. While there were eighty of them, the king still commanded an army. He could have put them to death. There was a precedent for this when Ahimelech the priest helped David against King Saul (1 Sam. 21–22). Saul called on Doeg the Edomite to attack the priests after the king's own servants refused: "And Doeg the Edomite turned around and attacked the priests, and he killed that day eighty-five who wore the linen ephod" (1 Sam. 22:18). Doeg the Edomite had no qualms about killing the priests. King Uzziah had Saul's hate in his eye: "Uzziah, with a censer in his hand for burning incense, was enraged" (2 Chron. 26:19).

There have been times when the Church has forgotten its God-ordained jurisdictional role. The Church can deny its prophetic ministry when it is seduced by politics, that is, to see politics as the sole way to advance God's kingdom. Isn't this what happened when the people wanted to crown Jesus as King, to make Him their political ruler? (John 6:15). They showed their true allegiance when Jesus refused to accept their view of what they thought God's kingdom should be like. "The distribution of bread moved the crowd to acclaim Jesus as the New Moses, the provider, the Welfare King whom they had been waiting for."[24] When Jesus did not satisfy their false conception of salvation, they turned elsewhere: "We have no king but Caesar" (John 19:15). They denied the transforming work of the Holy Spirit to regenerate the dead heart of man. For them and for many today, man's salvation comes through political power. Jesus, however, is not a political savior, but His saving work should impact politics, because civil government is ordained by God.

Understanding the First Amendment

How many times have you heard someone say the reason Christians cannot be involved in proposing public policy from a biblical perspective is due to the fact that the Constitution mandates a "separation between Church and State"? The separation between Church and State language translates into, "Religion can have nothing to do with politics." Few Americans have actually studied the Constitution, so it's not surprising that many people, Christians included, fail to recognize the following constitutional language:

> Congress shall make no law respecting an establishment of religion, or prohibiting the free exercise thereof; or abridging the freedom of speech or of the press; or the right of the people peaceably to assemble, and to petition the Government for a redress of grievances.

The following points can be made about the First Amendment: First, this amendment makes no mention of Church or State or a separation between the two jurisdictions. Church-State separation was an operating principle in the colonies. A number of colonial constitutions prohibited ministers from simultaneously holding ministerial credentials and running for political office. For example, Delaware's constitution (1776) established the Christian religion (Art. 22) while not elevating "one religious sect" in the "State in preference to another" (Art. 29).[25] A jurisdictional separation between Church and State was maintained by prohibiting a "clergyman or preacher of the gospel, of any denomination" from "holding any civil office" in the state, "or of being a member of either of the branches of the legislature, while they continue in the exercise of the pastoral function" (Art. 29).[26]

Second, included in the amendment are items which relate to "the free exercise" of religion clause: the right to talk about religion (freedom of speech), the right to publish religious works (freedom of the press), the right of people to worship publicly, either individually or in groups (freedom of assembly), and the right to petition the government when it goes beyond its delegated constitutional authority in these areas (the right of political involvement).

Third, the prohibition is addressed to *Congress*, the only national legislative body. Individual states are not included in the prohibition. If a state wanted the same freedoms that are included in the Bill of Rights, they had to write them into their own constitution, which they did.[27]

Fourth, there is no mention of a freedom *from* religion, that is, people cannot protest and ask for the national government to outlaw religion just because it exists in the society in which they live and offends those of a different religion or who have no religion at all (atheists). "Being offended" is not a constitutional issue.

The Amendment's History

With this introduction, let's look into the history and meaning of this much referenced but usually misquoted, misunderstood, and misapplied amendment. When the Constitution was sent to the states for ratification, there was fear that the new national government still had too much power. It was then proposed that specific prohibitions should be listed in the Constitution to add further restrictions on the national government's power and jurisdiction.

The area of religion was important since a number of the states had established churches, that is, churches that were supported with taxes. There was concern that a *national* church (e.g., Anglican, Presbyterian, or Congregational) would be funded by tax dollars thereby disestablishing the different religious expressions in the various state constitutions. So then, the First Amendment was designed to protect the *states* against the very thing that is happening today—a federalization of issues related to religion. The amendment was not designed to disestablish the Christian religion which was predominate in the colonies. Justice Joseph Story (1779–1845), a Supreme Court justice of the nineteenth century, offers the following commentary on the amendment's meaning.

> [T]he real object of the [F]irst Amendment was not to countenance, much less to advance Mohammedanism, or Judaism, or infidelity, by prostrating Christianity, but to exclude all rivalry among Christian sects [denominations] and to prevent any national ecclesiastical establishment which would give to an hierarchy the exclusive patronage of the national government.[28]

Story's comments are important. He states that the amendment's purpose was "to exclude all rivalry among Christian sects." This presupposes that Christianity was the accepted religion of the colonies but that no single denomination should be supported by the national government. The amendment was not designed to make all religions equal by excluding everything religious from civil government. To do this would mean the establishment of atheism as America's official religion.

If the amendment was constructed to remove religion from having even the slightest impact on civil governmental issues, then it seems rather strange that on September 24, 1789, the same day that it approved the First Amendment, members of Congress called on President Washington to proclaim a national day of prayer and thanksgiving, a recommendation that had nearly unanimous support:

> That a joint committee of both Houses be directed to wait upon the President of the United States to request that he would recommend to the people of the United States a day of public thanksgiving and prayer, to be observed by acknowledging, with grateful hearts, the many signal favors of Almighty God, especially by affording them an opportunity peaceably to establish a Constitution of government for their safety and happiness.

Washington issued the proclamation on October 3, 1789. The Virginia assembly resolved on November 19 that the chaplain "to this House, be accordingly requested to perform divine service, and to preach a sermon in the Capitol, before the General Assembly, suitable to the importance and solemnity of the occasion, on the said 26th day of November." Most newspapers printed the proclamation and announced plans for public functions in honor of the day. How is it possible that the men who were involved in drafting the First Amendment would then call on the President to issue a proclamation thanking God to exclude Him from government, especially when the Proclamation stated the following?: "[I]t is the duty of all Nations to acknowledge the providence of Almighty God, to obey his will, to be grateful for his benefits, and humbly to implore his protection and favor. . . ." "All nations" included the United States of America.

That Congress also established the Congressional chaplain system where official daily prayers to God are still offered. In the entire debate on the First Amendment, not one word was said by any Congressman about a "wall of separation between church and state." At the time of the drafting of the First Amendment, a number of the thirteen colonies had established churches.

> At the beginning of the Revolution established churches existed in nine of the colonies. . . . The first amendment in large part was a guarantee to the states which insured that the states would be able to continue whatever church-state relationship existed in 1791. Maryland, Virginia, North Carolina, South Carolina, and Georgia all shared Anglicanism as the established religion common to those colonies. Congregationalism was the established religion in Massachusetts, New Hampshire, and Connecticut. New York, on the other hand, allowed for the establishment of Protestant religions. Only in Rhode Island and Virginia were all religious sects disestablished. But all of the States still retained the Christian religion as the foundation stone of their social, civil, and political institutions. Not even Rhode Island and Virginia renounced Christianity, and both states continued to respect and acknowledge the Christian religion in their system of law.[29]

Older versions of state constitutions were explicit about the Christian faith. For example, up until it was changed in the second half of the nineteenth century, North Carolina's Constitution read: "That no person who shall deny the being of God, or the truth of the Protestant religion, or the divine authority of the Old or New Testaments, or who shall hold religious principles incompatible with the freedom and safety of the State, shall be capable of holding any office or place of trust or profit in the civil department within this State."

Since the First Amendment prohibits *Congress* from establishing a religion, the states were free from national control when it came to religious issues. That's why there was nothing unconstitutional about North Carolina's provision. Today's courts have reinterpreted the First Amendment to mean that any law that has any religious reference is unconstitutional. For example, if a school teaches that abstinence is the best method to prevent pregnancy, or that premarital sex is immoral, and such views are the teaching of any religious group, then abstinence cannot be taught in public schools.

Historical Fiction

The present Church/State debate is based on a bit of historical fiction. The origin of separating the *jurisdictions* of Church and State has a long and respected history within Christendom. "Martin Luther (1483–1546) wrote of a 'paper wall' between the 'spiritual estate' and the 'temporal estate.' In his *Institutes of the Christian Religion,* John Calvin (1509–1564) asserted that the 'spiritual kingdom' and the 'political kingdom' 'must always be considered separately' because there is a great 'difference and unlikeness . . . between ecclesiastical and civil power,' and it would be unwise to 'mingle these two, which have a completely different nature.'"[30] So then, it wasn't secularists who proposed that Church and State should be *jurisdictionally* separate, it was Christian theologians.

Long before Thomas Jefferson used the phrase in his 1802 letter to a group of Baptist pastors in Danbury, Connecticut, Anglican divine and theologian Richard Hooker (1554–1600) described "walls of separation between . . . the Church and the Commonwealth" in his *Of the Laws of Ecclesiastical Polity.* While no one can be sure whether Jefferson borrowed the phrase from Hooker, we do know that Jefferson owned a copy of *Ecclesiastical Polity,* and "it was among the volumes he sold to the Library of Congress."[31] The phrase was also used by Roger Williams (1603?–1683), the founder of Rhode Island, and the Scottish schoolmaster James Burgh (1714–1775).[32]

Jefferson's use of the phrase, which has been described as "a mere metaphor too vague to support any theory of the Establishment Clause,"[33] has been adopted by secularists as substitute language for the actual text of the First Amendment. If Jefferson's letter was so important in understanding the First Amendment, why did it take until 1946, in *Everson v. Board of Education* (1947), for a court to make it the basis for its decision? Our founders, Jefferson included, never supposed that moral precepts founded on religion were to be excluded from policy making.

> Jefferson's own conception of the wall of separation between church and state did not prevent him from advocating and implementing government for religious education in the state of Virginia. After he retired as President, Jefferson wrote a bill for Virginia providing for the creation of public elementary schools, which the state passed in 1817. The bill provided that "no religious reading, instruction or exercise, shall be prescribed or practiced *inconsistent with the tenets of any religious sect or denomination*." This law still allowed nondenominational religious activities.[34]

"Jefferson's Bible," officially titled by Jefferson as "The Morals of Jesus," was a compilation of "the very words of Jesus." Jefferson stated that "there will be found remaining the most sublime and benevolent code of morals which has ever been offered to man."[35] So, what was designed to keep the national government from establishing a national church is now being interpreted to keep all moral precepts based on religion from entering the realm of politics. This is a misreading of history and dangerous to the future of our republic.

Conclusion

The most basic and legitimate definition of "separation of Church and State," is that the *institution* of the Church is separate from the *institution* of civil government. The Church as an institution cannot mingle in the *institutional* affairs of civil government. Neither can its officers. In the same way, civil government cannot disturb the ministry and operation of the church. This does not mean that laws having a religious foundation cannot be adopted and implemented by the State. For example, biblical laws against theft, murder, polygamy, abortion, homosexuality, and perjury have been accepted by civil governments as having a civil application with no transgression of the First Amendment. The State, however, does not have the jurisdictional right to compel people to believe the gospel, confess the true religion, pay tithes, or attend church. Neither can the civil magistrate declare any single Christian denomination to be the nationally established denomination.

Notes

1. Joseph Story, *Commentaries on the Constitution* (1833). Quoted in Peter J. Ferrara, *Religion and the Constitution: A Reinterpretation* (Washington, DC: The Free Congress Research and Education Foundation, 1983), 31.

2. In addition to the Ten Commandments, the monument also includes quotations from the Declaration of Independence ("Laws of Nature and of Nature's God"); our national motto ("In God We Trust"); the Pledge of Allegiance ("One Nation under God, Indivisible, with Liberty and Justice for all"); and Section 7 of the Judiciary Act of 1789 ("So Help Me God"). In addition, there are statements from presidents (George Washington, James Madison, and Thomas Jefferson) acknowledging our nation's religious foundation; the preamble to the Alabama Constitution which invokes "the favor and guidance of Almighty God"; words from the National Anthem "In God is our trust"; George Mason's statement that "The laws of nature are the laws of God; whose authority can be superseded by no power on earth"; and the classic declaration on natural law by English Jurist William Blackstone: "This law of nature, being co-eval with mankind and dictated by God Himself, is of course superior in obligation to any other. It is binding over all the globe, in all countries, and at all times: no human laws are of any validity, if contrary to this; upon these two foundations, the law of nature and the law of revelation, depend all human laws; that is to say, no human laws should be suffered [permitted] to contradict these." This quotation, along with Blackstone himself, is painted on a mural that occupies a wall in the Pennsylvania State Supreme Court building in Harrisburg (www.courts.state.pa.us/Index/Supreme/photogallery8.asp). For further study of this topic, see Gary DeMar, *The Case for America's Christian Heritage* (Powder Springs, GA: American Vision, 2009).

3. George Wharton Pepper quoted in Violet Oakley, *The Holy Experiment: Our Heritage from William Penn—1644-1944* (Philadelphia: Gogslea Studio Publications, 1950), 106. Also see *A Sacred Challenge: Violet Oakley and the Pennsylvania Capitol Murals* (Harrisburg, PA: Pennsylvania Capitol Preservation Committee, 2003).

4. Oakley, *The Holy Experiment,* 106.

5. Oakley, *The Holy Experiment,* 106.

6. Gary DeMar, "Mount Rushmore and the Christian Entablature," *The Biblical Worldview* (September 2003), 19–20. Also see http://www.americanvision.org/article/mount-rushmore-and-the-vanishing-entablature/

7. Benjamin Weiss, *God in American History: A Documentation of America's Religious Heritage* (Grand Rapids, MI: Zondervan, 1966), 208–241.

8. Some dismiss these displays of the Ten Commandments because they are part of a historical montage that includes other lawgivers "such as Hammurabi, Solon, Confucius and Muhammad." (David Rensberger, "Commandments force-fed," *Atlanta Journal-Constitution* [October 3, 2003], A19). The problem with this argument is that our legal system does not reference the Code of Hammurabi, the Koran, or the writings of Confucius.

9. A photograph of the image appears in Fred J. Maroon, *The Supreme Court of the United States* (New York: Thomasson-Grant & Lickle, 1996), 50–51.

10. A photograph of the image appears in Maroon, *The Supreme Court of the United States*, 141.

11. A photograph of the image appears in Maroon, *The Supreme Court of the United States*, 149. It's the fifth image from the left. For a more detailed look, see Gary DeMar, *America's Christian Heritage* (Nashville: Broadman & Holman, 2003), 73.

12. A photograph of the image appears in Maroon, *The Supreme Court of the United States*, 148–149. A detail of the image is found on page 149.

13. U.S. Supreme Court *Lynch v. Donnelly*, 465 U.S. 668 (March 5, 1984), II.C.

14. David Barton, "The Ten Commandments: A Part of America's Legal System for Almost 400 years!" Prepared and presented in response to multiple ACLU lawsuits against public displays of the Ten Commandments, United States District Court, Eastern District Court, Eastern District of Kentucky, London Division (March 2001).

15. George Gurney, *Sculpture and the Federal Triangle* (Washington, D.C.: Smithsonian Institution Press, 1985), 177.

16. "The only days to be declared, treated, and considered as religious holidays shall be the first day of each week, called Sunday" (Unannotated Code 1–4–2) and "Any superintendent, warden, or other correctional official who causes any inmate to do any work on Sunday, except works of necessity, shall be guilty of a misdemeanor" (General Assembly Unannotated Code 42–5–40).

17. Francis Newton Thorpe, *The Federal and State Constitutions, Colonial Charters, and Other Organic Laws of the States, Territories, and Colonies Now or Heretofore Forming the United States of America*, 7 vols. (Washington, D.C.: Government Printing Office, 1909).

18. Public Law 97–280, 96 Stat. 1211, approved October 4, 1982.

19. Max I. Dimont, *Jews, God, and History* (New York: Simon and Schuster, 1962), 47.

20. Gary DeMar, *God and Government*, 3 vols. (Powder Springs, GA: American Vision, 1982—1986).

21. For an opposing view, see Gary North, *Political Polytheism* (Tyler, TX: Institute for Christian Economics, 1990).

22. Daniel Dreisbach, "The Constitution's Forgotten Religion Clause: Reflections on the Article VI Religious Test Ban," *Journal of Church and State* 38:2 (Spring 1996), 289.

23. Dreisbach, "The Constitution's Forgotten Religion Clause," 288–289. The word "affirm" was most likely "added to accommodate the religious sensibilities

of Quakers, Moravians, and Mennonites who take literally the Biblical injunction, 'swear not at all.' Matthew 5:33–37" (290, note 157).

24. John Howard Yoder, *The Politics of Jesus: Vicit Agnus Noster* (Grand Rapids, MI: Eerdmans, 1972), 42.

25. Thorpe, *The Federal and State Constitutions, Colonial Charters, and Other Organic Laws of the States, Territories, and Colonies. . . .*, 1:566.

26. Thorpe, *The Federal and State Constitutions, Colonial Charters, and Other Organic Laws of the States, Territories, and Colonies. . . .*, 1:567–568.

27. See Thorpe, *The Federal and State Constitutions, Colonial Charters, and Other Organic Laws of the States, Territories, and Colonies, ...*

28. Quoted by Judge Brevard Hand, in *Jaffree v. Board of School Commissioners of Mobile County*, 544 F. Supp. 1104 (S. D. Ala. 1983) in Russell Kirk, ed., *The Assault on Religion: Commentaries on the Decline of Religious Liberty* (Lanham, NY: University Press of America, 1986), 84.

29. Hand, *Jaffree v. Board of School Commissioners of Mobile County*, 22–23.

30. Daniel L. Dreisbach, *Thomas Jefferson and the Wall of Separation Between Church and State* (New York: New York University Press, 2002), 72.

31. Dreisbach, *Thomas Jefferson and the Wall of Separation Between Church and State*, 76.

32. Dreisbach, *Thomas Jefferson and the Wall of Separation Between Church and State*, 76–82.

33. Peter J. Ferrara, *Religion and the Constitution: A Reinterpretation* (Washington, DC: The FreeCongress Research and Education Foundation, 1983), 34–35.

34. Ferrara, *Religion and the Constitution*, 36. For a comprehensive study of the historical meaning of the separation of Church and State, see Philip Hamburger, *Separation of Church and State* (Cambridge, MA: Harvard University Press, 2002).

35. From a letter to John Adams (October 13, 1813).

PART FOUR

Christians and the Kingdom

12

"God's Kingdom is Not of This World"

Myth, Lie, or Half-Truth?: Christians must await Jesus' future heavenly kingdom where He will serve as a true king. Any sort of kingdom activity this side of heaven is illegitimate.

By 'not of this world' we are to understand that the nature and origin of His kingdom are not of this world, not that His kingdom will not extend in this world. In the world's sense of king and kingdom, in the sense in which the Roman empire claimed to rule the world, He had no kingdom.[1]

"Cousin America has eloped with a Presbyterian parson," Horace Walpole wrote in 1775. While Walpole does not name the parson who was fanning the flames of discontentment in the colonies, many believe that he had John Witherspoon in mind. Witherspoon, a Presbyterian minister and president of the College of New Jersey (later to be named Princeton), was also a member of the provincial congress and the only clergyman to sign the Declaration of Independence. Like all Christians of his era, Witherspoon regarded civil government to be a subordinate institution under God's all-embracing kingdom and government (Isa. 9:6–7).

Witherspoon and other Christian patriots of his era had no delusions about "bringing in God's kingdom" through political maneuvering. They recognized, as Benjamin Franklin so eloquently stated in his address to the Constitutional Convention, "God governs in the affairs of men." God governs because He is King, and this world is part of His universal kingdom. While His kingdom is not "*of* this world," it certainly operates *in* and *over* this world. Franklin continued: "And if a sparrow cannot fall to the ground without his notice, is it probable that an empire can rise without his aid? We have been assured . . . in the sacred writings that 'except the Lord build the house, they labor in vain that build it' [Ps. 127:1]. I firmly believe this, and I also believe that without his concurring aid we shall succeed in this political building no better than the builders of Babel." The kingdoms of men are dependent upon the operation of the Kingdom of God *in and over this world*. Birds do not fall and kingdoms do not rise without the overruling of God's providential hand.

More than a century before the drafting of the Declaration of Independence, John Eliot (*c.* 1604–1690), the Puritan missionary to the Indians, wrote in his *The Christian Commonwealth* (a document intended as a plan of government for the Natick Indian community), that it is not for man "to search humane Polities and Platformes of Government, contrived by the wisdom of man; but as the Lord hath carried on their works for them, so they ought to go unto the Lord, and enquire at the Word of his mouth, what Platforme of Government he hath therein commanded; and humble themselves to embrace that as the best. . . . [The] written Word of God is the perfect System or Frame of Laws, to guide all the Moral actions of man, either towards God or man."[2] Because we are living in God's kingdom, Eliot taught, it is our duty to follow the King's rules.

It was still the responsibility of the citizenry, as subjects of the King of heaven, to bring about a civil government that met the conditions of heaven.

> I would neither have you trust in an arm of flesh nor sit with folded hands and expect miracles should be wrought in your defence. This is a sin which is in Scripture styled tempting God.[3]

To trust in politics—"an arm of flesh"—was to trust in a kingdom that derived its power from this world. It was this condition, a preoccupation of pagan Rome, that led Jesus to proclaim, "My kingdom is not *of* this world" (John 18:36). God's kingdom should not be made in the image of Roman political theory or any modern representation of pluralistic political theory.

The Kingdom and the Kingdoms

If Jesus' kingdom is "not of this world," so the argument goes, then how can Christians claim to have a responsibility to be involved in kingdom work? Since God's kingdom is exclusively in the future and in heaven, as some assert, there can be no earthly manifestation of God's works other than redeeming the lost out of this world *for heaven*. God's kingdom has nothing to do with this world until He personally reigns on this earth in the "millennium," is the refrain of many. There is more to God's kingdom than an exclusively heavenly reign or even a literal thousand-year rule of Christ on the earth.

Some Christian writers are so extreme in their insistence that God's kingdom does not touch on earthly things that they are even denying that Jesus' millennial reign is the kingdom of God. Dave Hunt, a proponent of an any-moment rapture, wrote that "the millennial reign of Christ, *far from being the kingdom*, is actually the final proof of the incorrigible nature of the human heart."[4] Hunt later retracted this statement,[5] but his further writings on the same subject leave a clear impression: No aspect of God's kingdom can manifest itself in a world where sinners still have bodies of flesh and blood.

> While [the kingdom] does have an earthly manifestation during the millennium, the kingdom will not be

> realized in its eternal fullness—which "flesh and blood cannot inherit" (1 Corinthians 15:50)—except in the new indestructible and incorruptible universe that will be created after the present one is destroyed.[6]

Dave Hunt and others appeal to John 18:36 ("My kingdom is not of this world") to establish that the kingdom is essentially (exclusively?) heavenly.[7] David Wilkerson quotes this passage favorably and adds, "That settles it for me, as it should for all believers who tremble at His Word."[8] We must, as Wilkerson says, take Jesus' words with the utmost seriousness and veracity. The question is, *what* does Jesus' statement mean? What is settled by a recitation of a single verse? Satan knew the Bible as well as anyone. He was quick to quote it when it suited him. Of course, his favorite tactic was to quote it out of context to support his twisted worldview. The Bible is not a series of incantations that can be repeated to bring about miraculous results. The Bible was written in book and letter form. The context of every sentence is important.

What does Jesus mean when He tells Pilate that His kingdom is not *of* this world? Does He mean that His kingdom is like the invisible ether that scientists a century ago believed pervaded outer space? Does He mean that His kingdom has no effect on the course of history? Quoting the verse without explanation does little to enhance our understanding of the exchange of words between the prosecutor and the accused. A man on trial for murder who said in a police statement, "Yes, I killed the man," is not necessarily guilty of murder no matter how many times the prosecutor repeats the words back to the accused. Who did he kill and why? Was it in self-defense?

That Little Preposition

Several important issues need to be discussed in order to arrive at a proper interpretation of John 18:36. Perhaps the most important question to answer is in what way is "of" being used. Just think of how many different ways we use "of" in English: The Queen *of* England (tells us the Queen's domain), a stack *of* wood (tells what kind of stack), a box *of* cereal (tells the contents of the box), etc. Greek has the same kind of variety. Essentially, the Greek preposition *ek* means "out of," and it can have several shades of meaning: separation, the direction from which something comes, source or origin, as well as a host of minor meanings.[9] Many commentators agree that in John 18:36, *ek* has the sense of "source"; thus, Jesus' statement has to do with the *source* of His kingdom's authority and power. The French commentator Godet wrote, "The expression *ek tou kosmou, of this world,* is not synonymous with *en to kosmo, in this world.* For the kingdom of Jesus is certainly realized and developed here on earth; but it does not have its *origin* from earth, from the human will and earthly force."[10] This is an important distinction.

More recently, the Lutheran commentator R. C. H. Lenski has written, "The origin of Jesus' kingdom explains its unique character: it is 'not of this world.' . . . [All other kingdoms] sprang out of [*ek*] this world and had kings that corresponded to such an origin."[11] B. F. Westcott agrees that Jesus meant that His kingdom "does not derive its origin or its support from earthly forces. . . . At the same time Christ's kingdom is 'in the world,' even as His disciples are (xvii.11)."[12] Charles Ryrie's study Bible explains that Jesus meant that His kingdom is "not of human origin."[13] Robert Culver offers the following comments in *Toward a Biblical View of Civil Government:*

> The words "of this world" translate *ek tou kosmou toutou,* that is, out of this world. Source rather than realm is the sense. . . . The future consummation of the kingdom of Christ cannot rightly be said to be beyond history. No indeed! It will occur in history and is history's goal. . . . So Jesus very clearly is making no comment on either the nature of his kingdom or His realm, rather on the power and source of its establishment.[14]

Thus, when Jesus said that His kingdom is not "of" this world, He means that it does not *derive its authority and power from* our world. As He added, His kingdom is from another place. This verse refers to the *origin* of the kingdom, not to a restriction of where it operates. Jesus was not saying that His kingdom floats in the air, without touching the world. He did not mean that He rules heaven, but has left earth to be ruled by Satan. Rather, He means that the legitimacy of His rule has its *origin* in the eternality of heaven, not in the created world.

"In" But Not "Of" the World

Other passages are often quoted to support the view that the kingdom is exclusively an other-worldly kingdom, having no impact on this world.

- "If you were of (*ek*) the world, the world would love its own; but because you are not of (*ek*) the world, but I chose you out of (*ek*) the world, because of this the world hates you (John 15:19)."[15]
- "I manifested Thy name to the men whom thou gavest Me out of (*ek*) the world" (John 17:6).
- "I do not ask on behalf of the world, but of those whom thou hast given me" (John 17:9).
- "They are not of (*ek*) the world, even as I am not of (*ek*) the world (John 17:16)."

Again, we must be careful not to assume that we know what Jesus is talking about in these verses until we look at the fuller biblical context, taking all relevant passages into account. We must carefully examine what He says, and seek to understand it in the light of all Scripture.

Several points are clear. First, nearly the same phrase "out of the world" is used in John 18:36. We have already seen that "of" or "out of" refers to the *source* of Christ's kingdom. When Jesus says the same thing about His disciples ("They are not *of* the world"), we are justified in suspecting that it means the same thing. Though the disciples are *on* earth, they do not derive their power and authority as Jesus' kingdom representatives *from* earth.

As for the other passages, to be *chosen* "out of the world" does not mean "to be relieved of all responsibility in the world." The *ek* here quite obviously implies separation. It could mean separation from several things. It could mean simply that the disciples have been chosen out of the whole mass of humanity to be Christ's own people. Probably, it means that the disciples have been separated from the world-system that dominates unbelievers. Particularly in the book of John, "world" (*kosmos*) often refers to a system and world order under the control of Satanic forces. It refers to the "world below" in contrast to the "world above."[16] The word has ethical significance. It does not refer simply to the planet earth or to mankind. It refers to the *kingdom of darkness*. Thus, to be chosen "out of the world" means to be separated by the sovereign choice of Jesus from the world-system that is headed for destruction. It means that the disciples have been liberated from bondage to Satan.

The strongest point undergirding this interpretation is the parallel that Jesus draws between His relation to the world and the relation of His disciples to the world. Jesus says that the disciples are not of the world, "just as" He is not of the world. Now, in what sense was Jesus, during His earthly ministry, not "of the world"? What does it mean when we say that Jesus is not "of this world"? Does it mean that He didn't have any impact on history? Does it mean that He didn't have a physical body? No. Dave Hunt would certainly not say these things. But if we apply what Hunt is saying about the kingdom to Jesus (which is, in effect, what Jesus was doing), we would have to conclude that *Jesus never left heaven to take human flesh*. If "not of the world" refers to a location, a geographic position, then these verses imply that Jesus was never really incarnate on earth.[17]

Jesus was not "of the world" in the sense that He did not derive His authority, His power, His standards of conduct from the world. In the same sense, Christians are not of the world. Therefore, Christians are to be separated from the world morally. We are not to live by its standards or seek its power for kingdom work. In another sense, however, we are not to go "out of the world" (1 Cor. 5:9–10). Instead, we are to transform it as we bring the redeeming message of the gospel to all nations, and as we obediently implement Christ's spiritual dominion over the earth. Just as Jesus came from heaven to earth, so also the kingdom flows from heaven to earth. This is why we pray, "Thy will be done on *earth* as it is in *heaven*." John 17:15 is a good summary of this position: "I do not ask Thee to take them out of the world, but to keep them from the evil one."

Pilate's Perspective

Pontius Pilate's question about kingship and kingdoms concerned political power as he, an earthly ruler from Rome, understood it. Jesus was questioned from Pilate's perspective, and Jesus answered in a way that Pilate understood. Would Jesus bring an army? How large would it be? Since He was said to be "King of the Jews" (Luke 23:3), would Jesus incite a rebellion among the Jews to usurp Pilate's position of authority? What sort of weaponry would He use? Pilate believed, as did many Jews of that day, that armed conflict alone could extend a kingdom. It was a king's duty to use the power of the military against an enemy. Since Jesus was a king, Pilate assumed He must command His army in the same way as Rome did. This was the Roman way.

> The reader is presented with a dramatic scene, in which two types of kingships are contrasted; the kingship backed by the authority and might of imperial Rome represented by Pilate, a kingship *of this world* and upheld by this world's weapons, and the kingship of Jesus *not of this world*, in which the monarch is to reign by being

> lifted up on a cross ([John 18:]36). The narrative clearly presupposes that it had been intimated to Pilate that Jesus, by claiming kingship over Jewry, was in effect a political revolutionary and therefore a potential danger to Rome. . . .[18]

In John 18:37, Pilate asks, "So You are a king?" Jesus did not deny kingship. Jesus answered Pilate's question forthrightly: "You say correctly that I am a king. For this I have been born [Luke 1:32–33; 2:2], and for this I have come into the world, to bear witness to the truth. Every one who is of the truth hears My voice" (John 18:37).

Later, Jesus informed Pilate that his own position of political authority, and, by intimation, that of all who rule (cf. Rom. 13:1), was subject to God's kingly authority since Jesus is "ruler of the kings of the earth" (Rev. 1:5).

When Jesus kept silent regarding Pilate's question concerning His origin (John 19:9), Pilate grew indignant: "You do not speak to me? Do you not know that I have authority to release You, and I have authority to crucify you?" (19:10). Jesus' answer settled the matter about the operation of God's kingdom. Unless the kingdom of God operated *in* and *over* this world, what Jesus said next would be false: "You would have no authority over Me, unless *it had been given you from above. . .*" (19:11; cf. Rom. 13:1–4). So then, God's kingdom does operate in this world so that it influences the kingdoms of men: "The king's heart is like channels of water in the hand of the LORD; He turns it wherever He wishes" (Prov. 21:1). It's no wonder that Pilate said that he found no guilt in Jesus deserving death (Luke 23:22).

Confusion over Jesus' words develops from a false notion that the answer to man's problems is solely political. There were numerous occasions when the crowds wanted to make Jesus king (e.g., John 6:15). While there are political implications to Jesus' kingship, just as there are personal, familial, economic, business, ecclesiastical, and judicial implications, the kingdom of God is not brought about politically. Good laws do not make good people. Only the sovereign work of the Holy Spirit in regeneration makes people good. Civil government has a God-imposed jurisdiction to perform kingdom activities according to the specifics of God's Word as they relate to *civil* matters.

The people in Jesus' day saw the kingdom of God only in externals. They visualized the kingdom of God as coming, not through regeneration, but by revolution. Jesus said of His followers: "Truly, truly, I say to you, you seek Me, not because you saw signs, but because you ate of the loaves, and were filled" (John 6:26). It was Jesus' message about mankind's need for salvation and about Him as the Savior, the Messiah of God, that caused the religious and political establishments of the day to seek His death.

The kingdom of God does not advance by military power. Though power-directed, the kingdom's power comes from above and works on the heart of man: "I will give you a new heart and put a new spirit within you; and I will remove the heart of stone from your flesh and give you a heart of flesh. And I will put My Spirit within you and cause you to walk in My statutes, and you will be careful to observe My ordinances" (Ezek. 36:26–27). Self-government, wherein God subdues the heart to teachableness, leads to godly family, church, and civil governments under God (1 Tim. 3:1–13).

Implements of war can subdue a people, but they cannot regenerate those dead in their trespasses and sins (Eph. 2:1). God's Word, on the other hand, "is living and active and sharper than any two-edged sword, and piercing as far as the division of soul and spirit, of both joints and marrow, and able to judge the thoughts and intentions of the heart" (Heb. 4:12).

The supernatural power which energizes God's kingdom is never bound by political rhetoric: "For the kingdom of God does not consist in words, but in power" (1 Cor. 4:20). The battle against the kingdoms of this world is waged through the awesome power inherent in God's Word, energized by His Spirit: "For though we walk in the flesh, we do not war according to the flesh, for the weapons of our warfare are not of the flesh, but divinely powerful for the destruction of fortresses" (2 Cor. 10:3–4). It's the power of *regeneration*, not revolution, that advances the kingdom.

As Christians, "we are destroying speculations and every lofty thing raised up against the knowledge of God, and we are taking every thought captive to the obedience of Christ" (2 Cor. 10:5). This is kingdom living in the power of God's Spirit. The kingdom of God advances by changing the heart and mind of those who oppose Jesus Christ and His Word. The kingdoms of this world are at war with the kingdom of Jesus Christ, and it is the duty of all Christians to be involved in that war until the gates of Hades no longer stand (Matt. 16:18).

Restoration begins by realizing that we live in the midst of God's kingdom. God's pattern for godly living is established in heaven. In the Lord's Prayer we petition God, "Thy Kingdom come. Thy will be done, *on earth as it is in heaven*" (Matt. 6:10).

Some Objections

There are some Christians who maintain that the kingdom parables of Matthew 13 teach a different view of the kingdom from the one expressed above. They go to great lengths to try to prove that God's kingdom has little or virtually no positive effect on this world prior to Jesus' Second Coming. J. Dwight Pentecost, representing a school of interpretation known as dispensational premillennialism, believes that the kingdom loses its effectiveness over time, is a monstrosity, and is like evil. Let's put his views to a biblical test.

The Parable of the Sower and the Soils

In comments on the Parable of the Soils in Matthew 13:1–9, Pentecost states that "During the course of the age there will be a *decreasing* response to the sowing of the seed, from 'a hundredfold' to 'sixty' to 'thirty.'"[19] This is an odd interpretation seeing that one seed results in at least thirty *additional* seeds, not to mention an increase of sixty and one hundred. A thirty-to-one return on an investment is very impressive. Pentecost understands this parable to teach that the kingdom declines in influence over time. This is off the mark in terms of what the Bible actually states.

A careful reading of the text shows that the seeds are thrown at the same time (Matt. 13:4), and at maturation all the seeds produce in varying amounts—some produce a hundred more, some sixty more, and others "only" thirty more. The difference is in the abundance of growth. "The Lord is not informing His disciples of the *decline* of gospel influence, but of its *increase*,"[20] up to one hundred to one! History bears this out. From twelve disciples, there are now billions of Christians.

Pentecost sees something significant in the *order*, from an increase of one hundred to one to a decrease of thirty to one. But if we look at the same parable in Mark 4:1–9, we see that as the seeds "grew up and increased, they were yielding a crop and were producing thirty, sixty, and a hundredfold" (4:8). Here the order is reversed! If we assert that the order of increase tells us something about the maturation of the kingdom, then the parable in Mark tells us that the kingdom will advance beyond anything we could ever imagine, just the opposite of what Matthew teaches. The order is not the point; it's the amount of increase that God wants us to learn from the parable.

The Parable of the Mustard Seed

In this parable, Jesus contrasts the tiny mustard seed with its potential for growth: from "smaller than all other seeds" to "larger than the garden plants," large enough so "the birds of the air come and nest in its branches" (Matt. 13:31–32). Pentecost states, based on the teaching of this parable, that this age, prior to the return of Christ, "is characterized by an abnormal external growth. That which was to be an herb has become a tree—it has developed into a monstrosity."[21] This interpretation was included in an early printing of Pentecost's book *Thy Kingdom Come*. In a later printing, Pentecost changed his mind about the "abnormal external growth" that resulted in a "monstrosity" and wrote the following in a later printing:

> This part of the parable stresses the great growth of the kingdom when once it is introduced. The kingdom will grow from an insignificant beginning to great proportions. Historically the new form of the kingdom had its beginning with only a few to propagate it, but in spite of that it will reach to great size. In Daniel's prophecy (4:1–37) the tree represented Nebuchadnezzar's kingdom. The birds in the tree represented the peoples that received benefit from Nebuchadnezzar's kingdom (v. 12). Here the mustard [seed] reveals that the kingdom in its new form will have an insignificant beginning, but will grow to great size and multitudes will benefit from it.[22]

As Pentecost finally acknowledges, like the parable of the Sower and the Soils, this parable is comparing the relatively small seed with its enormous growth capacity, because it is a description of *God's kingdom*. We should expect big things to happen when God is the one who brings about the growth (1 Cor. 3:6–7). Jesus often used this type of comparative language to demonstrate how God uses the seemingly insignificant things to accomplish great things. Paul picks up on this theme when he describes how God "has chosen the foolish things of the world to shame the wise, and God chose the weak things of the world to shame the things that are strong" (1 Cor. 1:27). In another place, the apostle shows how weakness, when it is acknowledged before God, is actually strength: "For when I am weak, then I am strong" (2 Cor. 12:10) because "with God all things are possible" (Matt. 19:26; Mark 9:23; 10:27).

Jesus uses the mustard seed in another place to demonstrate the principle of smallness in nature but bigness in result: "For truly

I say to you, if you have faith as a mustard seed, you shall say to this mountain, 'Move from here to there,' and it shall move; and nothing shall be impossible" (Matt. 17:20).

The interpretation turns ridiculous when Pentecost wants us to believe that the birds in the parable are types of evil because in the first parable they ate the seeds that fell beside the road (Mark 4:4). But are birds always types of evil? God is said to feed the birds in Matthew 6:26. Does this mean that God is feeding evil? In the first parable the birds eat the seed; in this parable they nest in the tree's branches. These are two different actions. Nesting seems to be a good thing (Matt. 8:20). The imagery of birds nesting in the branches of a tree is based on Ezekiel 17:22–24. Birds nesting in the branches of a tree is a blessed thing: "And birds of every kind will nest under it; they will nest in the shade of its branches" (17:23).

The Parable of the Leaven

In order to avoid the implication that God's kingdom will advance in history prior to Jesus' second coming, the kingdom of God must become evil. Pentecost, in his early edition of *Things to Come,* stated that "the figure [of leaven] is used in Scripture to portray that which is evil in character."[23] He went on to argue that since Scripture says that "the kingdom of heaven is like leaven," and leaven is used to portray evil, then the parable must be teaching that the kingdom is like evil. There are a number of places in Scripture where leaven is a symbol of invisible evil influence (Matt. 16:6, 11; 1 Cor. 5:7–8; Gal. 5:9) and places where it is not.

Of course, leaven is not always a symbol of evil. A cake made with leaven was brought with the "peace offering for thanksgiving" in the Old Testament (Lev. 7:13), and the wave offering was made with leavened loaves of bread, "as first fruits to the LORD" (23:17). The context should determine what leaven is symbolizing. In Matthew 13:33, Jesus equates the kingdom of heaven with leaven, and there is nothing in this context to suggest that the leaven has an evil connotation since heaven is not evil. The kingdom of heaven expands in the world like leaven expands when put in dough.

To make interpretive matters even worse, Pentecost tells us that the woman in the parable is a symbol "of a false religious system (Rev. 2:20; 17:1–8)."[24] Are women *always* symbols of evil? Jesus makes mention of women in a favorable way in other parables (Matt. 25:1–2; Luke 15:8). Why does Jesus mention a woman in the context of this particular parable? As a description of evil? Hardly.

> It just so happens that women normally bake bread, as per the parable's demands (Lev. 26:26; 1 Sam. 28:24), much like the three measures being an amount which would be fitting (Gen. 18:6; Judg. 6:19; 1 Sam. 1:24). The woman *imports* the leaven *into* the meal, as Christ's kingdom comes from *without* (John 18:36; Rev. 21:2) and works *within* (Luke 17:20–21; Rom. 14:17).[25]

There is no getting around it. God's kingdom is with us, and it will continue with us: "For the earth will be full of the knowledge of the LORD as the waters cover the sea" (Isa. 11:9). Like the changes Pentecost made to his understanding of the mustard seed parable, he came to realize that leaven in this context does stand for the growth and expansion of the kingdom,[26] a very good thing.

Conclusion

When Christians read that the Bible's description of the kingdom is "heavenly," somehow this translates for many to mean a realm that is less "solid" than earth. This is a big misreading of Scripture, as Peter J. Leithart points out in his book *The Kingdom and the Power*:

> In the Bible, heaven is not an airy-fairy, ethereal place. C.S. Lewis was closer to the truth when, in *The Great Divorce*, he depicted heaven as *more* solid than earth, not less so. Angels are not chubby toddlers or winged androgynes.

> Angels are terrifying creatures and meeting an angel is a life-shattering experience (Judg. 6:22; 13:22).
>
> To say that the kingdom of God is heavenly, then, is not at all to detract from its reality or its "solidity" or its importance to our earthly lives. Jesus taught that the heavenly kingdom has come to earth in His person and work. Under the influence of the heavenly kingdom, the earth is to be transformed into a temple-city that reflects the glories of the heavenly city of God.[27]

This world is the realm of God's redemptive purposes. If God is king, then He is king of all that He has made. If His kingdom is universal, then the earth is part of His realm. "In the broadest sense God's kingdom refers to the most extended reaches of His sovereignty. As Psalm 103:19 puts it, 'The Lord hath prepared his throne in the heavens; and his kingdom ruleth over all.' God is sovereign and therefore He exercises full control over everything He has created."[28] J. I Packer offers a helpful summary of the nature of Jesus' kingdom:

> Jesus, the Spirit-anointed, Spirit-filled ruler-designate (Luke 3:21–22; 4:1, 18–21, 32–36, 41), died, rose, ascended, and is now enthroned in heaven as ruler over all things (Matt. 28:18; Col. 1:13), King of kings and Lord of lords (Rev. 17:14; 19:16). The golden age of blessing is an era of present spiritual benefit (salvation from sin and fellowship with God) leading to a future state of unmixed joy in a reconstructed universe. The kingdom is present in its beginnings though future in its fullness; in one sense it is here already, but in the richest sense it is still to come (Luke 11:20; 16:16; 17:21; 22:16, 18, 29–30).
>
> * * * * *
>
> The task of the church is to make the invisible kingdom visible through faithful Christian living and witness-bear-

> ing. The gospel of Christ is still the gospel of the kingdom (Matt. 4:23; 24:14; Acts 20:25; 28:23, 31), the good news of righteousness, peace, and joy in the Holy Spirit through entering a disciple's relationship to the living Lord (Rom. 14:17). The church must make its message credible by manifesting the reality of kingdom life.[29]

The kingdom is a present reality. Christians are to live out its principles in the here and now. To claim that God's kingdom is not of this world is to deny the kingdom altogether.

Notes

1. H. W. Watkins, "The Gospel According to John," *A New Testament Commentary for English Readers*, ed. Charles John Ellicott, 3 vols. (London: Cassell and Company, 1897), 1:532.

2. John Eliot, *The Christian Commonwealth: or, The Civil Policy of the Rising Kingdom of Jesus Christ* (1659). Quoted in John Eidsmoe, *Christianity and the Constitution: The Faith of Our Founding Fathers* (Grand Rapids, MI: Baker Book House, 1987), 23–34.

3. Quoted in Martha Lou Lemmon Stohlman, *John Witherspoon: Parson, Politician, Patriot* (Louisville, KY: Westminster/John Knox Press, 1976), 114.

4. From a taped interview with Peter Lalonde and Dave Hunt, "Dominion and the Cross," Tape #2 of *Dominion: The Word and New World Order*, distributed by the *Omega-Letter*, Ontario, Canada, 1987. Emphasis added. There is a similar quotation in Dave Hunt, *Beyond Seduction: A Return to Biblical Christianity* (Eugene, OR: Harvest House, 1987), 250.

5. In a letter to me (January 16, 1988), Hunt writes to clarify his position: "It is true that you have found a quote or two in which I was careless with my language." In this same letter, Hunt states that the future earthly millennium is "the temporary earthly manifestation of God's kingdom promised to Israel that becomes the final proof of the incorrigible nature of the human heart."

6. Dave Hunt, *Whatever Happened to Heaven?* (Eugene, OR: Harvest House, 1988), 255.

7. Dave Hunt and T. A. McMahon, *The Seduction of Christianity* (Eugene, OR: Harvest House, 1985), 224.

8. David Wilkerson, "The Laodicean Lie!," fourth page. Published by World Challenge, P.O. Box 260, Lindale, Texas 75771.

9. William F. Arndt and F. Wilbur Gingrich, *A Greek-English Lexicon of the New Testament and Other Early Christian Literature* (Chicago, IL: University of Chicago Press, 1957), 233–236. This lexicon, the standard work of New Testament Greek, has a two-and-one-half page discussion, in small print, of the various meanings of the two-letter preposition *ek*.

10. F. Godet, *Commentary on the Gospel of John*, trans. Timothy Dwight, 2 vols. (New York: Funk and Wagnalls, 1886), 2:369.

11. R.C.H. Lenski, *The Interpretation of St. John's Gospel* (Minneapolis, MN: Augsburg, [1943] 1961), p. 1229.

12. B.F. Westcott, *The Gospel According to St. John*, 260.

13. Quoted by John Lofton, "Our Man in Washington," Num. 18 (December 1986). Chalcedon Foundation, P.O. Box 158, Vallecito, California 95251.

14. Robert Duncan Culver, *Toward a Biblical View of Civil Government* (Chicago, IL: Moody, 1974), 195.

15. The New International Version captures the meaning of this verse: "If you belonged to the world, it would love you as its own. As it is, you do not belong to the world, but I have chosen you out of the world. That is why the world hates you" (John 15:19).

16. George Eldon Ladd, *A Theology of the New Testament* (Grand Rapids, MI: Eerdmans, 1974), 225. Ladd shows that while John often uses *kosmos* in a more general sense, he also uses the word to refer to "fallen humanity" which is "enslaved" to an "evil power."

17. I want to emphasize that this is *not* what Hunt is saying. We are trying to show inconsistencies in his interpretation of this text by pressing his position logically.

18. R.V.G. Tasker, *The Gospel According to John* (Grand Rapids, MI: Eerdmans, 1960), 201.

19. J. Dwight Pentecost, *Things to Come* (Grand Rapids, MI: Zondervan, 1958; early printing), 146. Emphasis added. A similar view can be found in *The New Scofield Reference Bible* (New York: Oxford University Press, 1967), 1015.

20. Kenneth L. Gentry, Jr., "Dispensational Dyslexia," *Dispensationalism in Transition* (October 1990), 1.

21. Pentecost, *Things to Come* (early printing), 147.

22. J. Dwight Pentecost, *Things to Come: A Study in Biblical Eschatology* (Grand Rapids, MI: Zondervan, [1964] 1987; later printing), 147–148. There is no indication that this printing is a "new edition," an acknowledgment that is usually made when substantive changes are made to a book. For a discussion of Pentecost's remodeling of his views, see Kenneth L. Gentry, Jr., "Things that Went," *Dispensationalism in Transition* (June 1992): http://tinyurl.com/yd67el6

23. Pentecost, *Things to Come* (early printing), 148.

24. Pentecost, *Things to Come*, 148.

25. Gentry, "Dispensational Dyslexia," 2.

26. Pentecost, *Things to Come* (later printing), 148.

27. Peter J. Leithart, *The Kingdom and the Power: Rediscovering the Centrality of the Church* (Phillipsburg, NJ: Presbyterian and Reformed, 1993), 79.

28. Raymond O. Zorn, *Church and Kingdom* (Nutley, NJ: Presbyterian and Reformed, 1962), 1. A revised edition was reprinted as *Christ Triumphant: Biblical Perspectives on His Church and Kingdom* (Edinburgh: Banner of truth Trust, 1997).

29. J. I. Packer, *Concise Theology: A Guide to Historic Christian Beliefs* (Carol Stream, IL: Tyndale House Publishers, 1993), 193–195.

13

"God's Kingdom Has Not Come"

Myth, Lie, or Half-Truth?: *Christians live in anticipation of God's future kingdom. This world belongs to the devil until God vanquishes him.*

> The presence and power of the kingdom was visible to all [the early church]. In spite of bitter persecution thousands were being converted to the Christian faith. They saw "greater works" than the physical miracles which Jesus Himself performed. The life-transforming evidence was before their eyes. Sane men do not dogmatically affirm to other sane men that there is a sun in the heavens. The gospel which the Baptist, Jesus, and Paul proclaimed was in the strictest sense the gospel of the kingdom which the Prophets spoke (cf. Acts 28:23, 31).[1]

A future kingdom means a future king. A future kingdom and an absent king means a future set of kingdom laws that have no present-day, this-world application. If this is what Christians mean by stating that God's kingdom is yet to come, then we are in a terrible dilemma. If God's kingdom can be expected solely future, then God has little or nothing to say about the way men and women should conduct their affairs in the here and now. This would mean, that while Jesus might be King of heaven where He rules over the angels and the invisible world, present earthly rulers are the sole and absolute kings of the earth. And for this Jesus died on the cross, rose from the dead, ascended into heaven, and took His seat on the throne? I don't think so.

To espouse the belief that God's kingdom will be manifested solely in the future means that we are living in a purely secular kingdom with purely secular laws cut off from the governance of heaven. This is the worldview of deism! If this is the view of any part of the church, then the secularists are right in condemning the mixing of any of God's laws with the State. How can God as a *future* King have any say in the affairs of a *present* kingdom under the rule of another king? This would be like a future presidential candidate telling the current president how to run his affairs. A future president has no legal standing to make such a demand.

The Kingdom Has Come

If the kingdom is defined in political and millennial terms, where Jesus personally and physically rules from Jerusalem in the midst of a rebuilt temple, a renewed sacrificial system, and the reestablishment of the Old Testament theocratic government, then God's kingdom has not yet come.[2] On the other hand, if the kingdom is defined as a spiritual manifestation of the work of Christ in this world that comes through the transforming and regenerating work of the Holy Spirit in the lives of sinners with Jesus enthroned at His Father's right hand, where presently He rules as "King of kings and Lord of lords" (Rev. 19:15), then it can be said that the kingdom has come. We should be reminded that the message of Jesus was quite clear on this issue: "The time is *fulfilled*," not postponed, "and the kingdom of God is at hand; repent and believe in the gospel" (Mark 1:15).

An objection often arises, however. Some maintain that only the kingdom fully realized attests to its inauguration. But does an inauguration of something have to be mature before it is that thing? For example, a tree that is four feet tall is still a tree. It will always be called a tree until it ceases to exist. A business that starts this year with only two employees may not realize a profit for three years, but it remains a business until it goes out of business. Fledgling as such operations may be at the beginning, it is still a business along with such conglomerates as IBM, General Electric, and Microsoft.

A Nation Producing the Fruit of It

Before we move into a study of the details of this view, it might prove profitable to deal with an important passage of Scripture that can shed a great deal of light on the subject of the present reality of God's kingdom. In the Parable of the Landowner, Jesus indicts the chief priests and Pharisees for their rejection of His Messiahship. He predicts that as the Heir of the Landowner, He will be cast out of the vineyard and be killed (Matt. 21:38). Jesus relates this to the kingdom in several ways. First, Israel had the kingdom, an extension of the Old Covenant kingdom, therefore, it was a present reality: "The kingdom of God *will be taken away from you,* and be given to a nation producing the fruit of it" (21:43). Jesus could not take from them what they did not have.

Second, there is no mention of a postponement or a parenthesis. Jesus does not say, "The coming of the kingdom will be delayed for another time." Third, the kingdom will "be given to a nation producing the fruit of it." The "deed" to the kingdom is transferred to a new "nation." Fourth, it is obvious from the apostles' question in Acts 1:6 that they believed the kingdom had been taken from Israel, because they ask, "Lord, is it at this time You are restoring the kingdom to Israel."

Where and when is the kingdom if it was taken from the unfaithful Jews of Jesus' day? According to Matthew 21:43, it resides with "a nation producing the fruit of it." And what is that nation? "But you [believers in Christ] are a chosen race, a royal priesthood, *a holy nation,* a people for God's own possession, that you may proclaim the excellencies of Him who has called you out of darkness into His marvelous light" (1 Cor. 2:9–11). As any student of Scripture will recognize, Peter's source for these descriptions is the Old Testament (Deut. 10:15; Isa. 43:20–21; 61:6; 66:21; Ex. 19:6; Deut. 7:6). These passages describe God's relationship with the *nation* of Israel. But with the coming of the Messiah, and the rejection of God's Heir by the unfaithful of that nation, the kingdom has been taken away and given to "a nation producing the fruit of it"—a reconstituted Israel, a people made up of believing Jews (Acts 2:5, 9–11, 37–42; 3:11–4:1–4) and Gentiles (10:34–45): "For you once were not a people, but now you are the people of God; you had not received mercy, but now you have received mercy" (1 Peter 2:10). And what follows? Peter exhorts them to produce the fruit commensurate with being "a holy nation": "Beloved, I urge you as aliens and strangers to abstain from fleshly lusts, which wage war against the soul. Keep your behavior excellent among the Gentiles, so that in the thing in which they slander you as evildoers, they may on account of your good deeds, as they observe them, glorify God in the day of visitation" (1 Peter 2:11–12). When will the kingdom be restored to Israel? It was restored to the "Israel of God" (Gal. 6:16) in its earthly manifestation soon after Pentecost.

The Need for Definitions

From a study of the Old Testament we realize that in some sense God's kingdom was a present reality even before Jesus came to earth. The New Testament does not indicate that it has somehow been interrupted or postponed for a distant future fulfillment. Even Nebuchadnezzar understood that God's "dominion is an everlasting dominion, and His kingdom endures from generation to generation" (Dan. 4:34). There is no "parenthesis," no gap of nearly two thousand years where God's "dominion" has somehow been put on hold.

First, it is equally obvious that the New Testament describes an approaching kingdom: "The kingdom of God is at hand" (Mark 1:14–15; cp. Matthew 4:12–17). This means that there is a fuller expression of that already present glorious kingdom approaching as God takes on human flesh and personally oversees the kingdom that brings with it the once-for-all sacrifice promised so long ago to Adam and Eve. The Seed of the woman, Jesus, has come to crush the head of the serpent (Gen. 3:15). "And when they had come to a place called Golgotha, which means Place of a Skull," they "crucified Him" (Matt. 27:33–35). The head of the serpent was definitely "crushed" as the stake of the cross penetrated the "skull" of the serpent. Because of the finished work of Jesus, through the power of His Spirit, Satan was crushed under *their* ("your") feet (Rom. 16:20). The inaugurated kingdom becomes the expanding kingdom in time and in history prior to Jesus' return. The gospel is to go into "all the world" (Matt. 28:18–20), a command not typical under the Old Covenant, although there were exceptions, as in Jonah preaching to the Ninevites and Daniel's message to Nebuchadnezzar. God's kingdom is not a political kingdom, and it will never be a political kingdom (John 18:36). Rather, the kingdom is "righteousness and peace and joy in the Holy Spirit" (Rom. 14:17). This kingdom is not devoid of authority in this age: "For the kingdom of God does not consist in words, but in power" (1 Cor. 4:20).

Second, there are verses that indicate that the kingdom *has come* and that it should affect the way we live in the world. (1) "For He delivered us from the domain of darkness, and *transferred* us to the kingdom of His beloved Son" (Col. 1:13); (2) "Therefore, since we receive a kingdom which cannot be shaken, let us show gratitude, by which we may offer to God an acceptable service with reverence and awe" (Heb. 12:28); (3) "I, John, your brother and fellow-partaker in the tribulation *and kingdom* and perseverance which are in Jesus, was on the island called Patmos, because of the word of God and the testimony of Jesus" (Rev. 1:9); (4) "And [Jesus] was saying to them, 'Truly I say to you, there are some of those who are standing here *who shall not taste of death* until *they* see the kingdom of God after it has come with power'" (Mark 9:1; cp. Matt. 16:27; Luke 9:27); (5) "But if I cast out demons by the Spirit of God, then the kingdom of God *has come* upon you" (Matt. 12:28). "The truth is, Jesus *did* cast out demons by the Spirit of God."[3] The conclusion that we should reach is the kingdom of God came upon the church of the first century, and there is no indication that it is being held in abeyance for a future millennium, often described as the "kingdom age."

Third, the kingdom requires the new birth and sanctification to enter in (John 3:3; Matt. 7:21; 18:3) and prevents the unrighteous from taking part (Matt. 5:20; 1 Cor. 6:9–10; Eph. 5:5). Yet, in another respect, in its earthly form, it contains even the wicked (Matt. 13:36–43). While the unrighteous live in the midst of God's kingdom, they do not have access to the King through His Mediator, Jesus Christ. Isn't this equally true of earthly kingships? While foreigners may reside within the borders of the United States, they do not have all the privileges of citizenship. For example, they cannot vote or run for political office. They do benefit, however, from the justice system under which citizens live.

Fourth, although Jesus states that the origination of His kingdom is heaven and not earth by declaring that His "kingdom is not of this world" (John 18:36), He nevertheless states that His kingdom is present. Jesus speaks of "my kingdom" (18:36a). He claims to have His own "servants" (even though they do not fight with sword to defend Him, 18:36b). Jesus clearly asserts: "I am a king" (18:37a). Finally, He confidently challenges Pilate: "For this I have been born, and for this I have come into the world, to bear witness to the truth" (18:37b).

Fifth, through Peter's Pentecost sermon we learn that Jesus suffered humiliation by enduring the "curse" of hanging "on a tree" (Gal. 3:13). But with His resurrection, He began His exaltation in preparation for His ascension to the right hand of the throne of His Father where He governs the universe with authority and power. There He was "crowned with glory and honor" (Heb. 2:9) to begin His rule as He sits "at the right hand of God" (Rom. 8:34; cf. Eph. 1:20; Col. 3:1; Heb. 12:2; 1 Peter 3:22; Rev. 3:21) by wielding "all authority and power" (Matt. 28:18). Through this authority, Jesus promises to assist His people through "tribulation, or distress, or persecution, or famine, or nakedness, or peril, or sword" (Rom. 8:34–35). In fact, He remains on that throne working for the collapse of all the works of His enemies (1 Cor. 15:23–24; Heb. 1:3, 13; 10:13).

Sixth, Christians have been raised up with Jesus as a testimony to our rule with Him (Eph. 2:6). "We are, in the eyes of God, seated with Christ in heavenly places (which, in essence, is the idea of Revelation 20:4–6), i.e., in regal position."[4]

Restricting the Kingdom

Some believe the kingdom can only be identified within the confines of the church, and kingdom activity cannot manifest itself outside the church. In this view, the kingdom *is* the church and nothing but the church. Since the church is "sacred" and the world "profane," as this position sees it, the church should not consider the world as an arena for kingdom activity. The world is the domain of the existing kingdoms that will only be judged when God's kingdom is inaugurated sometime in the future. Does this mean to hold a job "in the world" is to walk outside the kingdom?

> Perhaps the most common example of this restriction in Protestantism is found in *pietism*. Pietists restrict the kingdom of God to the sphere of personal piety, the inner life of the soul.... Other traditions curtail the scope of Christ's kingship by identifying the kingdom with the institutional church.... This view holds that only clergymen and missionaries engage in "full-time kingdom work" and that the laity are involved in kingdom activity only to the degree that they are engaged in church work. This restriction has given rise to the misleading phrase "church and world," which suggests that all of human affairs are in fact divided into two spheres.[5]

While the church has a particular function in the kingdom, the kingdom encompasses more than the church. "The institutional church is not to be equated with the kingdom of God. It is an agency of the kingdom, but it is not identical to the kingdom. The kingdom of God is as broad as the world."[6] When Jesus tells us to "seek first His kingdom and His righteousness" (Matt. 6:33), He reminds us that every earthly endeavor should be considered kingdom-activity, whether family, church, business, or politics. We are God's ambassadors, representing our King in His kingdom on earth (2 Cor. 5:20).

The Establishment of the Kingdom

Many Christians conclude that because the Bible describes a *future* kingdom that this is its sole emphasis. The kingdom cannot be presently with us if the kingdom is seen as only yet to come. Actually, the kingdom is more than just a future reality. First, it is *definitively* established in the life, death, resurrection, and ascension of Jesus Christ. Second, it increases and advances *progressively* from that time to the end of the world. Third, it is established *fully* at Christ's consummating coming.

The Present Status of the Kingdom

Let us first examine the definitive aspect of the kingdom. Even a superficial reading of the gospels shows that the kingdom of God is the major theme of the ministries of both John the Baptist and Jesus. In fact, this is what the gospels are all about: The King is coming to establish His kingdom. John the Baptist exhorted the people of Judea to repent because "the kingdom of heaven is *near*" (Matt. 3:2). From His very first sermon, Jesus preached a similar message: "Repent, for the kingdom of heaven is *near*" (4:17). When Jesus sent out the seventy-two disciples, He told them to preach that "The kingdom of God is *near*" (Luke 10:9).[7] The "synoptic" gospels—Matthew, Mark, and Luke—all declare that the content of Jesus' entire teaching ministry can be summed up as the "good news of the kingdom" (Matt. 4:23; Mark 1:14–15; Luke 4:16–30; 4:43; 8:1). These passages, along with many others, prove that the establishment of the kingdom was imminent. It was "near" already in the time of Jesus.[8]

There was, however, a very significant difference between the preaching of John the Baptist and the preaching of Jesus. They often used the same words. But we find in Mark 1:15 that Jesus not only proclaims that the kingdom is near, but announces that "the time is fulfilled."[9] Thus, while John prophesied that it was almost time for the Lord to visit His people, Jesus "asserted that this visitation was in actual progress, that God was already visiting his people."[10] Moreover, in Luke 17:21, Jesus tells the Pharisees that the "Kingdom of God is within you." The Greek word for "within" can also mean "in your midst." Since the Pharisees were not believers, the better translation seems to be "in your midst," right before your eyes. Whatever it means here, however, one thing is clear: Jesus was announcing that God's kingdom was *present*, not exclusively future.

In short, a great change had begun by virtue of Jesus' presence on earth. Jesus described this change in other terms as well. When the Pharisees complained that His disciples did not fast, He asked, "Can the children of the bridegroom mourn as long as the bridegroom is with them?" (Luke 5:33). The mere fact that Jesus was among them filled the disciples with joy, a sign of the kingdom (cf. Rom. 14:17). Herman Ridderbos notes that "this person is not only the announcer, but he himself is the center and the cause of the joy, the bliss, which has started with his coming."[11]

Jesus also was establishing the kingdom by His works of healing. The clearest passages in this regard are Luke 4:21 and Matthew 11:2–6. In each case, Jesus quoted from the Old Testament prophecies of Isaiah about the kingdom of God (Isa. 35:5; 61:2), and in each case Jesus applied the prophecy to His works of healing and His teaching. In other words, Jesus claimed to be fulfilling the prophecies of the Old Testament. When the Pharisees charged Jesus with casting out demons by the power of the devil, He denied it, and added, "But if it is by the Spirit of God that I cast out demons, *then the Kingdom of God has come upon you*." The verb used for "come upon" implies that something is present, not merely close by.[12] Jesus was saying that the casting out of demons demonstrated that the kingdom of God had arrived.

Jesus was establishing His rule by defeating the enemy of the kingdom, Satan. He gained the *definitive* victory over Satan supremely in His death and resurrection (Col. 2:15; 1 Cor. 15). But even during his earthly ministry, Jesus was winning early skirmishes with the ultimate victory, the cross, to come. The casting out of demons, a sign of the presence of the kingdom, was also a victory over Satan. As one scholar has put it, "In each act of exorcism Jesus saw a defeat of Satan."[13] Or, as Geerhardus Vos states, "The underlying principle is that in the world of spirits there is no neutral territory; where the demons depart, the divine Spirit enters."[14] Jesus even gave His disciples the authority to cast out demons. When they returned from their mission, Jesus told them that He had seen Satan fall as lightning from heaven (Luke 10:18).

In short, as George Eldon Ladd summarizes, "Jesus did not promise his hearers a better future or assure that they would soon enter the Kingdom. Rather he boldly announced that the Kingdom of God had come to them."[15] John Bright states, "It lies at the very heart of the gospel message to affirm that the Kingdom of God has in a real sense become a present fact, here and now."[16]

The definitive establishment of the kingdom takes place in several stages. Even in the initial establishment of the kingdom, a *principle of progress* is operating. The kingdom was dawning already when Jesus was born. Throughout His life He was routing enemy forces and extending His rule. His death was a triumph over Satan, and thus marked a further development in the founding of His kingdom. The Bible also says that Jesus' kingdom is established by His resurrection. This was part of Peter's Pentecost message (Acts 2:32–36). Paul implies the same in 1 Corinthians 15:23–25:

> But each in his own turn: Christ, the first fruits; then, when He comes, those who belong to Him. Then the end will come, when He hands over the kingdom to God the Father after He has destroyed all dominion, authority, and power. For He must reign until He has put all His enemies under His feet.

This passage speaks about Jesus' reign. The end will come *after* He has destroyed all His remaining enemies. He will reign *until* He has brought all things under His feet. In other words, the kingdom does not *begin* when Jesus returns. Jesus began reigning from the time of His resurrection. The kingdom *culminates* in His second coming.

Finally, Jesus' ascension is described in Scripture as an enthronement (Eph. 1:20–23; Phil. 2:9–11). In Ephesians 1:21, Paul states explicitly that Jesus has been placed "far above all rule and authority and power and dominion, and every name that is named, *not only in this age, but also in the one to come*." This happened after God raised Jesus from the dead and "seated Him at His right hand in the heavenly places" (Eph. 1:20). As A. A. Hodge wrote, "In the strictest sense we must date the actual and formal assumption of [Jesus'] kingly office, in the full and visible exercise thereof, from the moment of His ascension into heaven from this earth and His session at the right hand of the Father."[17]

The Progress of the Kingdom

The *progressive* aspect of the kingdom is seen most clearly in Jesus' parables. In fact, one of the dominant notes of many parables is the advancing nature of the kingdom. The kingdom of heaven is like a mustard seed that starts very small and grows into a huge tree, providing a resting place for the birds of the air (Matt. 13:31–32). The kingdom is also like leaven (yeast) placed in a loaf that eventually spreads throughout the loaf (13:33). The parable of the wheat and tares also implies a progressive development of the kingdom. This is again a central feature of the parable. The owner of the field knows there are weeds in his wheat field, but he delays the harvest. He lets the wheat and the weeds grow and mature before he sends his laborers to harvest them (13:24–30, 36–43).

What, then, did Jesus say would happen to the kingdom after its establishment? The parables cited above teach that the kingdom would grow. It began as a seed in a field, or as leaven in a loaf. Gradually, almost imperceptibly, it has grown into a tree and has leavened the whole lump. This same principle of permeation and growth is found in many of the Old Testament prophecies of the kingdom. Isaiah says that a *child* would be born a king, an obvious reference to the *first* advent of Jesus. Once His kingdom is established, there will be no end to the *increase* of His government (Isa. 9:2–7). It's not just that the *kingdom* is everlasting. Its *increase* is everlasting.

In Daniel 2, Nebuchadnezzar has a dream in which "the God of heaven [sets] up a kingdom which will never be destroyed" (Dan. 2:44–45). The kingdom is compared to a rock "cut without hands" that becomes "a great mountain" and fills "the whole earth" (2:31–34).

In the New Testament, in addition to the parables of Jesus, Paul says that the end will come *after* "He has put all His enemies under His feet" (1 Cor. 15:24), and that "the last enemy that will be abolished is death" (1 Cor. 15:26). In other words, *Jesus will return to a world in which nearly all His enemies have been conquered.* The only enemy that will remain is death, and even that will be defeated.

The Consummation of the Kingdom

The New Testament also teaches that we look for a future manifestation of the kingdom (1 Cor. 15:23–24; Rev. 21). In this sense, the kingdom refers to heaven and the fullness of the new heavens and new earth. Our true and permanent home is in the heavenly realm that Jesus has prepared for us. Our life here is a pilgrimage to that blessed land of rest. We look forward to heaven with joy and expectation, knowing that we shall be forever with our Savior and King in His perfect Kingdom. The hope of heaven helps us endure the trials of the present life. We look forward to the day when all believers from all lands will gather to worship the Lamb that was slain from the beginning of the world, and when we will live in perfect peace and love, free from the last remnants of sin. Any Christian who does not eagerly await his heavenly reward is grievously confused. Any Christian whose *sole* hope is an earthly reward has not understood Christianity.

But this does not relieve us of responsibility on earth. We will be judged according to our service on earth. Thus, we cannot sit on our laurels and wait for Jesus to come. We must be seeking and, by His grace, working in the midst of Jesus' kingdom throughout our lives as faithful kingdom subjects. Moreover, we do not look for a *new* kingdom. The heavenly kingdom is not something that God will establish for the first time at the end of history. It's simply the full and final and glorious manifestation of the kingdom that was first established two millennia ago. Since the coming of Jesus, therefore, we can say that the kingdom is both *already* present but *not yet* fully consummated.

Kingdom Implications

The very nature of Christianity implies that the rule of Jesus affects earthly history. Biblical Christianity has always been *historical.* The early creeds of the Church are simply recitals of the history of Jesus's birth, death, and resurrection. These all occurred on earth, in history (Luke 1:1–4; 2:1–2; 3:1–2). It would be more than strange if the King had come to earth, died on earth, rose from the dead so He could establish a kingdom that has nothing to do with the world He came to redeem. Why did Jesus become flesh and enter human history? The answer of Scripture is that He came to redeem what was fallen. He came into the world to redeem the world. He came into the world to establish His redemptive reign among men and women on earth who need redemption.

Moreover, several passages explicitly claim that Jesus exercises dominion on earth. Jesus claimed that He had been given all authority in heaven *and* on earth (Matt. 28:18–20). Paul wrote to the Colossians that Jesus, the Creator of all things, had come to earth to restore all things (Col. 1:16).[18] Jesus' rule is as extensive as creation itself. People enter the kingdom (1:13). When Jesus gave Peter the keys of the kingdom, He told him that they were for the binding and loosing of things both in heaven and *on earth* (Matt. 16:19). The signs of the coming of the kingdom in Jesus' ministry affected people this side of heaven. Jesus exhorted His followers to pursue the righteousness of the kingdom (6:33), a righteousness manifested visibly and historically in acts of charity and justice. Though the operation of the kingdom is Spiritual, and though our King sits on a heavenly throne, His rule nevertheless has visible, historical, and earthly implications.

But we cannot stop with individual submission to Jesus. We must also submit our families to His rule by acknowledging that Jesus rules our homes. Families that rebel against Him will be judged, unto the third and fourth generations. When families come under Jesus' gracious rule, they receive His blessing, and commit themselves to live by His standards for family life. Husbands must love their wives, wives must submit themselves to their husbands, and children must be obedient to their parents (Eph. 5:22–6:4). In this way, Jesus' rule is acknowledged and progressively manifested in our homes. As the gospel is preached to all creatures, more families will enjoy the blessings of Jesus' rule.

Jesus is King over all civil officials and their governments as "King of kings and the Lord of lords" (1 Tim. 6:15; Rev. 11:15; 19:16). Civil officials must acknowledge the Lordship of Jesus and obey His rules for civil governments (Psalm 2:10–12; Rom. 13:1–4). The blessings of the kingdom—peace, stability, and justice—will come to all nations that acknowledge the King and pattern their ways after His laws.

"Kings and Priests unto God"

The present reign of Jesus, of both heaven and earth, means, because Christians are "heirs of God and fellow-heirs with Christ"

(Rom. 8:17), they participate with Him in His reign. "Not only the Apostles, but all true Christians are spoken of as 'kings and priests unto God.' They are a 'royal priesthood.' They are now 'reigning with Christ,' even while they live in a sinful world."[19] Christians are "ambassadors for Christ" (2 Cor. 5:20), bringing the King's message of reconciliation, life, and love to a dead and dying world devoid of light. Believers reign with Jesus in the following ways, as Roderick Campbell summarizes:

(1) As "heirs of God and joint-heirs with Christ," they possess "all things" necessary for their highest well being (cf. Rom. 8:17; 1 Cor. 3:21–22; James 2:5).

(2) They reign, or rule, in the sense that all things in nature and in history are working together for their good (cf. Rom. 5:17; 8:28; 1 Peter 3:13).

(3) They rule in the sense that Christ has no other earthly instrumentality, or agency, for the propagation of His gospel and law—the only method by which true victory and lasting peace can be achieved on earth (cf. Mat. 28:19; 2 Cor. 6:1).

(4) By faith in the unlimited resources and powers of Christ, they triumph over the world, the flesh and the devil. They become "more than conquerors" over all their deadly foes (Rom. 8:37; cf. James 4:7; 1 Peter 5:9; 1 John 2:13–14; 3:8).

(5) They rule, or will rule, in the sense (which is everywhere implied in Scripture) that there can be no stable, peaceful, and righteous civil government except as it is administered by Christian men, or by rulers elected to office by Christian people. As, and when, these conditions are fulfilled, the saints will reign on earth in the most literal sense.

(6) In position and dignity, in the truest sense, and in the sight of God, they are higher than the kings and potentates of earth. All have freedom of access at all times to the presence of the King of kings and Lord of lords (cf. Eph. 2:6; Heb. 10:19–22; 1 Peter 2: 5, 9).

(7) As intercessors they plead with God on behalf of men. By their prayers they move the arm that controls the winds, the rain, all the potent forces of the physical world, and even the powers of wicked nations and men (cf. Jer. 1:10, 18; Mat. 7:7–8; 18:19; Acts 12:5; James 5:14–18).[20]

Conclusion

If we are not living in the midst of God's kingdom, then whose kingdom is it? Does the devil rule? Some Christians argue that God's kingdom cannot be present on earth because His throne is not physically present. When asked who is ruling, generally these same people claim that it's Satan. Using their line of reasoning, how can Satan be king when he does not have a physical throne set up on earth? Scripture tells us that if we resist the devil he will flee from us (James 4:7). A true king flees from no man. Is man the ruler of the kings of the earth? Hardly. "Stop regarding man, whose breath of life is in his nostrils; for why should he be esteemed?" (Isa. 2:22). What we believe about God's kingdom will impact how we live. If the kingdom has been postponed, then God is a bystander with His hands tied and our efforts hopeless.

Notes

1. Roderick Campbell, *Israel and the New Covenant* (Philadelphia, PA: Presbyterian and Reformed, 1954), 130–31.

2. This view of the kingdom is advocated by dispensational premillennialists. Dispensationalism asserts that Jesus offered to Israel a physical, political, earthly kingdom, but that the Jews rejected Jesus as their king, thus initiating the kingdom's "postponement." Such a view contradicts Scripture. First, Scripture nowhere states this. Second, Scripture tells a different story: "Jesus therefore perceiving that they were intending to come and take Him by force, to make

Him king, withdrew again to the mountain by Himself alone" (John 6:15). It was the idea of a political kingdom that Jesus rejected, the same type of kingdom that dispensationalists say is yet to be established during an earthly millennium. The observant reader will note that Revelation 20 makes no mention of Jesus' reigning on the earth, Jerusalem as a redemptive center, or the reinstitution of animal sacrifices and circumcision during the thousand-year period.

3. Greg L. Bahnsen and Kenneth L. Gentry, Jr., *House Divided: The Break-Up of Dispensational Theology* (Tyler, TX: Institute for Christian Economics, 1989), 181.

4. Bahnsen and, *House Divided,* 186.

5. Albert M. Wolters, *Creation Regained: Biblical Basics for a Reformational Worldview* (Grand Rapids, MI: Eerdmans, 1985), 65.

6. Gary North, *Unconditional Surrender: God's Program for Victory,* 2nd ed. (Tyler, TX: Institute for Christian Economics, 1983), 126. A new edition has been published by American Vision (Powder Springs, Georgia) in 2010.

7. The gospels say that "the kingdom of heaven" and "the kingdom of God" are near. The phrase "kingdom of heaven" appears only in Matthew. There is no distinction between these two phrases. Whatever distinctive shade of meaning Matthew might have given to "heaven," he uses the two phrases to refer to the same thing. See especially Matthew 19:23–24, where Jesus tells His disciples that it is hard for a rich man to enter the kingdom of heaven (19:23), and that it is easier for a camel to go through the eye of a needle than for a rich man to enter the kingdom of God (19:24). Clearly, the two phrases are parallel and, for all practical purposes, synonymous. For a discussion of this, see Oswald T. Allis, *Prophecy and the Church* (Philadelphia, PA: Presbyterian and Reformed, 1945), 299–301, notes 6–11 and Geerhardus Vos, *The Teaching of Jesus Concerning The Kingdom and the Church* (Grand Rapids, MI: Eerdmans, 1951), 23–26.

8. For further information on texts that use the words "near," "shortly," and "quickly," see Gary DeMar, *Last Days Madness: Obsession of the Modern Church,* 4th ed. (Powder Springs, GA: American Vision, 1999) and *Left Behind: Separating Fact from Fiction,* 2nd ed. (Powder Springs, GA: American Vision, 2009).

9. Herman Ridderbos, *The Coming of the Kingdom* (Philadelphia, PA: Presbyterian and Reformed, 1962), 48.

10. George Eldon Ladd, *Jesus and the Kingdom: The Eschatology of Biblical Realism,* 2nd ed. (Waco, TX: Word, 1964), 107.

11. Ridderbos, *The Coming of the Kingdom,* 51.

12. George Eldon Ladd, *A Theology of the New Testament* (Grand Rapids, MI: Eerdmans, 1974), 65–66. See 2 Corinthians 10:14, where the same verb is used.

13. Ladd, *A Theology of the New Testament,* 67.

14. Geerhardus Vos, *Biblical Theology: Old and New Testaments* (Carlisle, PA: The Banner of Truth Trust, [1948] 1975), 382.

15. Ladd, *Jesus and the Kingdom,* 107.

16. John Bright, *The Kingdom of God: The Biblical Concept and Its Meaning for the Church* (New York: Abingdon-Cokesbury, 1953), 216.

17. A. A. Hodge, *Evangelical Theology* (Edinburgh: Banner of Truth, [1890] 1976), 227.

18. See Greg L. Bahnsen, "The World and the Kingdom of God" in Gary DeMar and Peter Leithart, *The Reduction of Christianity: A Biblical Response to Dave Hunt* (Ft. Worth, TX: Dominion Press, 1988), appendix D.

19. Campbell, *Israel and the New Covenant*, 134.

20. Campbell, *Israel and the New Covenant*, 134–135.

PART FIVE

Christians and the Future

14

"We're Living in the Last Days"

Myth, Lie, or Half-Truth?: *The prophetic signs are around us and are evidence that we are living in the final days before Jesus' return, therefore, to be involved in issues beyond evangelism and church work seems pointless. Jesus is coming soon!*

> David was not a believer in the theory that the world will grow worse and worse, and that the dispensations will wind up with general darkness, and idolatry. Earth's sun is to go down amid tenfold night if some of our prophetic brethren are to be believed. Not so do we expect, but we look for a day when the dwellers in all lands shall learn righteousness, shall trust in the Saviour, shall worship thee alone, O God, *and shall glorify thy name*. The modern notion has greatly damped the zeal of the church for missions, and the sooner it is shown to be unscriptural the better for the cause of God. It neither consorts with prophecy, honours God, nor inspires the church with ardour. Far hence be it driven.[1]

Popular Bible teacher John MacArthur states that "'Reclaiming' the culture is a pointless, futile exercise."[2] He comes to this conclusion based on his reading of a section of 2 Timothy 3. He quotes selective verses (vv. 1–5, and 13) in an effort to support his belief that Paul is describing the inevitable triumph of evil prior to a "rapture." These verses, cut off from their immediate context, could lead almost anyone to adopt MacArthur's interpretation. A study of the entire passage, however, shows that Paul's message is not about the inevitability of evil triumphing over good. Paul compares the supposed progress of the ungodly in Timothy's day, the "last days" of the Old Covenant of Judaism (Heb. 1:1–2; 1 Cor. 10:11), to the overthrow of Jannes and Jambres in Moses' day (Ex. 7:11): "But *they* will not make further progress; for their folly will be obvious to all, as also that of those two [Jannes and Jambres] came to be" (2 Tim. 3:9).

Paul is forthright in encouraging Timothy that those who exhibit the deeds of wickedness will suffer the same fate as the two Egyptian sorcerers who confronted Moses and Aaron at the behest of the most powerful ruler of the day, Pharaoh. Paul backs up his claim of optimism not with a treatise on end-time speculation but from an incident recorded in the Bible that shows that God's people, through His providential care, triumph over wickedness:

> Then Pharaoh also called for the wise men and the sorcerers, and they also, the magicians of Egypt, did the same with their secret arts. For each one threw down his staff and they turned into serpents. *But Aaron's staff swallowed up their staffs* (Ex. 7:11–12).[3]

While it is true there is an attempt by the ungodly to dominate culture, and some are successful for a season, the fact is, that over time "they will not make further progress"; their fling with ungodliness is only temporary (cf. Rom. 1:18–32). Christians can be optimistic even if the actions of the ungodly increase in their own day. If Christians remain faithful in influencing their world with the gospel and applying a Christian worldview to every area of life, the world can and will change. History and God's providential care are on our side.[4]

Paul, however, does not allow Christians to remain passive as the ungodly self-destruct. Timothy has followed Paul's "teaching, conduct, purpose, faith, patience, love, perseverance, persecutions, [and] sufferings" (2 Tim. 3:10–11), and he calls on us to do the same. While the ungodly expend capital from their contrary and corrupted worldview on present-oriented living, the Christian is to develop future-oriented spiritual capital to replace the bankrupt culture of secularism, humanism, materialism, relativism, and hedonism.

Notice that the characteristics of the ungodly are all self-directed and short-lived, summarized by the phrase "lovers of pleasure rather than lovers of God" (2 Tim. 3:4). Sin has its pleasure for a short period of time: "He who loves pleasure will become a poor man; he who loves wine and oil will not become rich" (Prov. 21:17). The love of pleasure is no investment in the future.

The characteristics of the godly are directed toward the future, foregoing the lure of present pleasures for future blessings. Teaching, conduct, purpose, faith, patience, love and perseverance take time and energy from the present but result in lasting rewards. Moreover, even persecutions and sufferings should not deter future-oriented Christians because "out of them all the Lord" delivers His people (2 Tim. 3:11).

The ungodly are involved in a game of self-deception, so that even they are "being deceived" when they think their worldview will ultimately prevail. We also must remember the previous words of Paul: "But *they* will not make further progress; for *their* folly will be obvious to all." While the ungodly burn themselves out on present-oriented living, the faithful steadily influence their world: "You, however, *continue* in the things you have learned and become convinced of" (2 Tim. 3:14). In time, faithfulness will be rewarded: "And let us not lose heart in doing good, for in due time we shall reap if we do not grow weary" (Gal. 6:9).

Paul does not deny "persecutions" and "sufferings" (2 Tim. 3:11). In fact, his words echo those of Jesus: "In the world you have tribulation, but take courage; I have overcome the world" (John 16:33). Paul can tell Timothy, "out of them all the Lord delivered me!" (2 Tim. 3:11). If God delivered Paul and the Christian church of the first century from Jewish persecution and Roman tyranny, what leads us to believe that God cannot and will not do the same today? A belief in the inevitability of certain prophetic events, the belief that we are the terminal generation, can lead to a spirit of malaise, indifference, and despair.

Prophetic Déjà Vu

As early as the second century, prophets were suggesting dates for the second coming of Christ. The prophet Montanus in A.D. 156 was one of the first to suggest a date for the second coming. His failed attempts at predicting the end did not deter other date setters.

> In the third century, a prophet called Novatian gathered a huge following by crying, "Come, Lord Jesus!" Donatus, a fourth-century prophet, commanded attention when he stressed that only 144,000 people would be chosen by God. He found this magic figure in Revelation 14:1 (a verse which the Jehovah's Witnesses use to proclaim their own version of this heresy). Both Novatian and Donatus were branded as heretics by the church.[5]

As the last day of 999 approached, "the old basilica of St. Peter's at Rome was thronged with a mass of weeping and trembling worshipers awaiting the end of the world" believing that they were on the eve of the millennium.[6] Land, homes, and household goods were given to the poor as a final act of contrition to absolve the hopeless from sins of a lifetime. Some Europeans sold their goods to make the trip to Palestine to await the second coming. This mistaken application of biblical prophecy happened again in 1100, 1200, and 1245. Prophetic speculation continued. "In 1531, Melchoir Hofmann announced that the second coming would take place in the year 1533. . . . Nicholas

Cusa held that the world would not last past 1734."[7]

The Disappointed

Predictions of the impending return of Jesus have been rampant in the United States. William Miller (1782–1849), a farmer from Vermont, became an ardent Bible student, using only the marginal notes of his Bible and a *Concordance* to formulate a prophetical system that influenced tens of thousands of devotees. In 1831, Miller preached his first sermon and followed these with a series of messages on Daniel 7 and 8.

Miller's popularity increased, and so did opposition to his teachings. Miller finally set a date for Jesus' return: 1843. "He arrived at this date by interpreting Daniel's seventy weeks (i.e. 490 days) as meaning 490 years, on the principle that a 'day' means a year of time. From the 490 years he subtracted AD 33, the date of the crucifixion (on the premise that Christ's death marks the end of the seventy weeks or 490 year-days), leaving 457."[8] By subtracting this date from the 2,300 days (years) of Daniel 8:14, he was left with 1843 as the date of the second coming. When his prediction failed, Miller concluded that his date for the crucifixion was incorrect. After adjusting the date of the crucifixion, he predicted that the second coming would be on October 22, 1844. Nearly 50,000 persons (some estimates make it 100,000) left their churches to await the predicted event. "During the final week Millerites closed their stores, abandoned their crops and animals, and resigned from their posts."[9] The failed prophecies led to the "Great Disappointment," "when the movement collapsed, splintering into three main factions."[10] Tom Sine writes that "their eschatology had convinced them they couldn't make a difference in their world . . . and they didn't."[11] A similar "Great Disappointment" may meet today's church if more failed predictions of the end greet an already skeptical world.

Prophetic ideas based on a misreading of the Bible can have long lasting cultural, moral, political, and international consequences.

If enough people in our generation believe as the Millerites did, then what is to become of this world? Should it be abandoned to inevitable evil? Should we throw in the towel and await the second coming in passivity? If you are certain that Jesus is going to return in a few years, then this belief will have an impact on how you view this world, this present time, and what you do to effect any long-term change.

Some millennial adherents "found it difficult to adjust to the general enthusiasm for reform" in the nineteenth century "since it ran counter to the basic pessimism of their" end-time views.[12] This idea prevails today because of the claim that Jesus is coming "soon." Dave Hunt's book *When Will Jesus Come?* is a prime example of marking out this present generation as the final generation. He tells us in the subtitle that there is *Compelling Evidence for the Soon Return of Christ.*[13] If Jesus is coming "soon," why bother?

Will the Real Antichrist Please Stand Up?

In 1926, Oswald J. Smith first published *Is the Antichrist at Hand?—What of Mussolini?* Smith believed that the fascist dictator Benito Mussolini, who had ruled Italy since 1922, was the predicted antichrist. Ample biblical evidence was put forth by Smith in an effort to establish his claim.[14] Smith was not alone. In 1929, C. S. Tubby wrote *Mussolini: The Marvel-Man—Is He the Predicted Super Man?*:

> At no time during the history of the age, has any man become the center of such intense and widespread interest as Premier Benito Mussolini of Italy. He has astonished the whole world by his amazing accomplishments, his inexplicable force of personality, his uncanny measure of lion-like boldness and his startlingly sudden rise to power and prominence.
>
> * * * * *
>
> Along with other Bible teachers, the writer is con-

> vinced that Antichrist is now alive on the earth and will shortly be revealed as such. . . . Now we all believe that the apostasy is here. . . . [I]t is logical to conclude that Antichrist is right now somewhere in the world. If this is true, we are face to face with startling realities, and we may expect the Lord of glory to burst through the clouds at any moment, and we shall begin our eagle flight to the realms of eternal day.[15]

If Mussolini was the embodiment of the antichrist, and a whole series of end time events were to happen "shortly," then interest in a post-Mussolini world was not in view. Why care about the future of planet earth if the future is prophetically set and about to end in our day?

But something happened to Smith and other prophecy writers on their road to prophetic certainty. In April 1945, just before the Allied armies reached Milan, Italy, Mussolini was caught by Italian Communist partisans as he tried to escape to Switzerland. He and his mistress, Clara Patacci, were hanged.

In addition to making his predictions about Mussolini, Smith also believed that the Bible predicted a revived ten-nation Roman confederacy that was on the horizon. All the prophetic pieces were said to be in place, or so he thought. Smith was so sure of his views that in subsequent printings of his book, he included the following on the front cover:

> The fact that this book has run swiftly into a number of large editions bears convincing testimony to its intrinsic worth. There are here portrayed startling indications of the approaching end of the present age from the spheres of demonology, politics and religion. No one can read this book without being impressed with the importance of the momentous days in which we are living.

Smith was emphatic that "Ten nations, no more, no less, are to become allied and known as the Roman empire because Rome will be the centre, the capital, and it will be in Rome that the Emperor will reign."[16] Similar predictions were made by prophecy writers soon after the end of World War II.[17]

The speculation has continued. In his *Late Great Planet Earth* (1970), Hal Lindsey wrote about a "ten nation [European] confederacy" that would be in place by 1980. For support, he quoted Dr. William Hallstein, the former president of the European Economic Community, who described how a "Common Market could someday expand into a ten-nation economic entity whose industrial might would far surpass that of the Soviet Union." Lindsey remarked, "Imagine that. A 'ten-nation economic entity.'"[18]

Like Smith, Lindsey was wrong in his prophetic estimates. The European Union is much larger than ten nations and includes nations not originally part of the old Roman Empire and excludes the nations of northern Africa. Eight former Communist states and two island Mediterranean nations joined the European Union in 2004.[19] This brought the total to 25. Today, the number is 27 member states. So what happened to a literal ten-nation—no more, no less—Common Market? Lindsey fudges by revising his early comments by claiming that ten nations control the 27. Where does he find this in the Bible? Other prophecy writers understand the problem of maintaining that a modern-day ten-nation European confederacy is the fulfillment of Daniel 7:23–25 and Revelation 13:1–4. They are now using the phrase "ten regions of global governance."

For defending the faith against skeptics, prophetic certainty has proved to be a disastrous embarrassment as skeptics point out the repeated predictions, purportedly certain, that did not come to pass. John Warwick Montgomery's warning needs to be heeded:

> We are not saying that such efforts at end-time prophecy reach the level of the false prophets condemned in the Old Testament: those who "speak a vision out of

> their own heart, and not out of the mouth of the Lord" (Jer. 23:16). But we *are* saying that end-time prophecy lacks the necessary factual grounding to make it an effective apologetic to the unbeliever—and that it can be and often is in reality *counterproductive*, lowering rather than raising the credibility of Christianity in the eyes of the outsider.[20]

Does this mean that Christians should dismiss world events as outside the searching eye of Scripture? Not at all. There is enough non-prophetic teaching material in the Bible that can be used to analyze current social, moral, cultural, and political events. Consolidated political power is an issue that can be studied biblically (Ex. 18; 1 Sam. 8) without an appeal to prophecy. Christians can offer a reasonable voice without the dogmatism inherent in the ever-changing pronouncements made by prophetic speculators.

The Last Days

But aren't we living in the "last days"? A lot of confusion exists over what the Bible means by the "last days."[21] At least three views have been offered: (1) a concentrated period of time just prior to Jesus' second coming, making the time yet future; (2) the period of time between Jesus' first coming and second coming, what is typically and erroneously called the "church age"; (3) the forty year period from a point in time just prior to Jesus' death, resurrection, and ascension to the destruction of Jerusalem in A.D. 70, what the Bible describes as a generation (forty years) which constitutes the "last days" of the Old Covenant. Which is the biblical view? The first view finds little support in Scripture, since the writer to the Hebrews says:

> God, after He spoke long ago to the fathers in the prophets in many portions and in many ways, *in these last days* has spoke to us in His Son, whom He appointed heir of all

things, through whom also He made the world (Heb. 1:1–2).

It's obvious from this passage and others like it that the "last days" were operating in the first century. This immediately dismisses the futuristic view which concentrates the last days as a period of time just before Jesus returns. We are left with views 2 and 3. While position 2 has its adherents, position 3 seems to make more sense, since to extend the last *days* over two thousand *years* makes the phrase so imprecise that it loses any meaning. The "last days" refers to a period of time that was *about to* come to an end. The Apostle Paul tells the Corinthians that the *ends* of the ages had come upon them: "Now these things happened to [Israel] as an example, and they were written for our instruction, *upon whom the ends of the ages have come*" (1 Cor. 10:11).

The New Testament writers told their first readers that the "end of all things is at hand" (1 Peter 4:7), that is, the end of the Old Covenant with its types and shadows was about to pass away. These events were said to be "near" (James 5:7–9), near to those who first read the prophecies not near to people who wouldn't be around for 2000 years! There's no getting around the biblical language of nearness as it relates to Bible prophecy (e.g., Matt. 10:23; 16:27–28; 26:64; John 21:21–22; Rom. 13:11–12; 16:20; 1 Cor. 7:29, 31; 1 Cor. 10:11; 2 Thess. 2:6–7; Phil. 4:5; Heb. 9:26; 10:25; 10:37; James 5:7–9; 1 Peter 1:20; 4:7; 5:4; 1 John 2:18; Rev. 1:1; 1:3; 3:10–11; 11:14; 17:8; 22:6–7, 10, 12, 20).

How should we understand these time verses? Evangelical writers H. Wayne House and Gordon Carle "are convinced that the problem of the delay of the parousia [the return of Christ] is exaggerated.... Jesus did not say specifically when he would return, only that it was imminent—it could happen at any time."[22] Actually, Jesus did say when He would return *in judgment*: "This generation will not pass away until all these things take place" (Matt. 24:34).[23] The use of "this generation" in the gospels always refers to the generation then living. While His disciples would not know the "day and the hour" of His return to judge Jerusalem (24:36), they knew it would happen before the close of their generation *because Jesus said it would*. Some of them would be alive to see it (16:28; cf. John 21:18–23). The Bible never says that the return of Jesus is "imminent," that it could come at "any moment" over a period of thousands of years.[24] The words used to describe the judgment-coming of Jesus are "near," "shortly," "quickly," and "at hand." These words hardly qualify to extend time to nearly 2000 years as House, Carle, and other prophecy writers interpret them.[25]

The "last days" were the final days of the Old Covenant order that brought an end to the shedding of blood for atonement, the need for a physical temple, and an assembly of sinful priests to officiate in the temple. Jesus was the better and once-for-all sacrifice (Heb. 9:11–22; 10:10–18); His body became the new and everlasting temple (John 2:19; Heb. 9:11–12); and He was a better priest "after the order of Melchizedek" (Heb. 7).

The Effects of Prediction

Some of the Thessalonian Christians were "leading an undisciplined life, doing no work at all, but acting like busybodies" (2 Thess. 3:11). While this may have little to do with a preoccupation with "the day of the Lord" (1 Thess. 5:2), it reminds us that God requires us to work regardless of external circumstances. Faithfulness is evaluated in terms of kingdom work: "Who then is the faithful and sensible slave whom his master put in charge of his household to give them their food at the proper time? Blessed is that slave whom his master finds so doing when he comes" (Matt. 24:45–46). Jesus goes on to hint at the time and circumstances of His coming: "The master of that slave will come on a day *when he does not expect him and at an hour which he does not know*" (24:50). Nowhere does Scripture intimate that we should cease any aspect of kingdom work, even if we *think* Jesus' coming is near. "*The delay of the master made no difference to the true servant*: he busied himself about his Lord's business. . . . But the master's delay induced the false servant to a sinful course of action. *The Lord's delay brought out the true character of his servants.*"[26] In the years leading up to the destruction of Jerusalem, there didn't seem to be any social, political, or religious change until suddenly Jerusalem was surrounded by armies (Luke 21:20) and the temple was destroyed by the armies of Titus with not one stone "left upon another" (Matt. 24:2) as Jesus had predicted.

Jesus related a parable to His disciples when "they supposed that the kingdom of God was going to appear immediately" (Luke 19:11). In Jesus' day many assumed the kingdom would arrive through a cataclysmic event. Jesus told them through the parable to "do business until I come back" (19:13). When the master finally returns he will take an accounting. Those who made a profit on the money given by the master will "be in authority over" ten and five cities (19:17–19). Those who put the money "away in a handkerchief" (19:20), not being industrious enough to "put the money in the bank" to collect "interest" (19:23), lose everything (19:24).

For decades, prophecy writers have been making dire predictions about what the future might hold. Their regularity is only surpassed by their foolishness:

- "This world is not going to get any easier to live in. Almost unbelievably hard times lie ahead. Indeed, Jesus said that these coming days will be uniquely terrible. Nothing in all the previous history of the world can compare with what lies in store for mankind."[27]

- "What a way to live! With optimism, with anticipation, with excitement. We should be living like persons who don't expect to be around much longer."[28]

- "I don't like cliches but I've heard it said, 'God didn't send me to clean the fish bowl, he sent me to fish.' In a way there's a truth in that."[29]

- "The premillennial position sees no obligation to make distinctly Christian laws."[30]

Ted Peters writes that this type of prophetic futurism "functions to justify social irresponsibility," and many "find this doctrine a comfort in their lethargy."[31] While not everyone who believes in the end-time scenario outlined by Tim LaHaye and Jerry Jenkins in their multi-volume *Left Behind* series thinks this way,[32] there are too many who do. A form of "prophetic inevitability" has set in much of the church that "portrays the present evil world as beyond improvement or redemption, and predicts instead that it will deteriorate steadily until the coming of Jesus, who will then set up his millennial reign on earth. If the world is getting worse, and if only Jesus at his coming will put it right, the argument runs, there seems no point in trying to reform it meanwhile. Adopting political programs is 'like cleaning the staterooms on the Titanic after it has hit the iceberg. . . . It is far more important simply to preach the Gospel and to rescue souls for the next life.'"[33]

If this approach is taken, and a hundred or two hundred years pass without the return of Jesus, what will our world look like and how will Christians respond in the face of an even more degenerate world? Some might argue that no one really connects an end-time theology to present-day affairs. It's more prevalent than one might think, as Tom Sine observed:

> "Do you realize if we start feeding hungry people things won't get worse, and if things don't get worse, Jesus won't come?" interrupted a coed during a Futures Inter-term I recently conducted at a northwest Christian college. Her tone of voice and her serious expression revealed she was utterly sincere. And unfortunately I have discovered the coed's question doesn't reflect an isolated viewpoint. Rather, it betrays a widespread misunderstanding of biblical eschatology . . . that seems to permeate

> much contemporary Christian consciousness. . . . The response of the (student) . . . reflects what I call the Great Escape View of the future. . . .
>
> The irony of the Great Escape approach to the future is that, while it claims to take God seriously, it unwittingly moves God outside history, insisting that even he is powerless "in these last days" to feed the hungry, bring a global awakening, or change unjust economic structures. It portrays God as able to redeem sinners and to communicate with his children, but at the same time unintentionally fashions him into an impotent absentee landlord, who has lost control of his world and of human history. . . . The Great Escape becomes an incredible cop-out from all Christ called us to be and to do.[34]

Then there are the extremists. The FBI was unprepared for the end-time logic of Vicki and Randy Weaver in the Ruby Ridge disaster (1992). The Weavers were treated like fringe political extremists who were tied to white supremacist, anti-semitic, and Aryan Nation groups rather than believers in an imminent apocalypse that they (the Weavers) concluded would be led by governmental powers ("the Beast").

> The Weaver family's flight to Ruby Ridge was greatly influenced by *The Late Great Planet Earth*. Though Vicki Weaver, the family's spiritual leader, was also influenced by H. G. Wells and Ayn Rand, it was Lindsey's prophetic work, coupled with her home-spun visions, that convinced her to pack up her family and move to Ruby Ridge. She believed that the enemies of God predicted by Lindsey were prepared to strike at any moment.[35]

The Weavers mixed conspiracy theories, apocalypticism, and paranoia to conclude that the end was near.[36] You can imagine what the Weavers thought as they saw armed soldiers attacking their homestead. Was this happening everywhere? Was this the prelude to the end that they read so much about in popular prophecy books and expected to take place in their lifetime? The events described in Revelation were being acted out right before their eyes, so they thought.

Walking by Faith, Not by Sight

God had promised to give the land of Canaan to Israel (Num. 13:1–2). Just as God was about to bring the Israelites into the land, He put forth one more test. Twelve men, twelve representatives of the nation, a representative for each tribe, were sent to spy out the land (13:2). They spent forty days at their task after which they returned with evidence of everything God had told them: "Indeed, it was a land flowing with milk and honey" (13:25–27). But they also brought back a report about giants (13:28, 31–33).

You know the story. The majority believed the report of the spies instead of the many promises made by God. Forty years were wasted in the wilderness because of unbelief. God's Word was evaluated in terms of external circumstances. The paganism of Canaan festered for forty more years because the salve of Israel could not be applied. A generation died in the wilderness because of the failure to believe God's promise. But the forty years did pass.

This time Israel would enter the land, but not before God set them straight on the difference between walking by sight and walking by faith. The previous generation chose to walk by sight: "We *became* like grasshoppers in our own sight, and so we *were* in their sight" (13:33). They acted on what they saw. Notice the promise about the land: "I am *going to give* [the land] to the sons of Israel" (13:2). Contrast the unbelieving response of the Israelites who *saw* God deliver them from every obstacle with that of Rahab who only *heard* about it:

> Now before [the two spies] lay down, she came up to them on the roof, and said to the men, "I know that the LORD has given you the land, and that the terror of you has fallen on us, and that all the inhabitants of the land have melted away before you. For we have heard how the LORD dried up the water of the Red Sea before you when you came out of Egypt, and what you did to the two kings of the Amorites who were beyond the Jordan, to Sihon and Og, whom you utterly destroyed. And when we heard it, our hearts melted and no courage remained in any man any longer because of you; for the LORD your God, he is God in heaven above and on earth beneath (Joshua 2:8–11).

Forty years before, current events gave the *impression* that they would be defeated by the Canaanites, by the cultural giants of their day. They were mistaken. The residents of the land thought of themselves as the grasshoppers and the Israelites as the giants. Forty years were wasted in the wilderness because what they saw—"There are giants in the land!"—obscured what God had promised. Circumstances are not always accurate indicators of what God is doing in the world (cf. John 9:1–12). Instead of the disintegration of the church, we may be witnessing the disintegration of humanism.

So What Does This Mean?

Our nation, and every nation, could go through the most tumultuous upheaval that history has ever experienced, and this still would not mean that Jesus was returning soon. For date setters, history is ignored with the result that the church experiences wild gyrations in the field of biblical prophecy. W. Ward Gasque, writing in *Christianity Today*, concludes:

> The problem with the evangelicals who turn the Bible into a kind of crystal ball is that they show very little his-

> torical awareness. They speak assuredly about the signs that are being fulfilled "right before your very eyes" and point to the impending end. [Hal] Lindsey confidently refers to our own as "the terminal generation." However, these writers do not seem to be aware that there have been many believers in *every* generation—from the Montanists of the second century through Joachin of Fiore (c. 1135–1202) and Martin Luther to those Russian Mennonites who undertook a "Great Trek" to Siberia in 1880–84 and the nineteenth-century proponents of dispensationalism—who have believed that *they* were living in the days immediately preceding the second coming of Christ. So far they have all been mistaken. How many people have lost confidence in clear doctrines of Scripture affecting eternal life because of misguided prophetic teaching is, unfortunately, not likely to be investigated?[37]

Gasque's admonition is borne out when one considers the religious and cultural conditions prior to the Reformation of the sixteenth century. Medieval life was dominated by a corrupt church which positioned itself to be the ruler of all of life, from personal thought and behavior to ecclesiastical and political power. The theology of the leadership in the church could be described as heretical. It's no wonder that the Reformers saw the Papacy as the embodiment of the "antichrist."[38]

In addition to apostasy, the outbreak of bubonic plague nearly decimated Medieval Europe. The Black Death, or "The Great Dying" as it was popularly known, had started its trek through the trade routes from the East in the fourteenth century. All ages and classes were affected, and death, when it came, struck fast. While estimates vary on the number of deaths—from one-third to one-half of Europe's population—no epidemic since has matched its scourge.

The plague reached Constantinople in 1347 and spread through Europe to England by late 1348. As one could imagine, all of society was affected. The burial of the dead was a major task since the living were often outnumbered by victims who had succumbed to the epidemic. Courts were closed. Food prices dropped because people were afraid to buy meat and other food stuffs. Crops lay in the field for want of workmen. Those laborers who would work demanded exorbitant wages.

The time was ripe for prophecy advocates predicting the near-demise of the times. John Wycliffe "describes the 'covetousness, sensuality, and fraud' of the clergy as infecting all of humanity, thus causing the chastisement under which Europe mourned."[39] In addition to plague, heresy, social unrest, monumental economic changes, and class conflict, there were "exaggerated forms of religious mysticism," and "the lack of educated clergy reduced the church's intellectual vigor."[40]

Then there was the Hundred Years War which could be described as years of peace interrupted by war, a series of invasions and treaties, challenged succession to the French throne, disputes over trade and ports, territorial claims, and counter claims. But this was not the end, although there were certainly enough people around making their predictions, using the same Bible verses and the same interpretive methodologies that are being used today.

Conclusion

Chuck Smith, pastor of Calvary Chapel in Costa Mesa, California, was convinced that the Lord would be "coming for His Church before the end of 1981." While he stated that he "could be wrong," he nevertheless stated his beliefs with certainty: "It's a deep conviction in my heart, and all my plans are predicated upon that belief."[41] Smith's views on the timing of the Lord's return demonstrate the danger of setting dates. His plans were predicated on the almost certain return of Jesus in his lifetime. Since he made the claim in 1978, this would mean that his temporal plans would extend no longer than *three years*! Rebuilding anything takes time, and this certainly includes rebuilding a civilization. But there is no time when the end is just three years off. Since Jesus did not return in 1981, Smith later wrote: "Date setting is wrong, and I was guilty of coming close to that. I did believe that Hal Lindsey could have been on track when he talked about the forty-year generation, the fig tree budding being the rebirth of Israel, and I was convinced in my own heart."[42]

We should be wary of allowing current events to shape the way Scripture is interpreted. There is a long history of failure.[43] In addition to the impact such end-time views have on Christian involvement, there is also the impact that predictive prophecy has on those who want to discredit the Bible. In his best-selling book *Misquoting Jesus*, Bart Ehrman, who is Professor and Chair of the Department of Religious Studies at the University of North Carolina at Chapel Hill, describes how he struggled to reconcile the inerrancy of the Bible with what he was taught about prophecy. His trek down the road toward skepticism and unbelief begins with what he describes as "one of the most popular books on campus" that was being read while he was a student at Moody Bible Institute in the 1970s, Hal "Lindsay's [sic] apocalyptic blueprint for our future, *The Late Great Planet Earth*."[44] Ehrman writes that he "was particularly struck by the 'when'" of Lindsey's prophetic outline of Matthew 24.

Lindsey followed a futuristic paradigm that assured his readers that Jesus would return within forty-years of 1948 (1948 + 40 = 1988), because, according to Lindsey and many others, the reestablishment of the nation of Israel is the prophetic key to Bible prophecy. (The New Testament does not say a single word said about Israel becoming a nation again.) Ehrman writes that "this message proved completely compelling to us. It may seem odd now—given the circumstances that 1988 has come and gone, with no Armageddon—but, on the other hand, there are millions of Christians who still believe that the Bible can be read literally as completely inspired in its predictions of what is soon to happen to bring history as we know it to a close."[45] Instead of questioning the exegetical work of Lindsey and other prophecy writers,

Ehrman rejects the authority of the Bible. This is akin to rejecting the study of biology because nearly all scientists once believed in spontaneous generation.[47]

As the chairman of the Department of Religious Studies at the University of North Carolina at Chapel Hill, and someone who is described as "an authority on the history of the New Testament, the early church, and the life of Jesus," Ehrman should know that the interpretation made popular by Lindsey, LaHaye, and others has a recent history when compared to the great Bible expositors of the past. The fourth-century historian Eusebius outlines the preterist interpretation of the Olivet Discourse in his *Ecclesiastical History* and *Proof of the Gospe*l. Ehrman seems oblivious to the preterist interpretation of the Olivet Discourse found in Matthew 24, Mark 13, and Luke 21. A "preterist" contends that Jesus, in answering His disciples' questions about the destruction of the temple and the "end of the age" (Matt. 24:1–3), was referring to His coming in judgment against Jerusalem that took place before that first-century generation passed away. So when Jesus said, "this generation will not pass away until all these things take place" (24:34), He had that generation in view.

Using Lindsey and LaHaye as New Testament authorities, as Ehrman does, is a sad commentary on the state of scholarship today. But Ehrman is simply "following the money" by pointing out that it seems that a majority of evangelicals believe LaHaye's views are true based on the millions of copies of the *Left Behind* series sold (current estimates put the number at around 65 million). "Witness the current craze," he writes, "for the Timothy LaHaye and Jerry Jenkins series *Left Behind*, another apocalyptic vision of our future based on a literalistic reading of the Bible, a series that has sold more than sixty million copies in our own day."[48] It's a shame that this type of prophetic nonsense is continually promoted by Christian publishers that know better[49] and Christian news sites that should know better.[50] Today's end-time preoccupied church and those who make millions of dollars off the nonsense of these prophetic novels and their supposed non-fiction counterparts are giving aid and comfort to the enemies of the gospel.

Notes

1. Charles H. Spurgeon, *The Treasury of David: Containing the Book of Psalms*, 7 vols. (New York: Funk & Wagnalls Co., [1869], 1881), 4:102.

2. John F. MacArthur, Jr., *The Vanishing Conscience: Drawing the Line in a No-Fault, Guilt-Free World* (Dallas, TX: Word Publishing, 1994), 12. Even Tim and Beverly LaHaye cannot agree with MacArthur on this point: "Personally, we have serious problems with that kind of thinking. No one knows for certain whether these are indeed the last days" (Tim and Beverly LaHaye, *A Nation Without a Conscience: Where Have all the Values Gone?* [Wheaton, IL: Tyndale, 1994], 243). Even so, LaHaye is convinced that the rapture "is near, even at the doors" (Tim LaHaye, "Twelve Reasons Why This Could be the Terminal Generation," *When the Trumpet Sounds*, eds. Thomas Ice and Timothy Demy [Eugene, OR: Harvest House Publishers, 1995], 429), that we are living "within the 'season,' or generation [of Christ's return]" (443). He states, "while we cannot say dogmatically that Jesus will return in our generation, we can say that our generation has more legitimate reasons for believing it than any previous generation. . . . [T]he coming of Christ could be at hand. . . . This is the first generation to see the possible fulfillment of that end-time prophecy" (429, 436, 442). The website promoting his Left Behind series states that "Biblical prophecies *are becoming reality*. Current events *are being shaped* by God's plan." For a refutation of LaHaye's views, see Gary DeMar, *Left Behind: Separating Fact from Fiction*, rev. ed. (Powder Springs, GA: American Vision [2001] 2009).

3. For a study of the "magic" used by the Egyptians, see Gary DeMar, *Thinking Straight in a Crooked World: A Christian Defense Manual* (Powder Springs, GA: American Vision, 2001), 252–254.

4. Francis Herbert Stead, *The Story of Social Christianity*, 2 vols. (London: James Clarke & Co., Limited, 1924), Phillips Brooks, *The Influence of Jesus* (New York: Dutton, 1980), and J. Wesley Bready, *England: Before and After Wesley—The Evangelical Revival and Social Reform* (London: Hodder and Stoughton, 1939).

5. John C. Souter, "The Sky is Falling," *Future* (Wheaton, IL: Tyndale, 1984), 6.

6. Richard Erdoes, *AD 1000: Living on the Brink of Apocalypse* (San Francisco: Harper & Row, 1988), 1.

7. Souter, *Future*, 6. For a comprehensive study of date setting, see Francis X. Gumerlock, *The Day and the Hour: Christianity's Perennial Fascination with Predicting the End of the World* (Powder Springs, GA: American Vision, 2000).

8. J.F.C. Harrison, *The Second Coming: Popular Millennialism, 1780–1850* (New Brunswick, NJ: Rutgers University Press, 1979), 194. For a detailed description of Miller's views from a Seventh-Day Adventist scholar, see Leroy Edwin Froom, *The Prophetic Faith of Our Fathers: The Historical Development of Prophetic Interpretation*, 4 vols. (Washington, DC: Review and Herald, 1954), 4:429–876.

9. Harrison, *The Second Coming*, 195.

10. Ronald L. Numbers and Jonathan M. Butler, eds., "Introduction," *The Disap-*

pointed: Millerism and Millenarianism in the Nineteenth Century (Bloomington, IN: Indiana University Press, 1987), xv.

11. Tom Sine, *The Mustard Seed Conspiracy: You Can Make a Difference in Tomorrow's Troubled World* (Waco, TX: Word, 1981), 70.

12. Winthrop S. Hudson, *Religion in America: An Historical Account of the Development of American Religious Life* (New York: Charles Scribner's Sons, 1965), 364.

13. Dave Hunt, *When Will Jesus Come?: Compelling Evidence for the Soon Return of Christ* (Eugene, OR: Harvest House, 2003).

14. Paul Boyer, *When Time Shall Be No More: Prophecy Belief in Modern American Culture* (Cambridge, MA: The Belknap Press of Harvard University Press, 1992), 108–109.

15. C. S. Tubby, *Mussolini: The Marvel-Man—Is He the Predicted Super Man?* (published by the author, 1929), 3, 24.

16. Oswald J. Smith, *Is the Antichrist at Hand?* (Harrisburg, PA: The Christian Alliance Publishing Co., [1926] 1927), 18.

17. Harry Rimmer, *The Shadow of Coming Events* (Grand Rapids, MI: Eerdmans, 1954), 141–207.

18. Hal Lindsey, *The Late Great Planet Earth* (Grand Rapids, MI: Zondervan, 1970), 96–97.

19. Daniel Rubin, "European Union close to adding 10 nations," *Atlanta Journal-Constitution* (October 13, 2002), B4.

20. John Warwick Montgomery, "Eschatology, and Apologetics," *Looking Into the Future: Evangelical Studies in Eschatology*, ed. David W. Baker (Grand Rapids, MI: Baker Academic, 2001), 366. Oswald J. Smith did what no modern-day prophetic speculator has dared to do. He apologized for his overly presumptive predictions. Montgomery adds: "I understand that after the fall of Mussolini, Smith himself tried to buy up all remaining copies of the book to destroy them" (366).

21. For a comprehensive study of the last days, see Gary DeMar, *Last Days Madness: Obsession of the Modern Church*, 4th ed. (Powder Springs, GA: American Vision, 1999).

22. H. Wayne House and Gordon Carle, *Doctrine Twisting: How Core Biblical Truths Are Distorted* (Downers Grove, IL: InterVarsity Press, 2003), 186.

23. For a detailed exposition of Matthew 24–25, see DeMar, *Last Days Madness* and *Is Jesus Coming Soon?* (Powder Springs, GA: American Vision, 2006).

24. House and Carle claim that Mark 9:1 and 13:30 are "passages that support the idea of imminence" (*Doctrine Twisting*, 186). "Any moment" hardly means 2000 years! But notice what Mark 9:1 actually says: "*There are some of those standing here* who shall not taste death until *they see* the kingdom of God after it has come with power." Mark 13:30 says: "Truly I say to you, *this* generation will not pass away until *all these things take place*." Once again, Jesus is telling His *present* audience what will happen to *their* generation.

25. Thomas Ice's attempts to get around the clear meaning of the time texts is baffling ("Preterist 'Time Texts,'" *The End Times Controversy: The Second Coming Under Attack*, eds. Tim LaHaye and Thomas Ice [Eugene, OR: Harvest House, 2003], 83–122). For a consideration of the time texts, see DeMar, *Last Days Madness*, 51–64, 379–395.

26. George Eldon Ladd, *The Blessed Hope* (Grand Rapids, MI: Eerdmans, 1956), 106.

27. Charles C. Ryrie, *The Living End* (Old Tappan, NJ: Revell, 1976), 21.

28. Lindsey, *Late Great Planet Earth*, 145.

29. Hal Lindsey, "The Great Cosmic Countdown," *Eternity* (January 1977), 21.

30. Norman L. Geisler, "A Premillennial View of Law and Government, *Moody Monthly* (October 1985), 129.

31. Ted Peters, *Futures: Human and Divine* (Atlanta, GA: John Knox, 1978), 28, 29.

32. DeMar, *Left Behind*.

33. John R. W. Stott, *Human Rights and Human Wrongs: Major Issues for a New Century* (Grand Rapids, MI: Baker Books, 1999), 23.

34. Sine, *The Mustard Seed Conspiracy*, 69–71.

35. Paul T. Coughlin, *Secrets, Plots & Hidden Agendas: What You Don't Know About Conspiracy Theories* (Downers Grove, IL: InterVarsity, 1999), 145–146.

36. Jess Walter, *Every Knee Shall Bow: The Truth and Tragedy of Ruby Ridge and the Randy Weaver Family* (New York: Regan Books/Harper Collins, 1995).

37. W. Ward Gasque, "Future Fact? Future Fiction?," *Christianity Today* (April 15, 1977), 40.

38. The belief that the Papacy is the antichrist has a long history. "In the centuries just preceding the Reformation an ever-increasing number of pious persons began openly to express the conviction that the dire prophecies concerning Antichrist were even then in the process of fulfillment. They felt that the 'falling away' had *already* taken place. They declared that Antichrist was *already* seated in the churchly temple of God, clothed in scarlet and purple." (Froom, *The Prophetic Faith of Our Fathers*, 2:66). For a modern statement of this position, see Ralph Woodrow, *Great Prophecies of the Bible* (Riverside, CA: Ralph Woodrow Evangelistic Association, 1971), 148–200 and Dave Hunt, *A Woman Rides the Beast: The Roman Catholic Church and the Last Days* (Eugene, OR: Harvest House, 1994) .

39. "Wycliffe's England: A Time of Turmoil," *Christian History* Issue 3 (1983), 8.

40. "Wycliffe's England," 8.

41. Chuck Smith, *Future Survival* (Costa Mesa, CA: Calvary Chapel, 1978), 20. Quoted in William M. Alnor, *Soothsayers of the Second Advent* (Old Tappan, NJ: Revell, 1989), 41.

42. Quoted in Alnor, *Soothsayers of the Second Advent*, 41.

43. Gary Friesen, "A Return Visit," *Moody Monthly* (May 1988), 31.

44. Bart D. Ehrman, *Misquoting Jesus: The Story Behind Who Changed the Bible and Why* (New York: HarperCollins, 2005), 12.

45. Ehrman, *Misquoting Jesus*, 13.

46. Philip Jenkins is as of 2009 the Edwin Erle Sparks Professor of Humanities at Pennsylvania State University (PSU). He has also been a Professor (from 1993) and a Distinguished Professor (from 1997) of History and Religious studies at the same institution; and also assistant, associate and then full professor of Criminal Justice and American Studies at PSU (1980–1993). He is the author of 24 books, including *The Next Christendom: The Rise of Global Christianity* (New York: Oxford University Press, 2002), *Hidden Gospels: How*

the Search for Jesus Lost Its Way (New York: Oxford University Press), 2001, and *The Jesus Wars: How Four Patriarchs, Three Queens, and Two Emperors Decided What Christians Would Believe for the Next 1,500 Years* (San Francisco: HarperOne, 2010).

47. For a study of some of the most frequently used passages to teach that prophecy is being fulfilled in our day, see Gary DeMar, *Why the End of the World is Not in Your Future* (Powder Springs, GA: American Vision, 2009).

48. Ehrman, *Misquoting Jesus*, 13.

49. Chuck Missler, *Prophecy 20/20: Profiling the Future Through the Lens of Scripture* (Nashville: Thomas Nelson, 2006) and David Jeremiah, *What in the World is Going On?: 10 Prophetic Clues You Cannot Afford to Ignore* (Nashville: Thomas Nelson, 2008).

50. Greg Laurie, "Signs of the Times" (November 4, 2006): http://tinyurl.com/yaac57n

15

"It's Never Right to Resist Authority"

Myth, Lie, or Half-Truth?: *Rendering to Caesar the things that are Caesar's means Christians must submit to every law and edict made through legislation or pronounced by a court.*

> First they came for the Communists, but I was not a Communist so I did not speak out. Then they came for the Socialists and the Trade Unionists, but I was neither, so I did not speak out. Then they came for the Jews, but I was not a Jew so I did not speak out. And when they came for me, there was no one to speak out for me.[1]

"In 1660 John Bunyan disobeyed the law of England by preaching without a license. He was arrested at a church meeting and put in a prison so damp that he said it was enough to 'make the moss grow on one's eyebrows.' There he converted his prison into a pulpit and wrote the greatest of all Christian classics, *Pilgrim's Progress*. He was told that he would be released if he promised not to further violate the law for which he was imprisoned, but he refused to do so. He was arrested two more times for the same act of disobedience."[2] Bunyan was in good company. Peter and John were arrested "because they were teaching the people and proclaiming in Jesus the resurrection of the dead" (Acts 4:2). Even after their release, like Bunyan, they continued to preach the gospel, "for we cannot stop speaking what we have seen and heard" (4:20).

During the Nazi reign of terror, Jews were hidden from German officials who were carrying out orders from their superiors to round up "non-Aryans," specifically Jews. Hiding these "enemies of the State" was a crime against "legal" Nazi orders. What would you have done? What would your pastor have done? Was it right to disobey a law of this type?

> It is 1942. The Nazis who control your nation militarily have just announced a new policy requiring all Jews to come to the local city hall and register. The most prominent church leader in your denomination has recommended obedience to all "lawful" directives of the German authorities. He has not recommended disobeying this new directive, and you have no reason to believe that he will. Your denomination will not speak directly to this issue, and you think the civil authorities will threaten to shut down churches or in other ways pressure the church's leadership to remain silent or even recommend compliance with the order. Then a Jew you know comes to you and asks for asylum. He wants you to hide him in your attic or barn. You know that this would be illegal. Will you hide him or turn him over to the Nazis?[3]

Was it wrong to disobey these laws? In terms of Nazi law, yes. But what about in terms of the Bible? How would your pastor respond if a similar law were passed today? Hate-crime legislation may put your pastor, church, and denomination to the test. Of course, there were consequences for defying Nazi law. People who hid Jews from the Nazis risked the loss of their property and the possibility of losing their own life.[4] Many who spoke out publicly against the Nazi regime were sent to concentration camps.[5]

Moral Justification

Resistance movements like those practiced by Christians during World War II have been accepted as morally justified by nearly all ethical thinkers. *The Diary of Anne Frank* and Thomas Kineally's *Schindler's Ark* (later made into the film *Schindler's List*) show the highest praise for those who defied what was a "lawful" government policy. In *Give Me the Children: How a Christian Woman Saved a Jewish Family During the Holocaust,* Pola Arbiser describes how her nanny defied the law and hid her and her sister from Nazi officers. The Jewish community of survivors has characterized these resistors as "righteous gentiles"[6] or simply "Christian rescuers."[7] As we will see, in biblical terms, these actions were considered to be moral even though they violated Nazi Reich law. The biblical ethic of "we must obey God rather than men" holds true in these situations."

Times Have Changed—Or Have They?

Examples of resistance and persecution hardly seem applicable to our day. We are not under Nazi, English, Roman, or Communist oppression. While no civil official is demanding that ministers obtain a license to preach the gospel, restrictions are being placed on what ministers and Christians in general can say on moral issues derived from the Bible:

- "In Canada, serious limits have been placed on Christian broadcasters who take a biblical stand against homosexual behavior. Focus on the Family, for instance, cannot air programs that might portray homosexual behavior in a negative light, or it will face sanctions from the Canadian Communications Commission."[8]

- Newspaper advertisers and billboard owners have been regulated when they make reference to the anti-biblical nature of homosexual acts by citing Bible verses.

- Schools in Canada have been threatened with a loss of accreditation if they discriminate in any way against homosexual students because of their aberrant behavior.

- Canada's House of Commons passed a bill on September 17, 2003, that criminalizes public expressions against homosexual behavior.

- The Swedish parliament approved an amendment that bans all speech and materials opposing homosexual behavior and other so-called alternative life-styles.

- "Hate speech" laws are being drafted in the United States. This would mean that sections of the Bible could not be read from the pulpit because of their potential to offend certain groups.

- A former lesbian who is now a Christian was ordered by a judge not to teach her daughter anything negative about the homosexual life-style.

- A minister might face criminal charges if he refuses to marry same-sex couples.[9]

- Court rulings have specifically singled out Christian beliefs and practices as being incompatible with our nation's educational and legal system.[10]

- In 2009, Pauline Howe suffered verbal abuse from homosexuals when she passed out Christian leaflets at a "gay pride" event in Norwich, England. She objected to the abuse by writing a letter to the city's top official. Police replied to her letter with a visit to her home. The officers explained that her letter was considered "homophobic" and could be treated as a hate incident. They also said she might be cited on criminal charges based on the country's hate crimes laws, the Human Rights Act.

Will our government plant "spies" in churches to catch ministers who preach from those parts of the Bible where the practice of homosexuality is condemned? It's happened before with Martin Niemöller, and there is a good likelihood that it will happen again:

> Now, the charge against [Martin] Niemoeller was based entirely on his sermons, which the Gestapo agents had taken down stenographically. . . . [W]ritten laws, no matter how explicitly they were worded, were subjected to the interpretation of judges. The totalitarian principle which governs Nazi Germany, as I have indicated before, includes religion as a function of State. Therefore, by recognizing Christ only as his Leader, Pastor Niemoeller was denying the right to divine leadership to Hitler. His offense was all the more serious because he had exhorted his followers to do likewise.[11]

What will be the response of churches in America if the increasingly secular and anti-Christian courts rule that "discriminating" against "legally married" homosexual couples is a criminal act punishable by a fine, loss of the church's tax-exempt status, or imprisonment?[12]

The Tyranny of the Courts

Roy Moore, the former Chief Justice of the Alabama State Supreme Court, was ordered by the Federal 11th District Court in July 2003 to remove a display of the Ten Commandments from the lobby of the state's courthouse. Justice Moore claims that since the state's constitution invokes "the favor and guidance of Almighty God,"[13] and he and other state officials took an oath to uphold the state's constitution, there is no violation in posting a copy of the law that Almighty God gave for that guidance. The fact that the Ten Commandments are posted in courthouses around the country, including the Supreme Court and other state court buildings,[14] lends legal and constitutional support to Moore's actions.

In addition, since Alabama has its own constitution, courts, judges, and laws, and given the constitutional freedoms specified in the Tenth Amendment to our federal constitution,[15] no constitutional law had been violated. The state of Alabama, as well as every other state, is an *imperium in emperio*, "a sovereignty within a sovereignty."[16] The First Amendment to the Constitution prohibits "Congress" from either establishing a religion or "prohibiting the free exercise" of religion. Placing the Ten Commandments in a court house is not "an establishment of religion," and even if it were, the United States Congress did not place the monument in the lobby of the courthouse. The justices of the 11th District Court, in misreading and misapplying the First Amendment, are "prohibiting the free exercise of religion" by their ruling and usurping the sovereignty of the state of Alabama.

In the eyes of the justices and some Christian leaders, Moore's actions constitute disobeying "those in authority." But as Chief Justice Moore has argued, he is a duly elected civil official operating in a governmental capacity also "established by God" (Rom. 13:1). He believes that his actions against a federal court ruling are in compliance with his state-held office and the specified directives of our constitutional system. There is a long history of a lesser magistrate, in this case a state government, legally and morally interposing[17] itself between unjust rulings of federal courts and a state government to protect the people from oppression.[18]

Let Justice Roll Down

The civil rights movement in the United States had its turning point when Martin Luther King, Jr., defied a court order because laws discriminating against blacks were considered to be immoral and unconstitutional. In his account of the civil rights campaign in Birmingham, Alabama, King "speaks of a court injunction obtained by the city administration on April 10, 1963, directing that demonstrations be halted until the right to such activities might be argued in court. Dr. King continues: 'Two days later, we did an audacious thing, something we had never done in any other crusade. We disobeyed a court order.'"[19]

The irony is that the Southern Poverty Law Center, which claims to support civil rights causes, represented the plaintiffs in the case *against* Chief Justice Moore in the Ten Commandments case. The Center's hypocrisy is evident when one sees the statement it chose for the Civil Rights Memorial "which celebrates the memory of those who died during the Civil Rights Movement." Carved into the memorial's granite face is a phrase taken from King's "I Have a Dream Speech" given on August 28, 1963 in Washington, D.C.: ". . . until justice rolls down like waters and righteousness like a mighty stream." Almost any Bible student will recognize that these words are from the Bible (Amos 5:24).

King defined justice and righteousness in terms of the Bible. The Bible gave King moral certainty that he was right to defy what he considered to be a series of unjust laws. King's use of Amos 5:24 was directed at the civil authorities who were discriminating in the way they dispensed justice.

If we take the position advocated by some that civil government is the final arbiter of what's legal, moral, just, and right, with no higher law binding the magistrate, there can be no higher court of appeal other than the one in power. The most oppressive tyranny must stand as the people turn a blind eye to injustice and retreat behind a doctrine of impotent quietude. As soon as this happens, the State, by default, has established itself as the new god to be honored, worshiped, and obeyed without debate or objection. Rousas J. Rushdoony describes the inescapable logic of denying a higher law ethic:

> The universe of evolution and humanism is a closed universe. There is no law, no appeal, no higher order, beyond and above the universe. Instead of an open window upwards, there is a closed cosmos. There is no ultimate law and decree beyond man and the universe. In practice,

> this means that the positive law of the state is absolute law. The state is the most powerful and most highly organized expression of humanistic man, and the state is the form and expression of humanistic law. Because there is no higher law of God as judge over the universe, over every human order, the law of the state is a closed system of law. There is no appeal beyond it. Man has no "right," no realm of justice, no source of law beyond the state, to which he can appeal against the state.[20]

The philosophy of Georg F. W. Hegel (1770–1831), adopted by Marxists, Fascists, and Nazis, expresses the argument with chilling consistency: "The Universal is to be found in the State. . . . The State is the Divine Idea as it exists on earth. . . . We must therefore worship the State as the manifestation of the Divine on earth. . . . [T]he State is the march of God through the world." After compiling these statements from Hegel's works, Karl Popper comments that Hegel's views mandate the "absolute moral authority of the state, which overrules all personal morality, all conscience."[21] Once this happens, there is no place to appeal for a redress of grievances.

In 1907, Supreme Court Justice Charles Evan Hughes said, "We are under a Constitution, but the Constitution is what the judges say it is."[22] Since the Constitution is the "supreme law of the land," it follows that the *supreme* law is what the judges say it is. In *Tropp v. Dulles* (1958), Judge Earl Warren stated that the Constitution must draw its meaning from the evolving standards of decency that mark the progress of a maturing society." Who decides when a standard has evolved into a new standard? Five members of the Supreme Court.

Resistance in the Old Testament

The place to begin in the development of a doctrine of resistance is with the Old Testament. "It is precisely because the state is a *divine*[23] institution that its authority is not absolute. . . . Once government oversteps those bounds—when it interferes with the life of the church or demands compliance with unjust laws, for example—it exceeds its God-ordained boundaries."[24] The Bible includes examples of faithful believers who resisted claims by civil magistrates to obey unjust laws that force them to sin if obeyed.

The Hebrew Midwives

The Hebrew midwives were commanded by "the king of Egypt" to put to death all the male children being born to the Hebrew women (Ex. 1:15–16). The Hebrew midwives disobeyed the edict of the king: "But the midwives feared God, and *did not do as the king of Egypt had commanded them*, but let the boys live" (1:17). The midwives had to make a choice. Did God's law overrule the command of a king, even "the king of Egypt"? God shows His approval of their actions: "So God was good to the midwives, and the people multiplied, and became very mighty. And it came about because the midwives feared God, that He established households for them" (1:20–21).

In 1560, the Geneva Bible was published. Between 1560 and 1644, at least 144 editions appeared. The Geneva Bible was also called the "Puritan Bible" because it was popular with Christians who opposed certain actions of the English monarchy. In addition to being a fresh English translation, the Geneva Bible included notes on certain texts. King James I, whose name is associated with a later popular translation of the Bible, the King James Version (1611), disliked the Geneva Bible because of the specific nature of some of its notes. "The later vilification of marginal notes," David Daniell writes in his history of the English Bible, "especially by the politicians controlling King James in the early 1600s, was from fear of the working of this sovereign God in places outside the fence of what was narrowly understood as the only apostolic Christianity."[25]

The king expressly disliked the way some of the notes condemned rulers who acted contrary to God's Word. For example, a marginal note for Exodus 1:19 stated that the Hebrew midwives were correct to disobey the Egyptian king's order to kill the Hebrew babies. The king reasoned that if it was legitimate to oppose a ruler on one decree, then it was legitimate to oppose him on others. This is why King James professed, "I could never yet see a Bible well translated in English; but I think that, of all, that of Geneva is worst."[26]

In 1982, Juvenile Court judge Randall J. Hekman, "in direct opposition to the law of the land, which said women cannot be denied an abortion," refused to grant permission for a pregnant thirteen-year-old to obtain an abortion. Was he wrong? His decision parallels that of the midwives who refused to follow the directive of the king of Egypt. In a letter to the editor of a Grand Rapids, Michigan, newspaper, Judge Hekman explained why he refused to grant the abortion to the thirteen-year-old:

> What if the law requires a judge to order the execution of a person known to be totally innocent? What if a judge is required by law to order Jewish people to concentration camps or gas chambers because the law says that Jews are non-persons?. . .
>
> Ten short years ago, a judge in Michigan would be guilty of a felony crime if he encouraged, much less ordered that a pregnant girl obtain an abortion. Then, in 1973, the Supreme Court ruled that all state laws making abortion a crime were unconstitutional. In one day, that which had been a reprehensible crime became a sacred right protected by the Constitution itself.[27]

"Hekman was severely criticized in the press and by judicial colleagues. The child is now in grade school and is presumably more supportive of the judge's decision!"[28] Hekman could not hold this belief unless he believed that there was a higher law that demanded such a decision.

Jochebed's Deception

Jochebed, Moses' mother, also disobeyed the edict of the king of Egypt by hiding her child and later creating a way of escape for him so he would not be murdered by the king's army: "But when she could hide him no longer, she got him a wicker basket and covered it over with tar and pitch. Then she put the child into it, and set it among the reeds by the bank of the Nile" (Ex. 2:3). Jochebed even deceived Pharaoh's daughter into believing that she, Jochebed, was in no way related to the child (2:7–9). Surely Jochebed was right in her defiance.

Of Lying and Spying

Rahab hid the spies of Israel and lied about their whereabouts. When a route for escape became available, she led them out another way from that of the pursuing soldiers. The king issued a command to Rahab: "Bring out the men who have come to you, who have entered your house, for they have come to search out all the land" (Josh. 2:3). She disobeyed a direct command of the "king of Jericho." Some want to maintain that Rahab was right in "welcoming the spies in peace" (Heb. 11:31) but wrong in lying about the whereabouts of the spies. The following is a representative example of this view:

> We see, therefore, that neither Scripture itself nor the theological inferences derived from Scripture provide us with any warrant for the vindication of Rahab's untruth and this instance, consequently, does not support the position that under certain circumstances we may justifiably utter an untruth.[29]

"Welcoming them in peace" means that they would not fall in the hands of the king of Jericho which would have meant certain death. Rahab had changed her allegiance from Jericho to Israel. Conditions of war were operating. If she had told the truth to the men seeking the two spies, then she would have been an accomplice in their deaths (cf. Psalm 50:18).

There is another point that is often missed in this story about Rahab's lie. "Joshua the son of Nun sent two men as *spies secretly* from Shittim. . . (Josh. 2:1). The text continues by telling us that "they went and came into the house of a harlot whose name was Rahab, and lodged there." Did they announce to city officials that they were Israelite spies? Joshua says the operation was to be done "secretly," that is, without revealing the truth of their mission. Are not "spies" in the business of lying? Why was Joshua right in sending men to spy out the land, while Rahab was wrong in lying about the route the spies took? Why were the spies right in hiding and Rahab wrong in not revealing where they were hiding? Is that not an act of deception? Why didn't they rebuke Rahab for lying? Why didn't the spies leave by the same route they entered the city? Instead, they were accomplices in Rahab's lie by allowing her to "let them down by a rope through the window" (2:15).

Rahab is praised by two New Testament writers for her actions: "By faith Rahab the harlot did not perish along with those who were disobedient, after she had welcomed the spies in peace" (Heb. 11:31). Rahab is listed with Abraham as one whose faith was reflected in her works: "And in the same way [as Abraham] was not Rahab the harlot also justified by works, when she received the messengers and sent them out by another way?" (James 2:25). By sending the spies out by another way, she subverted the king's desire to capture the spies. God commended Rahab for deception because she had made a change in covenantal allegiance. Again, the circumstances were atypical. "The critics of Rahab's lie apparently think her case is analogous to David's adultery with Bathsheba, a union which ultimately produced Solomon. We are not, of course, bound to praise David's action simply because Solomon's rule produced many desirable results (such as the construction of God's temple). We are *specifically told* that David's adultery was abhorrent in the eyes of God; we are *not* so informed about Rahab's actions."[30]

When you go out at night, do you keep a light on in the house? Some people purchase devices that turn lights on and off at random intervals to give the appearance that they are at home. This is done to mislead burglars. Isn't this deception? Are you not lying? Most every home has an answering machine. A message is left on the machine which says: "No one can come to the phone right now, but if you leave a message, someone will get back to you as soon as possible." You haven't said that you are not at home, but you are giving the impression that someone may be in the house when, in fact, no one is at home. Again, deception. Do these actions violate the ninth commandment prohibiting bearing false witness?

Are resistance movements during times of war biblical? Should we abolish the C.I.A. and counter-intelligence agencies? Is it wrong to send messages in code? Is it proper for soldiers to wear camouflage? Would it be wrong to send false messages to the enemy to lead them in a direction that would hinder their ability to attack? Truth-telling "does not apply to acts of war. Spying is legitimate, as are deceptive tactics in warfare. Protection from thieves requires concealment and walls."[31]

Saying No to a King

Shadrach, Meshach, and Abed-nego refused to follow the command of the king to worship the golden statue: "These men, O king, have disregarded you; they do not serve your gods or worship the golden image you have set up" (Dan. 3:12). When the three were thrown into the furnace, the angel of the Lord came to their aid (2:25). This shows that there may be negative consequences in opposing an edict of a ruler, but this does not negate the legitimacy of the act of defiance. Some have suffered martyrdom because of their refusal to obey. "In the year A.D. 165 Justin Martyr and his companions refused to yield to the command of the emperor and sacrifice to the pagan gods. 'Do what you will. For we are Christians and offer no sacrifice to idols.' Justin and his companions were beheaded for their faithfulness to the Savior."[32]

King Darius signed a document that prohibited anyone from making "a petition to any god or man besides" himself (Dan. 6:7). Anyone refusing to obey the order "shall be cast into the lion's den" (6:7). Daniel refused to heed the edict's restrictions. The Bible states that Daniel went out of his way to disobey the order: "Now when Daniel knew that the document was signed, he entered his house (now in his roof chamber he had windows open toward Jerusalem); and he continued kneeling on his knees three times a day, praying and giving thanks before his God, as he had been doing previously" (6:10). He opened the windows so he could be seen. He wanted to display his disobedience to the king's edict by his obedience to God.

Resistance in the New Testament

The New Testament has similar accounts of resistance to tyranny. King Herod had commanded the wise men to return to him and provide information about the new-born "king of the Jews" (Matt. 2:7–8). The magi had "been warned *by God* in a dream not to return to Herod" (2:12). Here we find that God Himself is directing the Magi not to obey Herod's request.

When Peter and John were ordered by the rulers and elders of the people to stop preaching in the name of Jesus (Acts 4:18), the two apostles refused to follow their command: "Whether it is right in the sight of God to give heed to you rather than to God, you be the judge; for we cannot stop speaking what we have seen and heard" (4:19–20). Peter and John could not stop speaking what they had seen and heard because they had been commanded by Jesus to preach in His name (cf. Matt. 28:18–20; Acts 1:8; 1 Cor. 9:16).

On another occasion, some of the apostles were arrested for preaching and healing in the name of Jesus. Again, they were put in a "public jail" (Acts 5:18). During the night, "an angel of the Lord . . . opened the gates of the prison" and commanded them to disobey the rulers of Israel: "Go your way, stand and speak to the people in the temple the whole message of life" (5:20). When the apostles again were confronted with the command not to preach and teach, their response was quick and sure: "We must obey God rather than men" (5:29).

The apostles' obedience to God conflicted with the desires of the State. This resulted in the first apostolic death at the hands of a civil authority: "Now about that time Herod the king [Agrippa I] laid hands on some who belonged to the church, in order to mistreat them. And he had James the brother of John put to death" (12:1–2). Peter was later arrested for similar "crimes" against the State (12:3). Obeying God rather than men is legitimate. God certainly set the example when He sent one of His angels to release Peter from prison (12:6–8).

Either God or man is ultimately sovereign. When these sovereignties clash and conflict, the Christian, first a citizen of heaven (Phil. 3:20), must obey God rather than men. "William Tyndale (1490) taught that the truths of Scripture had authority over both the state and the church. Partly for this 'heresy,' government authorities in England tried to capture him, but Tyndale evaded them for years. He was finally caught, tried as a heretic, and executed in 1536."[33]

Rendering Unto Caesar

No human authority is absolute. In Matthew 22:21, Jesus tells the Pharisees and the Herodians to "render to Caesar the things that are Caesar's." He does not say, "render to Caesar everything Caesar commands and demands." We are only to render those things that *are* Caesar's. This implies limitations, as Lord Acton argues:

> But when Christ said "Render unto Caesar the things that are Caesar's and unto God the things that are God's," He gave to the State a legitimacy it had never before enjoyed, and set bounds to it that had never yet been acknowledged. And He not only delivered the precept but He also forged the instrument to execute it. To limit the power of the State ceased to be the hope of patient,

> ineffectual philosophers and became the perpetual charge of a universal Church.[34]

There are restrictions on Caesar's sovereignty, as Old and New Testament examples demonstrate, and by extension the sovereignty of all rulers, because we are told to "render to God the things that are God's," and Caesar is under God and must render to Him. The things that are God's did not belong to Caesar, and what legitimate authority Caesar did possess had been given to him by God (Rom. 13:1). Did Jesus give Caesar, and by analogy all civil governments, unlimited authority to rule without regard to God's commandments? Whatever else Matthew 22:21 can tell us, and it can tell us a lot, we know that Scripture *limits* the sovereignty of Caesar.

Petitioning the Government

We in America do not live under Caesar, but we do have a Caesar principle, the Constitution of the United States. The First Amendment to the Constitution states as clearly as it can that the people have the right to "petition the government for a redress of grievances." Wrapped up in this constitutional right are additional rights regarding speech, press, and assembly. It's a package deal. We can petition in these several ways without hindrance and without violating any biblical or constitutional provision. Any attempt to "infringe" on these rights, including religion, is blatantly unconstitutional.

As a side note, for Christians who claim they must remain silent when government acts, keep in mind that the Constitution, our "Caesar" (Matt. 22:21), gives us the right and duty to question its decisions. The President of the United States took an oath before God to "preserve, protect and defend the Constitution of the United States." At the start of each new Congress, in January of every odd-numbered year, those newly elected or re-elected Congressmen—the entire House of Representatives and one-third of the Senate—must recite an oath:

> I do solemnly swear (or affirm) that I will support and defend the Constitution of the United States against all enemies, foreign and domestic; that I will bear true faith and allegiance to the same; that I take this obligation freely, without any mental reservation or purpose of evasion; and that I will well and faithfully discharge the duties of the office on which I am about to enter. So help me God.

In Book 1, Chapter 1 of William Blackstone's *Commentaries on the Laws of England* (1765–1769) the point is made that "every individual" has "the right of petitioning the king, or either house of parliament, for the redress of grievance." Eleven years later, the Declaration of Independence listed King George's failure to redress the grievances listed in colonial petitions, such as the Olive Branch Petition of 1775, as a legal justification to declare independence:

> In every stage of these Oppressions We have Petitioned for Redress in the most humble terms: Our repeated Petitions have been answered only by repeated injury. A Prince, whose character is thus marked by every act which may define a Tyrant, is unfit to be the ruler of a free people.

As far back as Magna Carta (1215) and the later Bill of Rights of 1689, which explicitly declared the "right of the subjects to petition the king," the people had a fundamental right to make their grievances known to those holding civil office. The provision in the First Amendment was put to the test over the issue of slavery:

> The right of petition recognized by the First Amendment first came into prominence in the early 1830's, when petitions against slavery in the District of Columbia began flowing into Congress in a constantly increasing stream, which reached its climax in the winter of 1835. Finally

> on January 28, 1840, the House adopted as a standing rule: '"That no petition, memorial, resolution, or other paper praying the abolition of slavery in the District of Columbia, or any State or Territories of the United States in which it now exists, shall be received by this House, or entertained in any way whatever." Because of efforts of John Quincy Adams, this rule was repealed five years later

Can you imagine what would have happened if Congress had taken these petitions seriously? America could have averted a bloody civil war and an increase in federal power that we are living with today.

Staging protests, throwing tea parties, and packing Town Hall meetings to ask questions and voice grievances about legislative policies are fundamental freedoms that go back hundreds of years. The Constitution codifies these freedoms. Of course, if our elected officials don't read the bills they vote on, what makes us think they've read the Constitution they took an oath to uphold? And even if they have read the Constitution, what makes us think they care what it says? The Constitution is a prop to keep the people in check—until they read it.

What About The War for Independence?

None of the above examples should lead Christians to assert that God has called His church to promote anarchy or revolution in the name of some "sacred cause." America's "revolutionary war" was neither anarchistic nor revolutionary in the modern sense. The thirteen colonies were operating civil governments, having a contractual relationship with the King of England. The king violated the terms of the agreement. The disputants were independent civil governments (colonial governments), not individuals or mobs. The war for independence "was not a lawless rebellion against authority, as some historians claim. Rather, it was a *legal interposition* of one lawfully elected level of government (the colonial legislatures) against a king who insisted in obdurately breaking his feudal contract with the colonies."[35] This understanding of our nation's constitutional beginnings has been lost on the modern mind.

> For years we have been taught that we are the product of a revolutionary generation who, because of religious, economic, and political disagreements, finally (through anarchistic and violent means) tore themselves from a loving and legally constituted government.[36]

Too often some Americans are quick to support every revolutionary uprising around the world because of the good result of America's "revolution." They fail to recognize that our "revolution" was different. America was a functioning government. Each of the thirteen colonies had a governor, a written constitution, laws, and courts. The colonial militia was commanded by General George Washington under the authority and supervision of the then existing colonial governments. "Not one State, or one nation, but in the plural *States*; and again, in the next breath, so this multiple birth could not be misunderstood, 'that as Free and Independent States, they have full Power to levy War, conclude Peace, contract Alliances, establish Commerce, and to do all other Acts and things which Independent States may of right do.'"[37]

As Fisher and Chambers point out in *The Revolution Myth*, the modern view of America's "revolution" is "at variance with the actions and beliefs of those who participated in the 'Revolution.'. . . The American colonists did not revolt against constitutional authority; they did not seek independence from the King of England. The king, instead, severed all ties with his American colonies. The Declaration of Independence was not written to gain independence but to maintain and define what had been forced upon the colonies."[38]

> The Declaration's purpose was to inform a "candid world" that an action of the King and Parliament had cast the thirteen colonies out of the British Empire. The

> document did not proclaim legal, formal severance from England; that had already been accomplished by George III and Parliament on Friday, December 22, 1775.[39]

The colonies wanted a dissolution only of the "political bands." The colonists and their colonial governments had kept their part of the contract with the Crown. Therefore, any discussion of the legitimacy or illegitimacy of the colonists' actions is best handled under the topic of war. While revolutions are generated by "the people" *against* existing civil governments (e.g., the French Revolution), wars are fought by one existing civil government against another existing civil government. The people are conscripted to defend their national sovereignty. Some Christian writers fail to understand the dynamics behind the colonial war with England. The following is a representative example:

> It is understandable that everyone would like to believe that the revolution in his country was just, even if those in other countries are not. But in all honesty, given the biblical criteria listed here, it is not possible to justify the American Revolution either.[40]

None of the "biblical criteria" that this author sets forth fits the circumstances surrounding the American "revolution." In his chapter on "War," the author summarizes his position by stating that "God has ordained government and given it the sword."[41] The thirteen colonies were sovereign civil governments that also had the right to "bear the sword" (Rom. 13:4). They had their own state constitutions, governors, civil officers, courts, and militia. Since individuals and churches are not given the sword, they cannot legitimately revolt against the existing civil powers. But legitimate civil governments can, and the colonies were legitimate civil governments.

Are There Ever Exceptions?

John MacArthur, pastor-teacher of Grace Community Church in

Sun Valley, California, and president of The Master's College and Seminary, disagrees with the above arguments. Based on his reading of Romans 13, he does not believe that America's war for independence was justified "politically and scripturally."[42] He contends that supporters of the conflict with Britain acted "contrary to the clear teachings and commands of Romans 13:1–7," and that "the United States was actually born out of a violation of New Testament principles, and any blessings God has bestowed on America have come in spite of that disobedience by the Founding Fathers."[43]

Because of its no exception tone, Romans 13 is seen as prohibiting *all* forms of resistance: "Let every person [soul] be in subjection to the governing authorities. . ." (13:1). The apostle lists no exceptions. Peter offers a similar obligation: "Submit yourselves for the Lord's sake to *every* human institution, whether to a king as the one in authority, or to governors as sent by him for the punishment of evildoers and the praise of those who do right" (1 Pet. 2:13–14). Again, no exceptions. The same Peter who admonished believers to "submit yourselves . . . to *every* human institution" also declared, "We must obey God rather than men" (Acts 5:29; cf. 4:19–20). How do we reconcile the *apparent* contradiction?

There are a number of places in Scripture where one verse speaks in absolute terms and another verse offers an exception. This is not unusual. If I tell my children to go outside and play until dinner is ready, I have spoken in absolute terms. They are not to come into the house until they are called. No exceptions are given. What if it rains? What if a large dog enters the yard? What if a stranger offers them candy or a ride in a car? Can they enter the house without violating my absolute and no exception command? They would not be violating my no exception command because there are unspoken or previously spoken exceptions. They are assumed to be operating without them having to be repeated each time a new command is given. They have been told on previous occasions to "come in when it's raining," "do not go near stray dogs that wander into the yard," and "don't talk to strangers."

The Bible operates in the same manner. In one place Jesus says, "All those who take up the sword shall perish by the sword" (Matt. 26:52). Does this include the civil magistrate? What about the person who strikes an assailant in self-defense? Is this not an exception to Jesus' no exception statement? Since the Bible already discusses self-defense (Ex. 21:23–25; Lev. 24:19–21; Deut. 19:21) and the role of the civil magistrate (e.g., Gen. 9:6), there is no need to repeat the exceptions since His hearers know that Jesus has anarchy and revolution in mind (e.g., Lev. 19:18), not *every use* of the sword. Romans 13:4 informs us that it is the *duty* of the civil magistrate to use the sword. Is this a contradiction? No.

So then, when we read passages like Romans 13:1 and 1 Peter 2:13–14, we must not neglect the rest of the Bible that is equally authoritative and explains these passages more fully.

> Many general statements of Scripture must be open to admitting exceptions even if those qualifications are not immediately spelled out. Why are so many generalizations stated without qualification? *Because the exact conditions restricting their applicability are not known, or because the "accidental" or providential circumstances that render them inapplicable occur so seldom as to be practically negligible, or because such qualification has already been stipulated in another inscripturated context.*[44]

Conclusion

We must recognize that as the State becomes more tyrannical and non-Christian in its moral, legal, social, and political policies, conflicts between the institutional church, individual Christians, and Christian moral precepts and the State and its agencies will multiply. These conflicts may make it necessary for Christians to say no to statist laws that will force them to violate the laws of God. There is an additional reason why Christians must understand the limits of civil jurisdiction *and* the limits of resistance. Because of a desire to see the current corruption in our own nation reversed, some Christians may take it upon themselves to bring about change by revolutionary means. This is an unbiblical agenda to pursue. There is no warrant in Scripture for a revolutionary spirit. In fact, there is no need for an armed revolt. If Christians would involve themselves in the political process, at least in the United States, the realm of civil government could be changed at the ballot box.

Notes

1. The exact phrasing of the cited quotation by Martin Niemöller (1892–1984) was supplied by Sibylle Sarah Niemöller von Sell, Martin Niemöller's wife. Early in Adolf Hitler's rise to power, Niemöller (1892–1984), a former U-Boat commander and pastor, supported the Nazi party. When he understood the true nature of the Nazi worldview, he spoke out against the Third Reich and spent nearly eight years in a concentration camp because of his opposition to Adolf Hitler's policies.

2. Randy C. Alcorn, *Is Rescuing Right?: Breaking the Law to Save the Unborn* (Downers Grove, IL: InterVarsity Press, 1990), 106.

3. Gary North, "Editor's Introduction," *Christianity and Civilization: Tactics of Christian Resistance* (Tyler, TX: Geneva Divinity School Press, 1983), xii.

4. Nechama Tec, *When Light Pierced the Darkness: Christian Rescue of Jews in Nazi-Occupied Poland* (New York: Oxford University Press, 1986).

5. Basil Miller, *Martin Niemöller: Hero of the Concentration Camp* (Grand Rapids, MI: Zondervan, 1942), 112.

6. As reported in Catherine E. Shoichet, "Christian nanny hid Jewish family from Nazis," *Atlanta Journal-Constitution* (August 27, 2003), E1 and E6. See Pola Arbiser, *Give Me the Children: How A Christian Woman Saved a Jewish Family During the Holocaust* (Altona, Manitoba, Canada: Friesens, 2003). "The story of the Righteous is the story of men and women who risked their lives and those of their families to help save Jewish lives: people who, in the words of Si Frumkin, a survivor of the Kovno ghetto, 'ignored the law, opposed popular opinion, and dared to do what was right'" (Martin Gilbert, *The Righteous: The Unsung Heroes of the Holocaust* [New York: Henry Holt and Company, 2003], xx-xxi).

7. David P. Gushee, "Christians as Rescuers During the Holocaust," *Must Christianity Be Violent?: Reflections on History, Practice, and Theology*, eds. Kenneth R. Chase and Alan Jacobs (Grand Rapids, MI: Brazos Press, 2003), 71.

8. Alan Sears and Craig Osten, *The Homosexual Agenda: Exposing the Principal Threat to Religious Freedom Today* (Nashville, TN: Broadman & Holman, 2003), 182.

9. Sears and Osten, *The Homosexual Agenda*, 182–186.

10. David Limbaugh, *Persecution: How Liberals are Waging War Against Christianity* (Washington, D.C.: Regnery, 2003).

11. Leo Stein, *I Was in Hell with Niemoeller* (New York: Fleming H. Revell, 1942), 175.

12. For what may be in store for American churches, see Chuck McIlhenny and Donna McIlhenny, *When the Wicked Seize a City: A Grim Look at the Future and a Warning to the Church* (Lafayette, LA: Huntington House, 1993).

13. Benjamin Weiss, *God in American History: A Documentation of America's Christian Heritage* (Grand Rapids, MI: Zondervan, 1966), 156.

14. Gary DeMar, "The Ten Commandments on Trial," *America's Christian Heritage* (Nashville, TN: Broadman & Holman, 2003), chap. 7.

15. "The powers not delegated to the United States by the Constitution, nor prohibited by it to the States, are reserved to the States respectively, or to the people." There is nothing in the United States Constitution that prohibits posting the Ten Commandments in government offices or its courtrooms. The Constitution sets "Sunday" aside as a day of rest for the President (Art. 1, sec. 7), a direct reference to the fourth commandment. Witnesses still take an oath to tell the truth (the ninth commandment) with their hand on a Bible which contains the Ten Commandments.

16. Forrest McDonald, *States Rights and the Union: Imperium in Imperio, 1776–1876 (American Political Thought)* (Lawrence, KS: University Press of Kansas, 2000).

17. The doctrine of "interposition" is defined in *Black's Law Dictionary* (4th ed.) as "The doctrine that a state, in the exercise of its sovereignty, may reject a mandate of the federal government deemed to be unconstitutional or to exceed the powers delegated to the federal government. . . . Implementation of the doctrine may be peaceable, as by resolution, remonstrance or legislation, or may proceed ultimately to nullification with forcible resistance." Also see Sotirios A. Barber, "Interposition," *Encyclopedia of the American Constitution*, ed. Leonard W. Levy, 2 vol. ed. (New York: Macmillan Publishing, 1986), 1:992.

18. See John Eidsmoe, "A Call to Stand with Chief Justice Moore," (2203) www.americanheritageresearch.com/JohnEidsmoe,ACalltoStand.PDF

19. Daniel B. Stevick, *Civil Disobedience and the Christian* (New York: Seabury Press, 1969), 1.

20. Rousas J. Rushdoony, "Humanistic Law, introduction to E. L. Hebden Taylor, *The New Legality* (Nutley, NJ: Craig Press, 1967), vi–vii. A revised version can be found in Gary North, *Marx's Religion of Revolution: The Doctrine of Creative Destruction* (Nutley, NJ: Craig Press, 1968), 118–119.

21. Karl R. Popper, *The Open Society and Its Enemies: The High Tide of Prophecy: Hegel, Marx, and the Aftermath*, 2 vols. 5th rev. ed. (Princeton, NJ: Princeton University Press, [1966] 1971), 2:31.

22. David J. Danelski and Joseph S. Tulchin, eds., *The Autobiographical Notes of Charles Evans Hughes* (Cambridge, MA: Harvard University Press, 1973), 143. Quoted in John W. Whitehead, *The Second American Revolution* (Elgin, IL: David C. Cook, 1982), 20.

23. The author is using the word "divine" to mean "divinely ordained."

24. H. Wayne House, "The Christian's Duty of Civil Disobedience to the Government: Contemporary Struggles Between Christians and the State," *The Christian and American Law: Christianity's Impact on America's Founding Documents and Future Direction*, ed. H. Wayne House (Grand Rapids, MI: Kregel Publications, 1998), 149.

25. David Daniell, *The Bible in English: Its History and Influence* (New Haven, CT: Yale University Press, 2003), 309.

26. See Gary DeMar, *Reformation to Colonization* (Powder Springs, GA: American Vision, 1997), 247. Also see Daniel J. Ford, *In the Name of God, Amen: Rediscovering Biblical and Historical Covenants* (St. Louis, MO: Lex Rex Publishing, 2003), 41.

27. Judge Randall Hekman, "Letter to the Editor," *Grand Rapids Press* (November 19, 1982). Quoted in Alcorn, *Is Rescuing Right?*, 79–80

28. Alcorn, *Is Rescuing Right?*, 79.

29. John Murray, *Principles of Conduct: Aspects of Biblical Ethics* (London, England: The Tyndale Press, 1957), 139.

30. Gary North, "In Defense of Biblical Bribery," in Rousas J. Rushdoony, *The Institutes of Biblical Law* (Phillipsburg, NJ: Presbyterian and Reformed, 1973), 841.

31. North, "In Defense of Biblical Bribery," 544.

32. John Jefferson Davis, *Evangelical Ethics: Issues Facing the Church Today*, rev. ed. (Phillipsburg, NJ: Presbyterian and Reformed, 1993), 192.

33. Alcorn, *Is Rescue Right?*, 104.

34. Gertrude Himmelfarb, *Lord Acton: A Study in Conscience and Politics* (London: 1952), 45. Quoted in E. L. Hebden Taylor, *The Christian Philosophy of Law, Politics, and the State* (Nutley, NJ: Craig Press, 1966), 445–446.

35. Tom Rose, "On Reconstruction and the American Republic," *Christianity and Civilization*, The Theology of Christian Resistance, ed. Gary North (Tyler, TX: Geneva Divinity School, (1983), 295–296.

36. Gene Fisher and Glen Chambers, *The Revolution Myth* (Greenville, SC: Bob Jones University Press, 1981), ix.

37. James Jackson Kilpatrick, *The Sovereign States: Notes of a Citizen of Virginia* (Chicago, IL: Henry Regnery Co., 1957), 5.

38. Fisher and Chambers, *The Revolution Myth*, ix-x.

39. Fisher and Chambers, *The Revolution Myth*, 62.

40. Norman L. Geisler, *Christian Ethics: Options and Issues* (Grand Rapids, MI: Baker Book House, 1989), 254. In a later book, Geisler seems to have backed away from the view that the American "Revolution" was "unbiblical." See *Legislating Morality* (Minneapolis, MN: Bethany House, 1998), 18–20.

41. Geisler, *Christian Ethics*, 237.

42. John F. MacArthur, Jr., *Why Government Can't Save You* (Nashville, TN: Word Publishing, 2000), 6.

43. MacArthur, *Why Government Can't Save You*, 6–7.

44. Jim West, "Rahab's Justifiable Lie," in *Christianity and Civilization: The Theology of Christian Resistance*, ed. Gary North (Tyler, TX: Geneva Divinity School Press, 1983), 68. Emphasis in original.

Conclusion

It makes a big difference that the Ten Commandments are found in the Supreme Court building instead of selections from the code of Hammurabi and that our coins say "In God We Trust" instead of "In Baal We Trust." It makes a big difference that the Library of Congress has a quotation from a Psalm, instead of a quotation from the Koran.[1]

The God of the Bible has been replaced by the word of man. Ours is a day of "Bible-phobia," even among Christians: The Bible is a religious book that only has a word for private morality, and only if a person *chooses* to follow its precepts. The Bible, we are told, does not speak to the world. Those evangelicals who contend that it does speak to the world assure us that it speaks solely in general terms. There is no *specific* word. As we have seen, this was not always the case.

While the Bible may be believed in principle, it is too often denied in practice. When we are told that "Christians must address 'issues' in the society," the following disclaimer is often given: "but not institutions." How does one address issues but not institutions since "issues arise within institutions and cannot be properly addressed unless one has some idea of what an institution in God's world should be like"?[2] The key to fighting any evil is to understand how God's world works. Without that understanding there is no possibility of changing anything. There must be a model. That model must come from the person who designed the model. God has designed the world, and the Bible is the Owner's Manual on how it works. "Without a model, we draw our options over issues from the alternatives presented by the society."[3] This is exactly what the church has done. Prevailing anti-Christian ideologies have shaped the church's view of the world. The world has become the measuring stick for change, all in the name of "the Bible cannot be used as a standard for cultural change." The following quotation is a representative example:

> The Christian life is life in the Holy Spirit, not life governed by detailed regulations as was the life of God's people in Old Testament times. The New Testament does contain a few rules (e.g., "Pay just wages"; "pay your taxes"), but the believer under the authority of Scripture is spiritually liberated to keep the moral law in good conscience in a diversity of cultural contexts and political structures.[4]

This approach leaves the Christian with few regulations. "A diversity of cultural contexts and political structures" mitigates the application of a narrowly focused law system, even if it's from God. The absence of specific biblical regulations means an ethical free-for-all. If the Christian's life is not regulated by "detailed regulations," then we can't expect much from the Bible to be applied to the world at large.

We have moved from specific guidelines to being "moved by the Holy Spirit." The Spirit and the Word are never in opposition. Much has been done in the name of the Holy Spirit, and not all of it can be supported by Scripture. But what does it mean, for example, to "pay your taxes"? Is the State free to tax citizens at any rate? Are there biblical norms for taxation? If there are no "detailed regulations," then the State is free to confiscate all our income by an appeal to the *general* law "pay your taxes." Keep in mind that the prohibition regarding abortion is found with those laws Dr. Henry says are no longer obligatory during the New Testament era (Ex. 21:22–25).[5] There's no direct prohibition of abortion in the New Testament, although it is certainly possible to infer such a prohibition (Luke 1:41), but only because the Old Testament is more specific. Neither will you find a prohibition of bestiality in the New Testament (cf. Ex. 22:19; Lev. 18:23–25).

The Stepchild of the Enlightenment

Western culture is no longer seen as the child of the Reformation but an heir of the Enlightenment.[6] Of course, in one sense Western culture is now Enlightenment culture, and abortion is evidence that the reformational worldview has been discarded. The question is: Should our nation follow the path laid down by the Enlightenment philosophers, or should we work to recover the worldview of the Reformation?

> The utopian dream of the Enlightenment can be summed up by five words: reason, nature, happiness, progress, and liberty. It was thoroughly secular in its thinking. The humanistic elements which had risen during the Renaissance came to flood tide in the Enlightenment. Here was man starting from himself absolutely. And if the humanistic elements of the Renaissance stand in sharp contrast to the Reformation, the Enlightenment was in total antithesis to it. The two stood for and were based upon absolutely different things in an absolute way, and they produced absolutely different results.[7]

Cotton Mather wrote a history of early New England which he entitled *Magnalia Christi Americana*, or *The Great Works of Christ in America*. "The sum of the matter," he explained, "is that from the beginning of the Reformation in the English nation, there had always been a generation of godly men, desirous to pursue the reformation of religion, according to the Word of God. . . ." But in England, there were others with "power . . . in their hands" who desired "not only to stop the progress of the desired reformation but also, with innumerable vexation, to persecute those that most heartily wish well unto it." These early Christian settlers were here "driven to seek a place for the exercise of the Protestant religion, according to the light of conscience, in the deserts of America." Their purpose was nothing less than to complete the Reformation, believing "that the first reformers never intended that what they did should be the absolute boundary of reformation . . . ."[8]

The reformation, while still influencing many in the church, has taken a back seat to the Enlightenment worldview that spawned the French Revolution, Darwinism, Marxism, National Socialism, today's abortion industry, and the call for homosexual marriage. The spirit of the French Declaration of the Rights of Man (August 26, 1789), where "'the Supreme Being' equaled 'the sovereignty of the nation'—that is, the general will of the people,"[9] has usurped the reformational and biblical view that sovereignty is God's alone, and He delegates a limited sovereignty to individuals and institutions (e.g., family, church, and State). Whether it's "we the people," the French "citizen," the Nazi *Volk*, or the Marxist "proletariat," man rules, and in such a world the lives of the weakest and most despised are always in jeopardy.

Modern man's ideological tool for change is evolution. Harold O. J. Brown writes that "our present 'abortion revolution' is possible only on the basis of the widespread replacement of our perception of ourselves as rational creatures made in the image of God, with the perception of ourselves as mere accidental by-products of what Jacques Monod calls 'chance and necessity,'—in other words, with the general triumph of social Darwinism."[10]

What "nature used to do by "chance," man now initiates by terroristic design. The evolutionary doctrine of the "survival of the fittest" has been commandeered by modern man for the "betterment" of society. A calculated show of force by the "mother," her "doctor," and the autonomous courts is used to eliminate the defenseless unborn for "high social reasons." After a debate on the abortion issue, a pro-life lawyer who had taken part had the opportunity to speak with some of the participants.

> [M]ost of the students *already* recognized that the unborn child is a human life. Nevertheless, certain social reasons are considered "high enough" to justify ending that life. According to some of the women, examples of "high enough" reasons include protecting pregnant teenagers from the psychological distress of bearing a child, helping poor women who aren't able to care adequately for a child, and preventing children from coming into the world "unwanted." Many charged that pro-life philosophies are not "socially acceptable" because they fail to deal realistically with these problems.[11]

Abortion is simply State-sanctioned Darwinism. The State reflects the views of those who vote for the prevailing leadership. "If man has no individual dignity, no immortal soul, no destiny outside political order, then abortion—like fornication, adultery, and sodomy—becomes a trivial matter."[12] There are enough people who have made their voices heard: They want abortion, no matter that it means taking a human life. "High social reasons" have become the moral touchstone for the nation.

Developing a Long-Term Strategy

Many Christian organizations exist exclusively as spiritual fire houses. When they see a fire, they send a fire engine to put it out. They then return to the fire house to polish the fire engine awaiting another call. There is certainly a need for fire engines and fire houses. But there is no real community if there are only fire houses. Most of the time, a fire house is inactive. Most of a fireman's time is spent waiting for a fire alarm to go off.

Christians must get into the building business without neglecting the construction of a few well-placed fire houses along the way.

Life is more than waiting for fires to break out. In order to build a Christian society, planners must acquire the skills to design and build what can be conceived. Unfortunately, most Christians are ill-equipped to do the necessary planning and building. We are woefully ignorant of how the "system" works. Few Christians have the necessary experience to fight Leviathan and Behemoth. Even fewer have the theology to know why.

The best legal technicians are those who deal with law and the courts on a daily basis. For them, law is their salvation. This is not an area where Christians have excelled. We've gone about our business while an entire legal culture with its own language and community of associates has grown up around us until we have become the new subculture. Our lives are regulated by lawyers and an entrenched, nearly autonomous, bureaucracy. The church of Jesus Christ is woefully ill-equipped to cope with the system. If we're going to survive and thrive, we better learn how the system works and then make it work for us.

Abortion is ingrained in our society because the tenets that spawned abortion are ingrained. Nearly every vehicle of expression in our society fosters the lie that abortion is a "right" granted by the Constitution, in fact, an "inalienable right," to use the language of the Declaration of Independence. The average American citizen is bombarded on a daily basis by films from Hollywood presenting abortion as a modern freedom, "sensitive" television specials portraying the "compassion" of abortion, and a daily inundation of media-biased reporting on the topic. Of course, we must not forget how the courts have consistently upheld the *Roe v. Wade* creed. Friends, this scenario did not drop out of the sky. There are people behind these views, and these people learned the system and used it to advance their worldview.

The acceptance of abortion is the manifestation of a greater problem: The American people, a great many of whom are professing Christians, live in terms of what they think they know. What they know comes from what they're taught and the sources of information with which they choose to inform themselves. They're taught that absolutes do not exist, convenience is preferred over responsibility, the individual has worth because he or she has rights, rights are defined as an individual expression of choice, and the State is designed to protect those rights no matter what the cost. In fact, the State is the grantor of those rights—"The State makes right."

Learning the system means recapturing the system. This will take time. It's not enough to gear up every four years to elect a "Christian" president. Christians must make a concerted effort to replace the humanists at all levels of society with competent Christians who understand the Bible and how it works in the world. In addition, we need to know how the world works. This means that science, technology, and the arts are important and God-sanctioned.

Defense is Not Enough

For the most part, Christians have been fighting a defensive war. The humanists act and Christians (sometimes) react. Certainly it's important to have a good defense, but there must be an offensive strategy, a proactive agenda to counter the effects of secularism. In a defensive-only game, the opposition only has to score one point to win the war. With their win, they are empowered to make decisions for those who lost.

An offensive strategy assumes a viable future. This will mean a change in the church's thinking about eschatology. The preoccupation with the "end" must be replaced with a preoccupation with the finished work of Christ, including His death, resurrection, and ascension. We should act in terms of the power of Jesus' resurrection rather than the power of evil in the world and the supposed approaching antichrist. We need to come to grips with the implications of Jesus' ascension and what it tells us about His present status as the "Ruler of the kings of the earth" and our rulership with Him.

Education

One of the immediate long-term solutions is how we view education. No, I don't mean better public schools. I have in mind the creation of a vast network of Christian schools that can operate in already-established classrooms that are used one Sunday morning each week. Our church buildings must be turned into educational facilities. The pro-abortion mentality (as well as Socialism, atheism, naturalism, and relativism) arose in the anti-Christian confines of public education. It's time that Christians made the costly commitment to reverse the trend.

From these schools our nation will be revitalized with Christian educators, doctors, lawyers, economists, civil servants, journalists, musicians, and artists. With additional Christian schools, there will be a need for real Christian universities to compete with the well-endowed humanist institutions. The once-Christian Harvard (1636), Yale (1701), and Princeton (1746) have endowments totaling in the billions of dollars. These humanist institutions continue to attract the best and the brightest to corrupt them in terms of humanist "enlightenment."

Media

Another area of needed change is the media. The media have a liberal,[13] anti-Christian bias. David Limbaugh makes a compelling case for the reality of anti-Christian bias in his book *Persecution*:

> In the documented bias against Christians and Christianity in our modern culture, Hollywood and Big Media play very major roles. Political correctness tells us that it is unthinkable to ridicule (almost any) group, but both of these major cultural power centers routinely disparage Christians and present them in a negative light. This anti-Christian bias manifests itself in unflattering portrayals of Christians in Hollywood films and entertainment

> television and also in the demonization of Christian conservatives in the media.[14]

This won't change unless the people who broadcast the news change or Christians begin to replace them. Journalism and film-making must be seen as missionary fields. Opinions are based upon what people hear and see. Allowing the secularism of our present system to go unchallenged is to allow the gospel to undergo further corruption. This will mean establishing television and radio stations that do more than play contemporary "Christian music" and replay last Sunday's church service of a "famous" teacher/preacher. There has to be competition in the marketplace of ideas. This will mean being more professional and objective than our non-Christian media counterparts. Of course, this will mean support from the Christian community for such enterprises.

The Arts

Few Christians consider how much art impacts our worldview.[15] Man as superman, a preoccupation with death, the breakdown of the biblical family, and a do-your-own-thingism fill nearly every frame of film. Glimpses of life and light shine through Hollywood. These are the exceptions in an environment where the Christian worldview raises its head for a last gasp of breath before it sinks for the last time. The dimmed rays of light are more cries of desperation than expressions of hope and meaning. There is a distinct contrast between older films with their rich and honest portrayals of human nature and faith and today's sex-filled, violence-saturated, occultic, and hopeless portrayals of what Hollywood perceives to be "normal."

Christian television has a very narrow focus as does Christian film-making (if there is such a thing in our day). Christians have ghettoized the arts. Looking at what Christians have done, one might never realize that God is creative (Gen. 1:1). As creatures created in His image, we have the creative gifts and talents to use the "stuff" of His creation to fashion interpretive recreations that reflect something of that divine image. Man's artistry is one attribute that separates man from the animals. As G. K. Chesterton wrote, "art is the signature of man."[16] Non-image bearers (animals) are not artists. Their designs are wholly instinctive and never change. Only man can be innovative and recreative. A Christian worldview ought to permeate our creative images. Instead, homoeroticism and defaced religious images are passed off as "art." Of course, such expressions of "art" are simply the implications of the debased worldview of humanism. The Bible tells us that we will know a tree by its fruit. The fruit of humanism is decadence. But what has the tree of Christianity produced?

There is a subliminal impression that abortion and other types of violence and perversion are right because of the images that come from the screen: human autonomy, death, debauchery, pornography, the occult, and a not too subtle meaninglessness that makes death a sometimes preferable consideration than the grandeur of what life can be when surrendered to the lordship of Jesus Christ.

A life-affirming worldview must come from the screens of America's theaters. Christian films, like the world in which we live, should be multi-dimensional, showing life, death, and redemption, not so much in words spoken but in scenes painted on celluloid. There's more than one way to make God known. Keep in mind that "the heavens are telling of the glory of God; and their expanse is declaring the work of His hands" (Psalm 19:1), therefore, a depiction of the created order in a biblical fashion tells us something about God. The Bible interprets and applies these images.

There is much more that could be said. The task before us is monumental. Every area of life needs to be evaluated and reclaimed with Christian values: politics, law, economics, business, journalism, medicine, and every other conceivable area of life. The humanists have adopted this world as their own. They will stop at nothing to establish their version of heaven on earth. If they get their way, it will be hell for all of us.

Notes

1. Peter J. Leithart and George Grant, *In Defense of Greatness: How Biblical Character Shapes A Nation's Destiny* (Ft. Lauderdale, FL: Coral Ridge Ministries, 1990), 4–5.

2. Robert Drake, "What Should the Kingdom of God Look Like?," a review of *Dominion Theology: Blessing or Curse?*, *World* (February 11, 1989).

3. Drake, "What Should the Kingdom of God Look Like?"

4. Carl F. H. Henry, *Twilight of a Great Civilization: The Drift Toward Neo-Paganism* (Westchester, IL: Crossway Books, 1988), 30.

5. H. Wayne House, "Miscarriage or Premature Birth: Additional Thoughts on Exodus 21:22–25," *Westminster Theological Journal* 41:1 (Fall 1978), 108–123.

6. Our "Western heritage," in the words of one social critic/historian, was "bequeathed by the Enlightenment." Anson Shupe, "Prophets of a Biblical America," *The Wall Street Journal* (April 12, 1989), 14A.

7. Francis A. Schaeffer, *How Should We Then Live?* in *The Complete Works of Francis A. Schaeffer*, 5 vols. (Westchester, IL: Crossway Books, 1982), 5:148.

8. Cotton Mather, *The Great Works of Christ in America*, 2 vols. (Edinburgh: The Banner of Truth Trust, [1702] 1979), 1:26.

9. Schaeffer, *How Should We Then Live?*, 5:149.

10. Harold O. J. Brown, "Hidden Roots: Cultural Presuppositions of the Abortion Revolution," *The Human Life Review* 8:1 (Winter 1981), 69.

11. "Students Defend Abortion For 'High' Social Reasons," *The Rutherford Institute* 1:2 (January/February 1984), 8.

12. Joseph Sobran, "The Non-Debate of 1988 is on Abortion," *The Conservative Digest* (October 1988), 98.

13. Bernard Goldberg, *Bias: CBS Insider Exposes How the Media Distort the News* (Washington, D.C.: Regnery Publishing, 2002), 5; Bernard Goldberg, *Arrogance: Rescuing American from the Media Elite* (New York: Warner Books, 2003); Laura Ingraham, *Shut Up and Sing: How Elites from Hollywood, Politics, and the UN are Subverting America* (Washington, D.C.: Regnery Publishing, 2003).

14. David Limbaugh, *Persecution: How Liberals are Waging War Against Christianity* (Washington, D.C.: Regnery Publishing, 2003), 265.

15. Brian Godawa, *Hollywood Worldviews: Watching Films with Wisdom and Discernment*, rev. ed. (Downers Grove, IL: InterVarsity Press, [2002] 2009); Gene Edward Veith, Jr., *State of the Arts: From Bezalel to Mapplethorpe* (Wheaton, IL: Crossway Books, 1991); Jerry Solomon, ed., *Arts, Entertainment, and Christian Values* (Grand Rapids, MI: Kregel Publications, 2000)

16. G. K. Chesterton, "The Everlasting Man," *Collected Works* (San Francisco, CA: Ignatius Press, 1985), 2:166.

Scripture Index

Old Testament

New Testament

Subject Index

C

D

E

I

J

K

M

T